# Deep Learning from Scratch
*Building with Python from First Principles*

*Seth Weidman*

Beijing · Boston · Farnham · Sebastopol · Tokyo

**Deep Learning from Scratch**

by Seth Weidman

Published by O'Reilly Media, Inc., 1005 Gravenstein Highway North, Sebastopol, CA 95472.

O'Reilly books may be purchased for educational, business, or sales promotional use. Online editions are also available for most titles (*http://oreilly.com*). For more information, contact our corporate/institutional sales department: 800-998-9938 or *corporate@oreilly.com*.

**Development Editor:** Melissa Potter
**Acquisitions Editors:** Jon Hassell and Mike Loukides
**Production Editor:** Katherine Tozer
**Copyeditor:** Arthur Johnson
**Proofreader:** Rachel Monaghan

**Indexer:** Judith McConville
**Interior Designer:** David Futato
**Cover Designer:** Karen Montgomery
**Illustrator:** Rebecca Demarest

September 2019:     First Edition

**Revision History for the First Edition**
2019-09-06:   First Release

See *http://oreilly.com/catalog/errata.csp?isbn=9781492041412* for release details.

978-1-492-04141-2

[LSI]

# Table of Contents

# Preface

If you've tried to learn about neural networks and deep learning, you've probably encountered an abundance of resources, from blog posts to MOOCs (massive open online courses, such as those offered on Coursera and Udacity) of varying quality and even some books—I know I did when I started exploring the subject a few years ago. However, if you're reading this preface, it's likely that each explanation of neural networks that you've come across is lacking in some way. I found the same thing when I started learning: the various explanations were like blind men describing different parts of an elephant (*https://oreil.ly/r5YxS*), but none describing the whole thing. That is what led me to write this book.

These existing resources on neural networks mostly fall into two categories. Some are conceptual and mathematical, containing both the drawings one typically finds in explanations of neural networks, of circles connected by lines with arrows on the ends, as well as extensive mathematical explanations of what is going on so you can "understand the theory." A prototypical example of this is the very good book *Deep Learning* by Ian Goodfellow et al. (MIT Press).

Other resources have dense blocks of code that, if run, appear to show a loss value decreasing over time and thus a neural network "learning." For instance, the following example from the PyTorch documentation does indeed define and train a simple neural network on randomly generated data:

```
# N is batch size; D_in is input dimension;
# H is hidden dimension; D_out is output dimension.
N, D_in, H, D_out = 64, 1000, 100, 10

# Create random input and output data
x = torch.randn(N, D_in, device=device, dtype=dtype)
y = torch.randn(N, D_out, device=device, dtype=dtype)

# Randomly initialize weights
w1 = torch.randn(D_in, H, device=device, dtype=dtype)
w2 = torch.randn(H, D_out, device=device, dtype=dtype)
```

```
learning_rate = 1e-6
for t in range(500):
    # Forward pass: compute predicted y
    h = x.mm(w1)
    h_relu = h.clamp(min=0)
    y_pred = h_relu.mm(w2)

    # Compute and print loss
    loss = (y_pred - y).pow(2).sum().item()
    print(t, loss)

    # Backprop to compute gradients of w1 and w2 with respect to loss
    grad_y_pred = 2.0 * (y_pred - y)
    grad_w2 = h_relu.t().mm(grad_y_pred)
    grad_h_relu = grad_y_pred.mm(w2.t())
    grad_h = grad_h_relu.clone()
    grad_h[h < 0] = 0
    grad_w1 = x.t().mm(grad_h)

    # Update weights using gradient descent
    w1 -= learning_rate * grad_w1
    w2 -= learning_rate * grad_w2
```

Explanations like this, of course, don't give much insight into "what is really going on": the underlying mathematical principles, the individual neural network components contained here and how they work together, and so on.[1]

What *would* a good explanation of neural networks contain? For an answer, it is instructive to look at how other computer science concepts are explained: if you want to learn about sorting algorithms, for example, there are textbooks that will contain:

- An explanation of the algorithm, in plain English
- A visual explanation of how the algorithm works, of the kind that you would draw on a whiteboard during a coding interview
- Some mathematical explanation of "why the algorithm works"[2]
- Pseudocode implementing the algorithm

One rarely—or never—finds these elements of an explanation of neural networks side by side, even though it seems obvious to me that a proper explanation of neural networks should be done this way; this book is an attempt to fill that gap.

---

1 To be fair, this example was intended as an illustration of the PyTorch library for those who already understand neural networks, not as an instructive tutorial. Still, many tutorials follow this style, showing only the code along with some brief explanations.

2 Specifically, in the case of sorting algorithms, why the algorithm terminates with a properly sorted list.

# Understanding Neural Networks Requires Multiple Mental Models

I am not a researcher, and I do not have a Ph.D. I have, however, taught data science professionally: I taught a couple of data science bootcamps with a company called Metis, and then I traveled around the world for a year with Metis doing one- to five-day workshops for companies in many different industries in which I explained machine learning and basic software engineering concepts to their employees. I've always loved teaching and have always been fascinated by the question of how best to explain technical concepts, most recently focusing on concepts in machine learning and statistics. With neural networks, I've found the most challenging part is conveying the correct "mental model" for what a neural network is, especially since understanding neural networks fully requires not just one but *several* mental models, all of which illuminate different (but still essential) aspects of how neural networks work. To illustrate this: the following four sentences are all correct answers to the question "What is a neural network?":

- A neural network is a mathematical function that takes in inputs and produces outputs.
- A neural network is a computational graph through which multidimensional arrays flow.
- A neural network is made up of layers, each of which can be thought of as having a number of "neurons."
- A neural network is a universal function approximator that can in theory represent the solution to any supervised learning problem.

Indeed, many of you reading this have probably heard one or more of these before, and may have a reasonable understanding of what they mean and what their implications are for how neural networks work. To fully understand them, however, we'll have to understand *all* of them and show how they are connected—how is the fact that a neural network can be represented as a computational graph connected to the notion of "layers," for example? Furthermore, to make all of this precise, we'll implement all of these concepts from scratch, in Python, and stitch them together to make working neural networks that you can train on your laptop. Nevertheless, despite the fact that we'll spend a substantial amount of time on implementation details, *the purpose of implementing these models in Python is to solidify and make precise our understanding of the concepts; it is not to write as concise or performant of a neural network library as possible.*

My goal is that after you've read this book, you'll have such a solid understanding of all of these mental models (and their implications for how neural networks should be *implemented*) that learning related concepts or doing further projects in the field will be much easier.

## Chapter Outlines

The first three chapters are the most important ones and could themselves form a standalone book.

1. In Chapter 1 I'll show how mathematical functions can be represented as a series of operations linked together to form a computational graph, and show how this representation lets us compute the derivatives of these functions' outputs with respect to their inputs using the chain rule from calculus. At the end of this chapter, I'll introduce a very important operation, the matrix multiplication, and show how it can fit into a mathematical function represented in this way while still allowing us to compute the derivatives we'll end up needing for deep learning.

2. In Chapter 2 we'll directly use the building blocks we created in Chapter 1 to build and train models to solve a real-world problem: specifically, we'll use them to build both linear regression and neural network models to predict housing prices on a real-world dataset. I'll show that the neural network performs better than the linear regression and try to give some intuition for why. The "first principles" approach to building the models in this chapter should give you a very good idea of how neural networks work, but will also show the limited capability of the step-by-step, purely first-principles-based approach to defining deep learning models; this will motivate Chapter 3.

3. In Chapter 3 we'll take the building blocks from the first-principles-based approach of the first two chapters and use them to build the "higher level" components that make up all deep learning models: Layers, Models, Optimizers, and so on. We'll end this chapter by training a deep learning model, defined from scratch, on the same dataset from Chapter 2 and showing that it performs better than our simple neural network.

4. As it turns out, there are few theoretical guarantees that a neural network with a given architecture will actually find a good solution on a given dataset when trained using the standard training techniques we'll use in this book. In Chapter 4 we'll cover the most important "training tricks" that generally increase the probability that a neural network will find a good solution, and, wherever possible, give some mathematical intuition as to why they work.

5. In Chapter 5 I cover the fundamental ideas behind convolutional neural networks (CNNs), a kind of neural network architecture specialized for understanding images. There are many explanations of CNNs out there, so I'll focus on explaining the absolute essentials of CNNs and how they differ from regular neural networks: specifically, how CNNs result in each layer of neurons being

organized into "feature maps," and how two of these layers (each made up of multiple feature maps) are connected together via convolutional filters. In addition, just as we coded the regular layers in a neural network from scratch, we'll code convolutional layers from scratch to reinforce our understanding of how they work.

6. Throughout the first five chapters, we'll build up a miniature neural network library that defines neural networks as a series of Layers—which are themselves made up of a series of Operations—that send inputs forward and gradients backward. This is not how most neural networks are implemented in practice; instead, they use a technique called *automatic differentiation*. I'll give a quick illustration of automatic differentiation at the beginning of Chapter 6 and use it to motivate the main subject of the chapter: *recurrent neural networks* (RNNs), the neural network architecture typically used for understanding data in which the data points appear sequentially, such as time series data or natural language data. I'll explain the workings of "vanilla RNNs" and of two variants: *GRUs* and *LSTMs* (and of course implement all three from scratch); throughout, I'll be careful to distinguish between the elements that are shared across *all* of these RNN variants and the specific ways in which these variants differ.

7. Finally, in Chapter 7, I'll show how everything we did from scratch in Chapters 1–6 can be implemented using the high-performance, open source neural network library PyTorch. Learning a framework like this is essential for progressing your learning about neural networks; but diving in and learning a framework without first having a solid understanding of how and why neural networks work would severely limit your learning in the long term. The goal of the progression of chapters in this book is to give you the power to write extremely high-performance neural networks (by teaching you PyTorch) while still setting you up for long-term learning and success (by teaching you the fundamentals before you learn PyTorch). We'll conclude with a quick illustration of how neural networks can be used for unsupervised learning.

My goal here was to write the book that I wish had existed when I started to learn the subject a few years ago. I hope you will find this book helpful. Onward!

# Conventions Used in This Book

The following typographical conventions are used in this book:

*Italic*

> Indicates new terms, URLs, email addresses, filenames, and file extensions.

`Constant width`

> Used for program listings, as well as within paragraphs to refer to program elements such as variable or function names, databases, data types, environment variables, statements, and keywords.

**`Constant width bold`**

> Shows commands or other text that should be typed literally by the user.

*`Constant width italic`*

> Used for text that should be replaced with user-supplied values or by values determined by context and for comments in code examples.

The Pythagorean Theorem is $a^2 + b^2 = c^2$.

 This element signifies a general note.

# Using Code Examples

Supplemental material (code examples, exercises, etc.) is available for download at the book's GitHub repository (*https://oreil.ly/deep-learning-github*).

This book is here to help you get your job done. In general, if example code is offered with this book, you may use it in your programs and documentation. You do not need to contact us for permission unless you're reproducing a significant portion of the code. For example, writing a program that uses several chunks of code from this book does not require permission. Selling or distributing a CD-ROM of examples from O'Reilly books does require permission. Answering a question by citing this book and quoting example code does not require permission. Incorporating a significant amount of example code from this book into your product's documentation does require permission.

We appreciate, but do not require, attribution. An attribution usually includes the title, author, publisher, and ISBN. For example: "*Deep Learning from Scratch* by Seth Weidman (O'Reilly). Copyright 2019 Seth Weidman, 978-1-492-04141-2."

If you feel your use of code examples falls outside fair use or the permission given above, feel free to contact us at *permissions@oreilly.com*.

## O'Reilly Online Learning

 For almost 40 years, *O'Reilly Media* has provided technology and business training, knowledge, and insight to help companies succeed.

Our unique network of experts and innovators share their knowledge and expertise through books, articles, conferences, and our online learning platform. O'Reilly's online learning platform gives you on-demand access to live training courses, in-depth learning paths, interactive coding environments, and a vast collection of text and video from O'Reilly and 200+ other publishers. For more information, please visit *http://oreilly.com*.

## How to Contact Us

Please address comments and questions concerning this book to the publisher:

O'Reilly Media, Inc.
1005 Gravenstein Highway North
Sebastopol, CA 95472
800-998-9938 (in the United States or Canada)
707-829-0515 (international or local)
707-829-0104 (fax)

We have a web page for this book, where we list errata, examples, and any additional information. You can access this page at *https://oreil.ly/dl-from-scratch*.

Email *bookquestions@oreilly.com* to comment or ask technical questions about this book.

For more information about our books, courses, conferences, and news, see our website at *http://www.oreilly.com*.

Find us on Facebook: *http://facebook.com/oreilly*

Follow us on Twitter: *http://twitter.com/oreillymedia*

Watch us on YouTube: *http://www.youtube.com/oreillymedia*

# Acknowledgments

I'd like to thank my editor, Melissa Potter, along with the team at O'Reilly, who were meticulous with their feedback and responsive to my questions throughout the process.

I'd like to give a special thanks to several people whose work to make technical concepts in machine learning accessible to a wider audience has directly influenced me, and a couple of whom I've been lucky enough to have gotten to know personally: in a randomly generated order, these people are Brandon Rohrer, Joel Grus, Jeremy Watt, and Andrew Trask.

I'd like to thank my boss at Metis and my director at Facebook, who were unreasonably supportive of my carving out time to work on this project.

I'd like to give a special thank you and acknowledgment to Mat Leonard, who was my coauthor for a brief period of time before we decided to go our separate ways. Mat helped organize the code for the minilibrary associated with the book—lincoln—and gave me very helpful feedback on some extremely unpolished versions of the first two chapters, writing his own versions of large sections of these chapters in the process.

Finally, I'd like to thank my friends Eva and John, both of whom directly encouraged and inspired me to take the plunge and actually start writing. I'd also like to thank my many friends in San Francisco who tolerated my general preoccupation and worry about the book as well as my lack of availability to hang out for many months, and who were unwaveringly supportive when I needed them to be.

# Foundations

*Don't memorize these formulas. If you understand the concepts, you can invent your own notation.*
—John Cochrane, *Investments Notes* (*https://oreil.ly/33CVXjg*) 2006

The aim of this chapter is to explain some foundational mental models that are essential for understanding how neural networks work. Specifically, we'll cover *nested mathematical functions and their derivatives*. We'll work our way up from the simplest possible building blocks to show that we can build complicated functions made up of a "chain" of constituent functions and, even when one of these functions is a matrix multiplication that takes in multiple inputs, compute the derivative of the functions' outputs with respect to their inputs. Understanding how this process works will be essential to understanding neural networks, which we technically won't begin to cover until Chapter 2.

As we're getting our bearings around these foundational building blocks of neural networks, we'll systematically describe each concept we introduce from three perspectives:

- Math, in the form of an equation or equations
- Code, with as little extra syntax as possible (making Python an ideal choice)
- A diagram explaining what is going on, of the kind you would draw on a whiteboard during a coding interview

As mentioned in the preface, one of the challenges of understanding neural networks is that it requires multiple mental models. We'll get a sense of that in this chapter: each of these three perspectives excludes certain essential features of the concepts we'll cover, and only when taken together do they provide a full picture of both how and why nested mathematical functions work the way they do. In fact, I take the uniquely strong view that any attempt to explain the building blocks of neural networks that excludes one of these three perspectives is incomplete.

With that out of the way, it's time to take our first steps. We're going to start with some extremely simple building blocks to illustrate how we can understand different concepts in terms of these three perspectives. Our first building block will be a simple but critical concept: the function.

# Functions

What is a function, and how do we describe it? As with neural nets, there are several ways to describe functions, none of which individually paints a complete picture. Rather than trying to give a pithy one-sentence description, let's simply walk through the three mental models one by one, playing the role of the blind men feeling different parts of the elephant.

## Math

Here are two examples of functions, described in mathematical notation:

- $f_1(x) = x^2$
- $f_2(x) = max(x, 0)$

This notation says that the functions, which we arbitrarily call $f_1$ and $f_2$, take in a number $x$ as input and transform it into either $x^2$ (in the first case) or $max(x, 0)$ (in the second case).

## Diagrams

One way of depicting functions is to:

1. Draw an $x$-$y$ plane (where $x$ refers to the horizontal axis and $y$ refers to the vertical axis).

2. Plot a bunch of points, where the x-coordinates of the points are (usually evenly spaced) inputs of the function over some range, and the y-coordinates are the outputs of the function over that range.

3. Connect these plotted points.

This was first done by the French philosopher René Descartes, and it is extremely useful in many areas of mathematics, in particular calculus. Figure 1-1 shows the plot of these two functions.

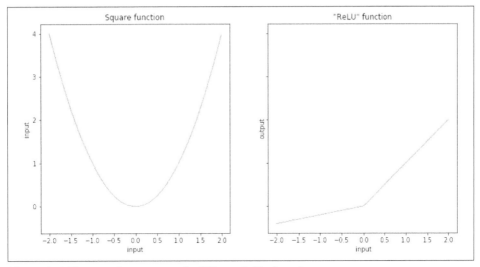

*Figure 1-1. Two continuous, mostly differentiable functions*

However, there is another way to depict functions that isn't as useful when learning calculus but that will be very useful for us when thinking about deep learning models. We can think of functions as boxes that take in numbers as input and produce numbers as output, like minifactories that have their own internal rules for what happens to the input. Figure 1-2 shows both these functions described as general rules and how they operate on specific inputs.

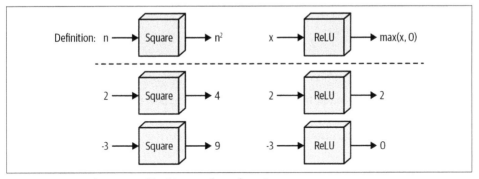

*Figure 1-2. Another way of looking at these functions*

# Code

Finally, we can describe these functions using code. Before we do, we should say a bit about the Python library on top of which we'll be writing our functions: NumPy.

### Code caveat #1: NumPy

NumPy is a widely used Python library for fast numeric computation, the internals of which are mostly written in C. Simply put: the data we deal with in neural networks will always be held in a *multidimensional array* that is almost always either one-, two-, three-, or four-dimensional, but especially two- or three-dimensional. The ndarray class from the NumPy library allows us to operate on these arrays in ways that are both (a) intuitive and (b) fast. To take the simplest possible example: if we were storing our data in Python lists (or lists of lists), adding or multiplying the lists element-wise using normal syntax wouldn't work, whereas it does work for ndarrays:

```
print("Python list operations:")
a = [1,2,3]
b = [4,5,6]
print("a+b:", a+b)
try:
    print(a*b)
except TypeError:
    print("a*b has no meaning for Python lists")
print()
print("numpy array operations:")
a = np.array([1,2,3])
b = np.array([4,5,6])
print("a+b:", a+b)
print("a*b:", a*b)

Python list operations:
a+b: [1, 2, 3, 4, 5, 6]
a*b has no meaning for Python lists

numpy array operations:
a+b: [5 7 9]
a*b: [ 4 10 18]
```

ndarrays also have several features you'd expect from an n-dimensional array; each ndarray has n axes, indexed from 0, so that the first axis is 0, the second is 1, and so on. In particular, since we deal with 2D ndarrays often, we can think of axis = 0 as the rows and axis = 1 as the columns—see Figure 1-3.

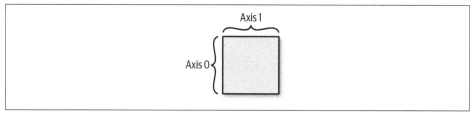

*Figure 1-3. A 2D NumPy array, with axis = 0 as the rows and axis = 1 as the columns*

NumPy's `ndarrays` also support applying functions along these axes in intuitive ways. For example, summing along axis 0 (the *rows* for a 2D array) essentially "collapses the array" along that axis, returning an array with one less dimension than the original array; for a 2D array, this is equivalent to summing each column:

```
print('a:')
print(a)
print('a.sum(axis=0):', a.sum(axis=0))
print('a.sum(axis=1):', a.sum(axis=1))

a:
[[1 2]
 [3 4]]
a.sum(axis=0): [4 6]
a.sum(axis=1): [3 7]
```

Finally, NumPy `ndarrays` support adding a 1D array to the last axis; for a 2D array `a` with `R` rows and `C` columns, this means we can add a 1D array `b` of length `C` and NumPy will do the addition in the intuitive way, adding the elements to each row of `a`:[1]

```
a = np.array([[1,2,3],
              [4,5,6]])

b = np.array([10,20,30])

print("a+b:\n", a+b)

a+b:
[[11 22 33]
 [14 25 36]]
```

## Code caveat #2: Type-checked functions

As I've mentioned, the primary goal of the code we write in this book is to make the concepts I'm explaining precise and clear. This will get more challenging as the book goes on, as we'll be writing functions with many arguments as part of complicated classes. To combat this, we'll use functions with type signatures throughout; for example, in Chapter 3, we'll initialize our neural networks as follows:

```
def __init__(self,
             layers: List[Layer],
             loss: Loss,
             learning_rate: float = 0.01) -> None:
```

This type signature alone gives you some idea of what the class is used for. By contrast, consider the following type signature that we *could* use to define an operation:

---

[1] This will allow us to easily add a bias to our matrix multiplication later on.

```
def operation(x1, x2):
```

This type signature by itself gives you no hint as to what is going on; only by printing out each object's type, seeing what operations get performed on each object, or guessing based on the names x1 and x2 could we understand what is going on in this function. I can instead define a function with a type signature as follows:

```
def operation(x1: ndarray, x2: ndarray) -> ndarray:
```

You know right away that this is a function that takes in two ndarrays, probably combines them in some way, and outputs the result of that combination. Because of the increased clarity they provide, we'll use type-checked functions throughout this book.

### Basic functions in NumPy

With these preliminaries in mind, let's write up the functions we defined earlier in NumPy:

```
def square(x: ndarray) -> ndarray:
    '''
    Square each element in the input ndarray.
    '''
    return np.power(x, 2)

def leaky_relu(x: ndarray) -> ndarray:
    '''
    Apply "Leaky ReLU" function to each element in ndarray.
    '''
    return np.maximum(0.2 * x, x)
```

 One of NumPy's quirks is that many functions can be applied to ndarrays either by writing np.*function_name*(ndarray) or by writing ndarray.*function_name*. For example, the preceding relu function could be written as: x.clip(min=0). We'll try to be consistent and use the np.*function_name*(ndarray) convention throughout—in particular, we'll avoid tricks such as *ndarray*.T for transposing a two-dimensional ndarray, instead writing np.trans pose(*ndarray*, (1, 0)).

If you can wrap your mind around the fact that math, a diagram, and code are three different ways of representing the same underlying concept, then you are well on your way to displaying the kind of flexible thinking you'll need to truly understand deep learning.

# Derivatives

Derivatives, like functions, are an extremely important concept for understanding deep learning that many of you are probably familiar with. Also like functions, they can be depicted in multiple ways. We'll start by simply saying at a high level that the derivative of a function at a point is the "rate of change" of the output of the function with respect to its input at that point. Let's now walk through the same three perspectives on derivatives that we covered for functions to gain a better mental model for how derivatives work.

## Math

First, we'll get mathematically precise: we can describe this number—how much the output of $f$ changes as we change its input at a particular value $a$ of the input—as a limit:

$$\frac{df}{du}(a) = \lim_{\Delta \to 0} \frac{f(a + \Delta) - f(a - \Delta)}{2 \times \Delta}$$

This limit can be approximated numerically by setting a very small value for $\Delta$, such as 0.001, so we can compute the derivative as:

$$\frac{df}{du}(a) = \frac{f(a + 0.001) - f(a - 0.001)}{0.002}$$

While accurate, this is only one part of a full mental model of derivatives. Let's look at them from another perspective: a diagram.

## Diagrams

First, the familiar way: if we simply draw a tangent line to the Cartesian representation of the function $f$, the derivative of $f$ at a point $a$ is just the slope of this line at $a$. As with the mathematical descriptions in the prior subsection, there are two ways we can actually calculate the slope of this line. The first would be to use calculus to actually calculate the limit. The second would be to just take the slope of the line connecting $f$ at $a - 0.001$ and $a + 0.001$. The latter method is depicted in Figure 1-4 and should be familiar to anyone who has taken calculus.

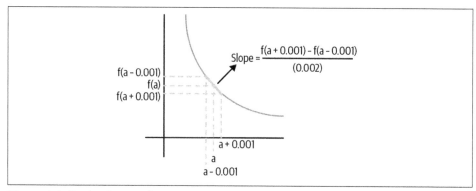

*Figure 1-4. Derivatives as slopes*

As we saw in the prior section, another way of thinking of functions is as mini-factories. Now think of the inputs to those factories being connected to the outputs by a string. The derivative is equal to the answer to this question: if we pull up on the input to the function *a* by some very small amount—or, to account for the fact that the function may be asymmetric at *a*, pull down on *a* by some small amount—by what multiple of this small amount will the output change, given the inner workings of the factory? This is depicted in Figure 1-5.

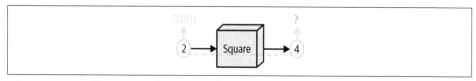

*Figure 1-5. Another way of visualizing derivatives*

This second representation will turn out to be more important than the first one for understanding deep learning.

## Code

Finally, we can code up the approximation to the derivative that we saw previously:

```
from typing import Callable

def deriv(func: Callable[[ndarray], ndarray],
        input_: ndarray,
        delta: float = 0.001) -> ndarray:
    '''
    Evaluates the derivative of a function "func" at every element in the
    "input_" array.
    '''
    return (func(input_ + delta) - func(input_ - delta)) / (2 * delta)
```

When we say that "something is a function of something else"—for example, that *P* is a function of *E* (letters chosen randomly on purpose), what we mean is that there is some function *f* such that *f(E)* = *P*—or equivalently, there is a function *f* that takes in *E* objects and produces *P* objects. We might also think of this as meaning that *P is defined as* whatever results when we apply the function *f* to *E*:

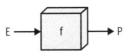

And we would code this up as:

```
def f(input_: ndarray) -> ndarray:
    # Some transformation(s)
    return output

P = f(E)
```

# Nested Functions

Now we'll cover a concept that will turn out to be fundamental to understanding neural networks: functions can be "nested" to form "composite" functions. What exactly do I mean by "nested"? I mean that if we have two functions that by mathematical convention we call $f_1$ and $f_2$, the output of one of the functions becomes the input to the next one, so that we can "string them together."

## Diagram

The most natural way to represent a nested function is with the "minifactory" or "box" representation (the second representation from "Functions" on page 2).

As Figure 1-6 shows, an input goes into the first function, gets transformed, and comes out; then it goes into the second function and gets transformed again, and we get our final output.

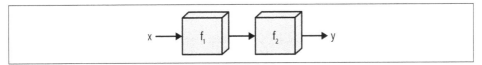

*Figure 1-6. Nested functions, naturally*

## Math

We should also include the less intuitive mathematical representation:

$$f_2(f_1(x)) = y$$

This is less intuitive because of the quirk that nested functions are read "from the out-side in" but the operations are in fact performed "from the inside out." For example, though $f_2(f_1(x)) = y$ is read "f 2 of f 1 of x," what it really means is to "first apply $f_1$ to $x$, and then apply $f_2$ to the result of applying $f_1$ to $x$."

## Code

Finally, in keeping with my promise to explain every concept from three perspectives, we'll code this up. First, we'll define a data type for nested functions:

```python
from typing import List

# A Function takes in an ndarray as an argument and produces an ndarray
Array_Function = Callable[[ndarray], ndarray]

# A Chain is a list of functions
Chain = List[Array_Function]
```

Then we'll define how data goes through a chain, first of length 2:

```python
def chain_length_2(chain: Chain,
                   a: ndarray) -> ndarray:
    '''
    Evaluates two functions in a row, in a "Chain".
    '''
    assert len(chain) == 2, \
    "Length of input 'chain' should be 2"

    f1 = chain[0]
    f2 = chain[1]

    return f2(f1(x))
```

## Another Diagram

Depicting the nested function using the box representation shows us that this composite function is really just a single function. Thus, we can represent this function as simply $f_1 f_2$, as shown in Figure 1-7.

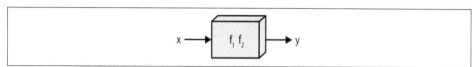

*Figure 1-7. Another way to think of nested functions*

Moreover, a theorem from calculus tells us that a composite function made up of "mostly differentiable" functions is itself mostly differentiable! Thus, we can think of

$f_1 f_2$ as just another function that we can compute derivatives of—and computing derivatives of composite functions will turn out to be essential for training deep learning models.

However, we need a formula to be able to compute this composite function's derivative in terms of the derivatives of its constituent functions. That's what we'll cover next.

# The Chain Rule

The chain rule is a mathematical theorem that lets us compute derivatives of composite functions. Deep learning models are, mathematically, composite functions, and reasoning about their derivatives is essential to training them, as we'll see in the next couple of chapters.

## Math

Mathematically, the theorem states—in a rather nonintuitive form—that, for a given value x,

$$\frac{df_2}{du}(x) = \frac{df_2}{du}(f_1(x)) \times \frac{df_1}{du}(x)$$

where $u$ is simply a dummy variable representing the input to a function.

 When describing the derivative of a function $f$ with one input and output, we can denote the *function* that represents the derivative of this function as $\frac{df}{du}$. We could use a different dummy variable in place of $u$—it doesn't matter, just as $f(x) = x^2$ and $f(y) = y^2$ mean the same thing.

On the other hand, later on we'll deal with functions that take in *multiple* inputs, say, both $x$ and $y$. Once we get there, it will make sense to write $\frac{df}{dx}$ and have it mean something different than $\frac{df}{dy}$.

This is why in the preceding formula we denote *all* the derivatives with a $u$ on the bottom: both $f_1$ and $f_2$ are functions that take in one input and produce one output, and in such cases (of functions with one input and one output) we'll use $u$ in the derivative notation.

## Diagram

The preceding formula does not give much intuition into the chain rule. For that, the box representation is much more helpful. Let's reason through what the derivative "should" be in the simple case of $f_1 f_2$.

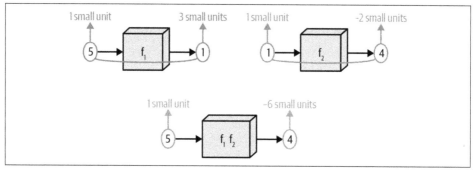

*Figure 1-8. An illustration of the chain rule*

Intuitively, using the diagram in Figure 1-8, the derivative of the composite function *should* be a sort of product of the derivatives of its constituent functions. Let's say we feed the value 5 into the first function, and let's say further that computing the *derivative* of the first function at $u = 5$ gives us a value of 3—that is, $\frac{df_1}{du}(5) = 3$.

Let's say that we then take the *value* of the function that comes out of the first box— let's suppose it is 1, so that $f_1(5) = 1$—and compute the derivative of the second function $f_2$ at this value: that is, $\frac{df_2}{du}(1)$. We find that this value is –2.

If we think about these functions as being literally strung together, then if changing the input to box two by 1 unit yields a change of –2 units in the output of box two, changing the input to box two by 3 units should change the output to box two by –2 × 3 = –6 units. This is why in the formula for the chain rule, the final result is ultimately a product: $\frac{df_2}{du}(f_1(x))$ *times* $\frac{df_1}{du}(x)$.

So by considering the diagram and the math, we can reason through what the derivative of the output of a nested function with respect to its input ought to be, using the chain rule. What might the code instructions for the computation of this derivative look like?

## Code

Let's code this up and show that computing derivatives in this way does in fact yield results that "look correct." We'll use the square function from "Basic functions in NumPy" on page 6 along with sigmoid, another function that ends up being important in deep learning:

```
def sigmoid(x: ndarray) -> ndarray:
    '''
    Apply the sigmoid function to each element in the input ndarray.
    '''
    return 1 / (1 + np.exp(-x))
```

And now we code up the chain rule:

```python
def chain_deriv_2(chain: Chain,
                  input_range: ndarray) -> ndarray:
    '''
    Uses the chain rule to compute the derivative of two nested functions:
    (f2(f1(x))' = f2'(f1(x)) * f1'(x)
    '''

    assert len(chain) == 2, \
    "This function requires 'Chain' objects of length 2"

    assert input_range.ndim == 1, \
    "Function requires a 1 dimensional ndarray as input_range"

    f1 = chain[0]
    f2 = chain[1]

    # df1/dx
    f1_of_x = f1(input_range)

    # df1/du
    df1dx = deriv(f1, input_range)

    # df2/du(f1(x))
    df2du = deriv(f2, f1(input_range))

    # Multiplying these quantities together at each point
    return df1dx * df2du
```

Figure 1-9 plots the results and shows that the chain rule works:

```python
PLOT_RANGE = np.arange(-3, 3, 0.01)

chain_1 = [square, sigmoid]
chain_2 = [sigmoid, square]

plot_chain(chain_1, PLOT_RANGE)
plot_chain_deriv(chain_1, PLOT_RANGE)

plot_chain(chain_2, PLOT_RANGE)
plot_chain_deriv(chain_2, PLOT_RANGE)
```

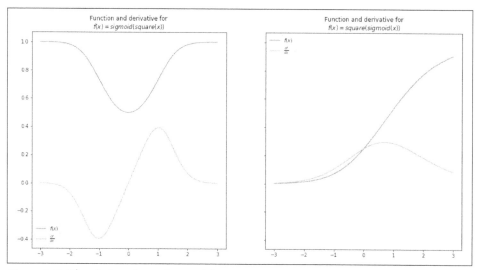

*Figure 1-9. The chain rule works, part 1*

The chain rule seems to be working. When the functions are upward-sloping, the derivative is positive; when they are flat, the derivative is zero; and when they are downward-sloping, the derivative is negative.

So we can in fact compute, both mathematically and via code, the derivatives of nested or "composite" functions such as $f_1 f_2$, as long as the individual functions are themselves mostly differentiable.

It will turn out that deep learning models are, mathematically, long chains of these mostly differentiable functions; spending time going manually through a slightly longer example in detail will help build your intuition about what is going on and how it can generalize to more complex models.

# A Slightly Longer Example

Let's closely examine a slightly longer chain: if we have three mostly differentiable functions—$f_1$, $f_2$, and $f_3$—how would we go about computing the derivative of $f_1 f_2 f_3$? We "should" be able to do it, since from the calculus theorem mentioned previously, we know that the composite of *any* finite number of "mostly differentiable" functions is differentiable.

## Math

Mathematically, the result turns out to be the following expression:

$$\frac{df_3}{du}(x) = \frac{df_3}{du}(f_2(f_1(x))) \times \frac{df_2}{du}(f_1(x)) \times \frac{df_1}{du}(x))$$

The underlying logic as to why the formula works for chains of length 2, $\frac{df_2}{du}(x) = \frac{df_2}{du}(f_1(x)) \times \frac{df_1}{du}(x)$, also applies here—as does the lack of intuition from looking at the formula alone!

## Diagram

The best way to (literally) see why this formula makes sense is via another box diagram, as shown in Figure 1-10.

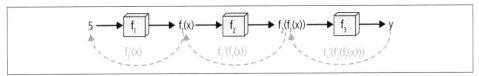

*Figure 1-10. The "box model" for computing the derivative of three nested functions*

Using similar reasoning to the prior section: if we imagine the input to $f_1 f_2 f_3$ (call it $a$) being connected to the output (call it $b$) by a string, then changing $a$ by a small amount $\Delta$ will result in a change in $f_1(a)$ of $\frac{df_1}{du}(x))$ times $\Delta$, which will result in a change to $f_2(f_1(x))$ (the next step along in the chain) of $\frac{df_2}{du}(f_1(x)) \times \frac{df_1}{du}(x))$ times $\Delta$, and so on for the third step, when we get to the final change equal to the full formula for the preceding chain rule times $\Delta$. Spend a bit of time going through this explanation and the earlier diagram—but not too much time, since we'll develop even more intuition for this when we code it up.

## Code

How might we translate such a formula into code instructions for computing the derivative, given the constituent functions? Interestingly, already in this simple example we see the beginnings of what will become the forward and backward passes of a neural network:

```
def chain_deriv_3(chain: Chain,
                  input_range: ndarray) -> ndarray:
    '''
    Uses the chain rule to compute the derivative of three nested functions:
    (f3(f2(f1)))' = f3'(f2(f1(x))) * f2'(f1(x)) * f1'(x)
    '''

    assert len(chain) == 3, \
    "This function requires 'Chain' objects to have length 3"
```

```
f1 = chain[0]
f2 = chain[1]
f3 = chain[2]

# f1(x)
f1_of_x = f1(input_range)

# f2(f1(x))
f2_of_x = f2(f1_of_x)

# df3du
df3du = deriv(f3, f2_of_x)

# df2du
df2du = deriv(f2, f1_of_x)

# df1dx
df1dx = deriv(f1, input_range)

# Multiplying these quantities together at each point
return df1dx * df2du * df3du
```

Something interesting took place here—to compute the chain rule for this nested function, we made two "passes" over it:

1. First, we went "forward" through it, computing the quantities f1_of_x and f2_of_x along the way. We can call this (and think of it as) "the forward pass."

2. Then, we "went backward" through the function, using the quantities that we computed on the forward pass to compute the quantities that make up the derivative.

Finally, we multiplied three of these quantities together to get our derivative.

Now, let's show that this works, using the three simple functions we've defined so far: sigmoid, square, and leaky_relu.

```
PLOT_RANGE = np.range(-3, 3, 0.01)
plot_chain([leaky_relu, sigmoid, square], PLOT_RANGE)
plot_chain_deriv([leaky_relu, sigmoid, square], PLOT_RANGE)
```

Figure 1-11 shows the result.

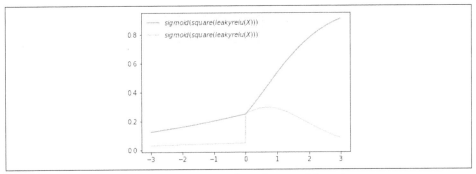

*Figure 1-11. The chain rule works, even with triply nested functions*

Again, comparing the plots of the derivatives to the slopes of the original functions, we see that the chain rule is indeed computing the derivatives properly.

Let's now apply our understanding to composite functions with multiple inputs, a class of functions that follows the same principles we already established and is ultimately more applicable to deep learning.

# Functions with Multiple Inputs

By this point, we have a conceptual understanding of how functions can be strung together to form composite functions. We also have a sense of how to represent these functions as series of boxes that inputs go into and outputs come out of. Finally, we've walked through how to compute the derivatives of these functions so that we understand these derivatives both mathematically and as quantities computed via a step-by-step process with a "forward" and "backward" component.

Oftentimes, the functions we deal with in deep learning don't have just one input. Instead, they have several inputs that at certain steps are added together, multiplied, or otherwise combined. As we'll see, computing the derivatives of the outputs of these functions with respect to their inputs is still no problem: let's consider a very simple scenario with multiple inputs, where two inputs are added together and then fed through another function.

## Math

For this example, it is actually useful to start by looking at the math. If our inputs are $x$ and $y$, then we could think of the function as occurring in two steps. In Step 1, $x$ and $y$ are fed through a function that adds them together. We'll denote that function as $\alpha$ (we'll use Greek letters to refer to function names throughout) and the output of the function as $a$. Formally, this is simply:

$$a = \alpha(x, y) = x + y$$

Step 2 would be to feed $a$ through some function $\sigma$ ($\sigma$ can be any continuous function, such as sigmoid, or the square function, or even a function whose name doesn't start with $s$). We'll denote the output of this function as $s$:

$$s = \sigma(a)$$

We could, equivalently, denote the entire function as $f$ and write:

$$f(x, y) = \sigma(x + y)$$

This is more mathematically concise, but it obscures the fact that this is really two operations happening sequentially. To illustrate that, we need the diagram in the next section.

## Diagram

Now that we're at the stage where we're examining functions with multiple inputs, let's pause to define a concept we've been dancing around: the diagrams with circles and arrows connecting them that represent the mathematical "order of operations" can be thought of as *computational graphs*. For example, Figure 1-12 shows a computational graph for the function $f$ we just described.

*Figure 1-12. Function with multiple inputs*

Here we see the two inputs going into $\alpha$ and coming out as $a$ and then being fed through $\sigma$.

## Code

Coding this up is very straightforward; note, however, that we have to add one extra assertion:

```
def multiple_inputs_add(x: ndarray,
                        y: ndarray,
                        sigma: Array_Function) -> float:
    '''
    Function with multiple inputs and addition, forward pass.
    '''
    assert x.shape == y.shape

    a = x + y
    return sigma(a)
```

Unlike the functions we saw earlier in this chapter, this function does not simply operate "elementwise" on each element of its input ndarrays. Whenever we deal with an operation that takes multiple ndarrays as inputs, we have to check their shapes to ensure they meet whatever conditions are required by that operation. Here, for a simple operation such as addition, all we need to check is that the shapes are identical so that the addition can happen elementwise.

# Derivatives of Functions with Multiple Inputs

It shouldn't seem surprising that we can compute the derivative of the output of such a function with respect to both of its inputs.

## Diagram

Conceptually, we simply do the same thing we did in the case of functions with one input: compute the derivative of each constituent function "going backward" through the computational graph and then multiply the results together to get the total derivative. This is shown in Figure 1-13.

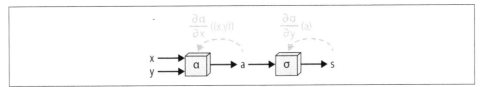

*Figure 1-13. Going backward through the computational graph of a function with multiple inputs*

## Math

The chain rule applies to these functions in the same way it applied to the functions in the prior sections. Since this is a nested function, with $f(x, y) = \sigma(\alpha(x, y))$, we have:

$$\frac{\partial f}{\partial x} = \frac{\partial \sigma}{\partial u}(\alpha(x, y)) \times \frac{\partial \alpha}{\partial x}((x, y)) = \frac{\partial \sigma}{\partial u}(x + y) \times \frac{\partial \alpha}{\partial x}((x, y))$$

And of course $\frac{\partial f}{\partial y}$ would be identical.

Now note that:

$$\frac{\partial \alpha}{\partial x}((x, y)) = 1$$

since for every unit increase in *x*, *a* increases by one unit, no matter the value of *x* (the same holds for *y*).

Given this, we can code up how we might compute the derivative of such a function.

## Code

```
def multiple_inputs_add_backward(x: ndarray,
                                 y: ndarray,
                                 sigma: Array_Function) -> float:
    '''
    Computes the derivative of this simple function with respect to
    both inputs.
    '''
    # Compute "forward pass"
    a = x + y

    # Compute derivatives
    dsda = deriv(sigma, a)

    dadx, dady = 1, 1

    return dsda * dadx, dsda * dady
```

A straightforward exercise for the reader is to modify this for the case where x and y are multiplied instead of added.

Next, we'll examine a more complicated example that more closely mimics what happens in deep learning: a similar function to the previous example, but with two *vector* inputs.

# Functions with Multiple Vector Inputs

In deep learning, we deal with functions whose inputs are *vectors* or *matrices*. Not only can these objects be added, multiplied, and so on, but they can also combined via a dot product or a matrix multiplication. In the rest of this chapter, I'll show how the mathematics of the chain rule and the logic of computing the derivatives of these functions using a forward and backward pass can still apply.

These techniques will end up being central to understanding why deep learning works. In deep learning, our goal will be to fit a model to some data. More precisely, this means that we want to find a mathematical function that maps *observations* from the data—which will be inputs to the function—to some desired *predictions* from the data—which will be the outputs of the function—in as optimal a way as possible. It turns out these observations will be encoded in matrices, typically with row as an observation and each column as a numeric feature for that observation. We'll cover this in more detail in the next chapter; for now, being able to reason about the derivatives of complex functions involving dot products and matrix multiplications will be essential.

Let's start by defining precisely what I mean, mathematically.

## Math

A typical way to represent a single data point, or "observation," in a neural network is as a row with $n$ features, where each feature is simply a number $x_1$, $x_2$, and so on, up to $x_n$:

$$X = \begin{bmatrix} x_1 & x_2 & \cdots & x_n \end{bmatrix}$$

A canonical example to keep in mind here is predicting housing prices, which we'll build a neural network from scratch to do in the next chapter; in this example, $x_1$, $x_2$, and so on are numerical features of a house, such as its square footage or its proximity to schools.

# Creating New Features from Existing Features

Perhaps the single most common operation in neural networks is to form a "weighted sum" of these features, where the weighted sum could emphasize certain features and de-emphasize others and thus be thought of as a new feature that itself is just a combination of old features. A concise way to express this mathematically is as a *dot product* of this observation, with some set of "weights" of the same length as the features, $w_1$, $w_2$, and so on, up to $w_n$. Let's explore this concept from the three perspectives we've used thus far in this chapter.

## Math

To be mathematically precise, if:

$$W = \begin{bmatrix} w_1 \\ w_2 \\ \vdots \\ w_n \end{bmatrix}$$

then we could define the output of this operation as:

$$N = v(X, W) = X \times W = x_1 \times w_1 + x_2 \times w_2 + \ldots + x_n \times w_n$$

Note that this operation is a special case of a *matrix multiplication* that just happens to be a dot product because $X$ has one row and $W$ has only one column.

Next, let's look at a few ways we could depict this with a diagram.

## Diagram

A simple way of depicting this operation is shown in Figure 1-14.

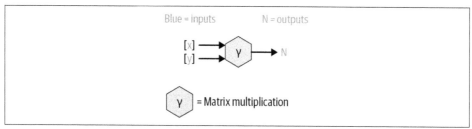

*Figure 1-14. Diagram of a vector dot product*

This diagram depicts an operation that takes in two inputs, both of which can be ndarrays, and produces one output ndarray.

But this is really a massive shorthand for many operations that are happening on many inputs. We could instead highlight the individual operations and inputs, as shown in Figures 1-15 and 1-16.

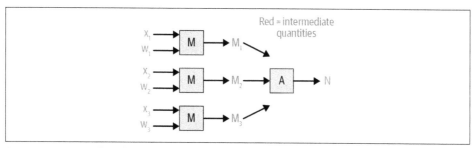

*Figure 1-15. Another diagram of a matrix multiplication*

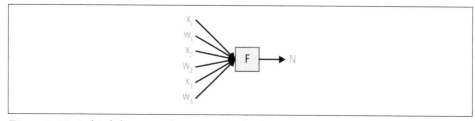

*Figure 1-16. A third diagram of a matrix multiplication*

The key point is that the dot product (or matrix multiplication) is a concise way to represent many individual operations; in addition, as we'll start to see in the next section, using this operation makes our derivative calculations on the backward pass extremely concise as well.

## Code

Finally, in code this operation is simply:

```
def matmul_forward(X: ndarray,
                   W: ndarray) -> ndarray:
    '''
    Computes the forward pass of a matrix multiplication.
    '''

    assert X.shape[1] == W.shape[0], \
    '''
    For matrix multiplication, the number of columns in the first array should
    match the number of rows in the second; instead the number of columns in the
    first array is {0} and the number of rows in the second array is {1}.
    '''.format(X.shape[1], W.shape[0])

    # matrix multiplication
    N = np.dot(X, W)

    return N
```

where we have a new assertion that ensures that the matrix multiplication will work. (This is necessary since this is our first operation that doesn't merely deal with ndarrays that are the same size and perform an operation elementwise—our output is now actually a different size than our input.)

# Derivatives of Functions with Multiple Vector Inputs

For functions that simply take one input as a number and produce one output, like $f(x) = x^2$ or $f(x) = \text{sigmoid}(x)$, computing the derivative is straightforward: we simply apply rules from calculus. For vector functions, it isn't immediately obvious what the derivative is: if we write a dot product as $v(X, W) = N$, as in the prior section, the question naturally arises—what would $\frac{\partial N}{\partial X}$ and $\frac{\partial N}{\partial W}$ be?

## Diagram

Conceptually, we just want to do something like in Figure 1-17.

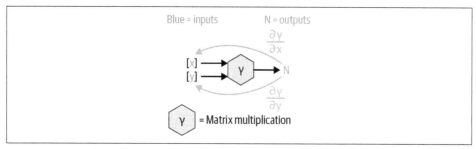

*Figure 1-17. Backward pass of a matrix multiplication, conceptually*

Calculating these derivatives was easy when we were just dealing with addition and multiplication, as in the prior examples. But how can we do the analogous thing with matrix multiplication? To define that precisely, we'll have to turn to the math.

## Math

First, how would we even define "the derivative with respect to a matrix"? Recalling that the matrix syntax is just shorthand for a bunch of numbers arranged in a particular form, "the derivative with respect to a matrix" really means "the derivative with respect to each element of the matrix." Since $X$ is a row, a natural way to define it is:

$$\frac{\partial v}{\partial X} = \begin{bmatrix} \frac{\partial v}{\partial x_1} & \frac{\partial v}{\partial x_2} & \frac{\partial v}{\partial x_3} \end{bmatrix}$$

However, the output of $v$ is just a number: $N = x_1 \times w_1 + x_2 \times w_2 + x_3 \times w_3$. And looking at this, we can see that if, for example, $x_1$ changes by $\epsilon$ units, then $N$ will change by $w_1 \times \epsilon$ units—and the same logic applies to the other $x_i$ elements. Thus:

$$\frac{\partial v}{\partial x_1} = w_1$$

$$\frac{\partial v}{\partial x_2} = w_2$$

$$\frac{\partial v}{\partial x_3} = w_3$$

And so:

$$\frac{\partial v}{\partial X} = \begin{bmatrix} w_1 & w_2 & w_3 \end{bmatrix} = W^T$$

This is a surprising and elegant result that turns out to be a key piece of the puzzle to understanding both why deep learning works and how it can be implemented so cleanly.

Using similar reasoning, we can see that:

$$\frac{\partial v}{\partial W} = \begin{bmatrix} x_1 \\ x_2 \\ x_3 \end{bmatrix} = X^T$$

## Code

Here, reasoning mathematically about what the answer "should" be was the hard part. The easy part is coding up the result:

```
def matmul_backward_first(X: ndarray,
                          W: ndarray) -> ndarray:
    '''
    Computes the backward pass of a matrix multiplication with respect to the
    first argument.
    '''

    # backward pass
    dNdX = np.transpose(W, (1, 0))

    return dNdX
```

The dNdX quantity computed here represents the partial derivative of each element of $X$ with respect to the sum of the output $N$. There is a special name for this quantity that we'll use throughout the book: we'll call it the *gradient* of $X$ with respect to $X$. The idea is that for an individual element of $X$—say, $x_3$—the corresponding element in dNdx (dNdX[2], to be specific) is the partial derivative of the output of the vector dot product $N$ with respect to $x_3$. The term "gradient" as we'll use it in this book simply refers to a multidimensional analogue of the partial derivative; specifically, it is an array of partial derivatives of the output of a function with respect to each element of the input to that function.

# Vector Functions and Their Derivatives: One Step Further

Deep learning models, of course, involve more than one operation: they include long chains of operations, some of which are vector functions like the one covered in the last section, and some of which simply apply a function elementwise to the ndarray they receive as input. Therefore, we'll now look at computing the derivative of a composite function that includes *both* kinds of functions. Let's suppose our function takes in the vectors $X$ and $W$, performs the dot product described in the prior section—which we'll denote as $v(X, W)$—and then feeds the vectors through a function $\sigma$. We'll express the same objective as before, but in new language: we want to compute the gradients of the output of this new function with respect to $X$ and $W$. Again, starting in the next chapter, we'll see in precise detail how this is connected to what neural networks do, but for now we just want to build up the idea that we can compute gradients for computational graphs of arbitrary complexity.

## Diagram

The diagram for this function, shown in Figure 1-18, is the same as in Figure 1-17, with the $\sigma$ function simply added onto the end.

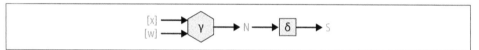

*Figure 1-18. Same graph as before, but with another function tacked onto the end*

## Math

Mathematically, this is straightforward as well:

$$s = f(X, W) = \sigma(v(X, W)) = \sigma(x_1 \times w_1 + x_2 \times w_2 + x_3 \times w_3)$$

## Code

Finally, we can code this function up as:

```
def matrix_forward_extra(X: ndarray,
                         W: ndarray,
                         sigma: Array_Function) -> ndarray:
    '''
    Computes the forward pass of a function involving matrix multiplication,
    one extra function.
    '''
    assert X.shape[1] == W.shape[0]

    # matrix multiplication
```

```
N = np.dot(X, W)

# feeding the output of the matrix multiplication through sigma
S = sigma(N)

return S
```

# Vector Functions and Their Derivatives: The Backward Pass

The backward pass is similarly just a straightforward extension of the prior example.

## Math

Since $f(X, W)$ is a nested function—specifically, $f(X, W) = \sigma(v(X, W))$—its derivative with respect to, for example, $X$ should conceptually be:

$$\frac{\partial f}{\partial X} = \frac{\partial \sigma}{\partial u}(v(X, W)) \times \frac{\partial v}{\partial X}(X, W)$$

But the first part of this is simply:

$$\frac{\partial \sigma}{\partial u}(v(X, W)) = \frac{\partial \sigma}{\partial u}(x_1 \times w_1 + x_2 \times w_2 + x_3 \times w_3)$$

which is well defined since $\sigma$ is just a continuous function whose derivative we can evaluate at any point, and here we are just evaluating it at $x_1 \times w_1 + x_2 \times w_2 + x_3 \times w_3$.

Furthermore, we reasoned in the prior example that $\frac{\partial v}{\partial X}(X, W) = W^T$. Therefore:

$$\frac{\partial f}{\partial X} = \frac{\partial \sigma}{\partial u}(v(X, W)) \times \frac{\partial v}{\partial X}(X, W) = \frac{\partial \sigma}{\partial u}(x_1 \times w_1 + x_2 \times w_2 + x_3 \times w_3) \times W^T$$

which, as in the preceding example, results in a vector of the same shape as $X$, since the final answer is a number, $\frac{\partial \sigma}{\partial u}(x_1 \times w_1 + x_2 \times w_2 + x_3 \times w_3)$, times a vector of the same shape as $X$ in $W^T$.

## Diagram

The diagram for the backward pass of this function, shown in Figure 1-19, is similar to that of the prior example and even higher level than the math; we just have to add one more multiplication based on the derivative of the $\sigma$ function evaluated at the result of the matrix multiplication.

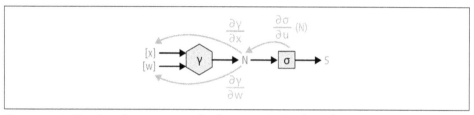

*Figure 1-19. Graph with a matrix multiplication: the backward pass*

## Code

Finally, coding up the backward pass is straightforward as well:

```
def matrix_function_backward_1(X: ndarray,
                               W: ndarray,
                               sigma: Array_Function) -> ndarray:
    '''
    Computes the derivative of our matrix function with respect to
    the first element.
    '''
    assert X.shape[1] == W.shape[0]

    # matrix multiplication
    N = np.dot(X, W)

    # feeding the output of the matrix multiplication through sigma
    S = sigma(N)

    # backward calculation
    dSdN = deriv(sigma, N)

    # dNdX
    dNdX = np.transpose(W, (1, 0))

    # multiply them together; since dNdX is 1x1 here, order doesn't matter
    return np.dot(dSdN, dNdX)
```

Notice that we see the same dynamic here that we saw in the earlier example with the three nested functions: we compute quantities on the forward pass (here, just N) that we then use during the backward pass.

## Is this right?

How can we tell if these derivatives we're computing are correct? A simple test is to perturb the input a little bit and observe the resulting change in output. For example, *X* in this case is:

```
print(X)

[[ 0.4723  0.6151 -1.7262]]
```

If we increase $x_3$ by *0.01*, from -1.726 to -1.716, we should see an increase in the value produced by the forward function of *the gradient of the output with respect to $x_3$* × *0.01*. Figure 1-20 shows this.

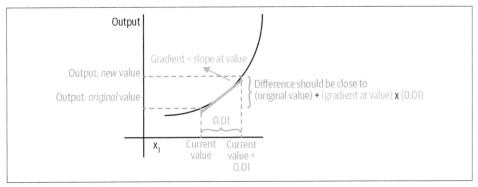

*Figure 1-20. Gradient checking: an illustration*

Using the `matrix_function_backward_1` function, we can see that the gradient is -0.1121:

```
print(matrix_function_backward_1(X, W, sigmoid))
```

```
[[ 0.0852 -0.0557 -0.1121]]
```

To test whether this gradient is correct, we should see, after incrementing $x_3$ by 0.01, a corresponding decrease in the *output* of the function by about `0.01 × -0.1121 = -0.001121`; if we saw an decrease by more or less than this amount, or an increase, for example, we would know that our reasoning about the chain rule was off. What we see when we do this calculation,[2] however, is that increasing $x_3$ by a small amount does indeed decrease the value of the output of the function by `0.01 × -0.1121`— which means the derivatives we're computing are correct!

To close out this chapter, we'll cover an example that builds on everything we've done so far and directly applies to the models we'll build in the next chapter: a computational graph that starts by multiplying a pair of two-dimensional matrices together.

# Computational Graph with Two 2D Matrix Inputs

In deep learning, and in machine learning more generally, we deal with operations that take as input two 2D arrays, one of which represents a batch of data $X$ and the other of which represents the weights $W$. In the next chapter, we'll dive deep into why this makes sense in a modeling context, but in this chapter we'll just focus on the

---

2 Throughout I'll provide links to relevant supplementary material on a GitHub repo that contains the code for the book, including for this chapter (*https://oreil.ly/2ZUwKOZ*).

mechanics and the math behind this operation. Specifically. we'll walk through a simple example in detail and show that even when multiplications of 2D matrices are involved, rather than just dot products of 1D vectors, the reasoning we've been using throughout this chapter still makes mathematical sense and is in fact extremely easy to code.

As before, the math needed to derive these results gets…not difficult, but messy. Nevertheless, the result is quite clean. And, of course, we'll break it down step by step and always connect it back to both code and diagrams.

## Math

Let's suppose that:

$$X = \begin{bmatrix} x_{11} & x_{12} & x_{13} \\ x_{21} & x_{22} & x_{23} \\ x_{31} & x_{32} & x_{33} \end{bmatrix}$$

and:

$$W = \begin{bmatrix} w_{11} & w_{12} \\ w_{21} & w_{22} \\ w_{31} & w_{32} \end{bmatrix}$$

This could correspond to a dataset in which each observation has three features, and the three rows could correspond to three different observations for which we want to make predictions.

Now we'll define the following straightforward operations to these matrices:

1. Multiply these matrices together. As before, we'll denote the function that does this as $v(X, W)$ and the output as $N$, so that $N = v(X, W)$.

2. Feed $N$ result through some differentiable function $\sigma$, and define $(S = \sigma(N)$.

As before, the question now is: what are the gradients of the output $S$ with respect to $X$ and $W$? Can we simply use the chain rule again? Why or why not?

If you think about this for a bit, you may realize that something is different from the previous examples that we've looked at: $S$ *is now a matrix*, not simply a number. And what, after all, does the gradient of one matrix with respect to another matrix mean?

This leads us to a subtle but important idea: we may perform whatever series of operations on multidimensional arrays we want, but for the notion of a "gradient" with respect to some output to be well defined, we need to *sum* (or otherwise aggregate into a single number) the final array in the sequence so that the notion of "how much will changing each element of $X$ affect the output" will even make sense.

So we'll tack onto the end a third function, *Lambda*, that simply takes the elements of $S$ and sums them up.

Let's make this mathematically concrete. First, let's multiply $X$ and $W$:

$$X \times W = \begin{bmatrix} x_{11} \times w_{11} + x_{12} \times w_{21} + x_{13} \times w_{31} & x_{11} \times w_{12} + x_{12} \times w_{22} + x_{13} \times w_{32} \\ x_{21} \times w_{11} + x_{22} \times w_{21} + x_{23} \times w_{31} & x_{21} \times w_{12} + x_{22} \times w_{22} + x_{23} \times w_{32} \\ x_{31} \times w_{11} + x_{32} \times w_{21} + x_{33} \times w_{31} & x_{31} \times w_{12} + x_{32} \times w_{22} + x_{33} \times w_{32} \end{bmatrix} = \begin{bmatrix} XW_{11} & XW_{12} \\ XW_{21} & XW_{22} \\ XW_{31} & XW_{32} \end{bmatrix}$$

where we denote row $i$ and column $j$ in the resulting matrix as $XW_{ij}$ for convenience.

Next, we'll feed this result through $\sigma$, which just means applying $\sigma$ to every element of the matrix $X \times W$:

$$\sigma(X \times W) = \begin{bmatrix} \sigma(x_{11} \times w_{11} + x_{12} \times w_{21} + x_{13} \times w_{31}) & \sigma(x_{11} \times w_{12} + x_{12} \times w_{22} + x_{13} \times w_{32}) \\ \sigma(x_{21} \times w_{11} + x_{22} \times w_{21} + x_{23} \times w_{31}) & \sigma(x_{21} \times w_{12} + x_{22} \times w_{22} + x_{23} \times w_{32}) \\ \sigma(x_{31} \times w_{11} + x_{32} \times w_{21} + x_{33} \times w_{31}) & \sigma(x_{31} \times w_{12} + x_{32} \times w_{22} + x_{33} \times w_{32}) \end{bmatrix}$$

$$= \begin{bmatrix} \sigma(XW_{11}) & \sigma(XW_{12}) \\ \sigma(XW_{21}) & \sigma(XW_{22}) \\ \sigma(XW_{31}) & \sigma(XW_{32}) \end{bmatrix}$$

Finally, we can simply sum up these elements:

$$L = \Lambda(\sigma(X \times W)) = \Lambda\left(\begin{bmatrix} \sigma(XW_{11}) & \sigma(XW_{12}) \\ \sigma(XW_{21}) & \sigma(XW_{22}) \\ \sigma(XW_{31}) & \sigma(XW_{32}) \end{bmatrix}\right) = \sigma(XW_{11}) + \sigma(XW_{12}) + \sigma(XW_{21})$$

$$+ \sigma(XW_{22}) + \sigma(XW_{31}) + \sigma(XW_{32})$$

Now we are back in a pure calculus setting: we have a number, $L$, and we want to figure out the gradient of $L$ with respect to $X$ and $W$; that is, we want to know how much changing *each element* of these input matrices ($x_{11}$, $w_{21}$, and so on) would change $L$. We can write this as:

$$\frac{\partial \Lambda}{\partial u}(X) = \begin{bmatrix} \frac{\partial \Lambda}{\partial u}(x_{11}) & \frac{\partial \Lambda}{\partial u}(x_{12}) & \frac{\partial \Lambda}{\partial u}(x_{13}) \\ \frac{\partial \Lambda}{\partial u}(x_{21}) & \frac{\partial \Lambda}{\partial u}(x_{22}) & \frac{\partial \Lambda}{\partial u}(x_{23}) \\ \frac{\partial \Lambda}{\partial u}(x_{31}) & \frac{\partial \Lambda}{\partial u}(x_{32}) & \frac{\partial \Lambda}{\partial u}(x_{33}) \end{bmatrix}$$

And now we understand mathematically the problem we are up against. Let's pause the math for a second and catch up with our diagram and code.

## Diagram

Conceptually, what we are doing here is similar to what we've done in the previous examples with a computational graph with multiple inputs; thus, Figure 1-21 should look familiar.

*Figure 1-21. Graph of a function with a complicated forward pass*

We are simply sending inputs forward as before. We claim that even in this more complicated scenario, we should be able to calculate the gradients we need using the chain rule.

## Code

We can code this up as:

```
def matrix_function_forward_sum(X: ndarray,
                                W: ndarray,
                                sigma: Array_Function) -> float:
    '''
    Computing the result of the forward pass of this function with
    input ndarrays X and W and function sigma.
    '''
    assert X.shape[1] == W.shape[0]

    # matrix multiplication
    N = np.dot(X, W)
```

```
# feeding the output of the matrix multiplication through sigma
S = sigma(N)

# sum all the elements
L = np.sum(S)

return L
```

# The Fun Part: The Backward Pass

Now we want to "perform the backward pass" for this function, showing how, even when a matrix multiplication is involved, we can end up calculating the gradient of N with respect to each of the elements of our input ndarrays.[3] With this final step figured out, starting to train real machine learning models in Chapter 2 will be straightforward. First, let's remind ourselves what we are doing, conceptually.

## Diagram

Again, what we're doing is similar to what we've done in the prior examples from this chapter; Figure 1-22 should look as familiar as Figure 1-21 did.

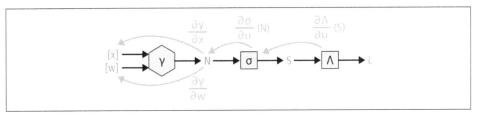

*Figure 1-22. Backward pass through our complicated function*

We simply need to calculate the partial derivative of each constituent function and evaluate it at its input, multiplying the results together to get the final derivative. Let's consider each of these partial derivatives in turn; the only way through it is through the math.

## Math

Let's first note that we could compute this directly. The value $L$ is indeed a function of $x_{11}$, $x_{12}$, and so on, all the way up to $x_{33}$.

However, that seems complicated. Wasn't the whole point of the chain rule that we can break down the derivatives of complicated functions into simple pieces, compute

---

3 In the following section we'll focus on computing the gradient of N with respect to X, but the gradient with respect to W could be reasoned through similarly.

each of those pieces, and then just multiply the results? Indeed, that fact was what made it so easy to code these things up: we just went step by step through the forward pass, saving the results as we went, and then we used those results to evaluate all the necessary derivatives for the backward pass.

I'll show that this approach only *kind of* works when there are matrices involved. Let's dive in.

We can write $L$ as $\Lambda(\sigma(v(X, W)))$. If this were a regular function, we would just write the chain rule:

$$\frac{\partial \Lambda}{\partial X}(X) = \frac{\partial v}{\partial X}(X, W) \times \frac{\partial \sigma}{\partial u}(N) \times \frac{\partial \Lambda}{\partial u}(S)$$

Then we would compute each of the three partial derivatives in turn. This is exactly what we did before in the function of three nested functions, for which we computed the derivative using the chain rule, and Figure 1-22 suggests that approach should work for this function as well.

The first derivative is the most straightforward and thus makes the best warm-up. We want to know how much $L$ (the output of $\Lambda$) will increase if each element of $S$ increases. Since $L$ is the sum of all the elements of $S$, this derivative is simply:

$$\frac{\partial \Lambda}{\partial u}(S) = \begin{bmatrix} 1 & 1 \\ 1 & 1 \\ 1 & 1 \end{bmatrix}$$

since increasing any element of $S$ by, say, 0.46 units would increase $\Lambda$ by 0.46 units.

Next, we have $\frac{\partial \sigma}{\partial u}(N)$. This is simply the derivative of whatever function $\sigma$ is, evaluated at the elements in $N$. In the "$XW$" syntax we've used previously, this is again simple to compute:

$$\begin{bmatrix} \frac{\partial \sigma}{\partial u}(XW_{11}) & \frac{\partial \sigma}{\partial u}(XW_{12}) \\ \frac{\partial \sigma}{\partial u}(XW_{21}) & \frac{\partial \sigma}{\partial u}(XW_{22}) \\ \frac{\partial \sigma}{\partial u}(XW_{31}) & \frac{\partial \sigma}{\partial u}(XW_{32}) \end{bmatrix}$$

Note that at this point we can say for certain that we can multiply these two derivatives together *elementwise* and compute $\frac{\partial L}{\partial u}(N)$:

---

$$\frac{\partial \Lambda}{\partial u}(N) = \frac{\partial \Lambda}{\partial u}(S) \times \frac{\partial \sigma}{\partial u}(N) = \begin{bmatrix} \frac{\partial \sigma}{\partial u}(XW_{11}) & \frac{\partial \sigma}{\partial u}(XW_{12}) \\ \frac{\partial \sigma}{\partial u}(XW_{21}) & \frac{\partial \sigma}{\partial u}(XW_{22}) \\ \frac{\partial \sigma}{\partial u}(XW_{31}) & \frac{\partial \sigma}{\partial u}(XW_{32}) \end{bmatrix} \times \begin{bmatrix} 1 & 1 \\ 1 & 1 \\ 1 & 1 \end{bmatrix} = \begin{bmatrix} \frac{\partial \sigma}{\partial u}(XW_{11}) & \frac{\partial \sigma}{\partial u}(XW_{12}) \\ \frac{\partial \sigma}{\partial u}(XW_{21}) & \frac{\partial \sigma}{\partial u}(XW_{22}) \\ \frac{\partial \sigma}{\partial u}(XW_{31}) & \frac{\partial \sigma}{\partial u}(XW_{32}) \end{bmatrix}$$

Now, however, we are stuck. The next thing we want, based on the diagram and applying the chain rule, is $\frac{\partial v}{\partial u}(X)$. Recall, however, that $N$, the output of $v$, was just the result of a matrix multiplication of $X$ with $W$. Thus we want some notion of how much increasing each element of $X$ (a $3 \times 3$ matrix) will increase each element of $N$ (a $3 \times 2$ matrix). If you're having trouble wrapping your mind around such a notion, that's the point—it isn't clear at all how we'd define this, or whether it would even be useful if we did.

Why is this a problem now? Before, we were in the fortunate situation of $X$ and $W$ being transposes of each other in terms of shape. That being the case, we could show that $\frac{\partial v}{\partial u}(X) = W^T$ and $\frac{\partial v}{\partial u}(W) = X^T$. Is there something analogous we can say here?

## The "?"

More specifically, here's where we're stuck. We need to figure out what goes in the "?":

$$\frac{\partial \Lambda}{\partial u}(X) = \frac{\partial \Lambda}{\partial u}(\sigma(N)) \times ? = \begin{bmatrix} \frac{\partial \sigma}{\partial u}(XW_{11}) & \frac{\partial \sigma}{\partial u}(XW_{12}) \\ \frac{\partial \sigma}{\partial u}(XW_{21}) & \frac{\partial \sigma}{\partial u}(XW_{22}) \\ \frac{\partial \sigma}{\partial u}(XW_{31}) & \frac{\partial \sigma}{\partial u}(XW_{32}) \end{bmatrix} \times ?$$

## The answer

It turns out that because of the way the multiplication works out, what fills the "?" is simply $W^T$, as in the simpler example with the vector dot product that we just saw! The way to verify this is to compute the partial derivative of $L$ with respect to each element of $X$ directly; when we do so,[4] the resulting matrix does indeed (remarkably) factor out into:

$$\frac{\partial \Lambda}{\partial u}(X) = \frac{\partial \Lambda}{\partial u}(S) \times \frac{\partial \sigma}{\partial u}(N) \times W^T$$

---

4  We do this in "Matrix Chain Rule" on page 221.

where the first multiplication is elementwise, and the second one is a matrix multiplication.

This means that *even if the operations in our computational graph involve multiplying matrices with multiple rows and columns, and even if the shapes of the outputs of those operations are different than those of the inputs, we can still include these operations in our computational graph and backpropagate through them using "chain rule" logic*. This is a critical result, without which training deep learning models would be much more cumbersome, as you'll appreciate further after the next chapter.

## Code

Let's encapsulate what we just derived using code, and hopefully solidify our understanding in the process:

```python
def matrix_function_backward_sum_1(X: ndarray,
                                    W: ndarray,
                                    sigma: Array_Function) -> ndarray:
    '''
    Compute derivative of matrix function with a sum with respect to the
    first matrix input.
    '''
    assert X.shape[1] == W.shape[0]

    # matrix multiplication
    N = np.dot(X, W)

    # feeding the output of the matrix multiplication through sigma
    S = sigma(N)

    # sum all the elements
    L = np.sum(S)

    # note: I'll refer to the derivatives by their quantities here,
    # unlike the math, where we referred to their function names

    # dLdS - just 1s
    dLdS = np.ones_like(S)

    # dSdN
    dSdN = deriv(sigma, N)

    # dLdN
    dLdN = dLdS * dSdN

    # dNdX
    dNdX = np.transpose(W, (1, 0))

    # dLdX
    dLdX = np.dot(dSdN, dNdX)
```

```
    return dLdX
```

Now let's verify that everything worked:

```
np.random.seed(190204)
X = np.random.randn(3, 3)
W = np.random.randn(3, 2)

print("X:")
print(X)

print("L:")
print(round(matrix_function_forward_sum(X, W, sigmoid), 4))
print()
print("dLdX:")
print(matrix_function_backward_sum_1(X, W , sigmoid))

X:
[[-1.5775 -0.6664  0.6391]
 [-0.5615  0.7373 -1.4231]
 [-1.4435 -0.3913  0.1539]]
L:
2.3755

dLdX:
[[ 0.2489 -0.3748  0.0112]
 [ 0.126  -0.2781 -0.1395]
 [ 0.2299 -0.3662 -0.0225]]
```

As in the previous example, since dLdX represents the gradient of $X$ with respect to $L$, this means that, for instance, the top-left element indicates that $\frac{\partial \Lambda}{\partial x_{11}}(X, W) = 0.2489$.

Thus, if the matrix math for this example was correct, then increasing $x_{11}$ by 0.001 should increase $L$ by 0.01 × 0.2489. Indeed, we see that this is what happens:

```
X1 = X.copy()
X1[0, 0] += 0.001

print(round(
        (matrix_function_forward_sum(X1, W, sigmoid) - \
         matrix_function_forward_sum(X, W, sigmoid)) / 0.001, 4))

0.2489
```

Looks like the gradients were computed correctly!

### Describing these gradients visually

To bring this back to what we noted at the beginning of the chapter, we fed the element in question, $x_{11}$, through a function with many operations: there was a matrix multiplication—which was really shorthand for combining the nine inputs in the matrix $X$ with the six inputs in the matrix $W$ to create six outputs—the sigmoid function, and then the sum. Nevertheless, we can also think of this as a single function called, say, "*WNSL*, "as depicted in Figure 1-23.

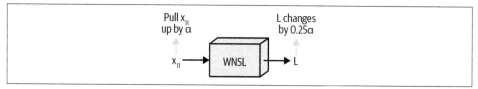

*Figure 1-23. Another way of describing the nested function: as one function, "WNSL"*

Since each function is differentiable, the whole thing is just a single differentiable function, with $x_{11}$ as an input; thus, the gradient is simply the answer to the question, what is $\frac{dL}{dx_{11}}$? To visualize this, we can simply plot how $L$ changes as $x_{11}$ changes. Looking at the initial value of $x_{11}$, we see that it is -1.5775:

```
print("X:")
print(X)

X:
[[-1.5775 -0.6664  0.6391]
 [-0.5615  0.7373 -1.4231]
 [-1.4435 -0.3913  0.1539]]
```

If we plot the value of $L$ that results from feeding $X$ and $W$ into the computational graph defined previously—or, to represent it differently, from feeding X and W into the function called in the preceding code—changing nothing except the value for $x_{11}$ (or X[0, 0]), the resulting plot looks like Figure 1-24.[5]

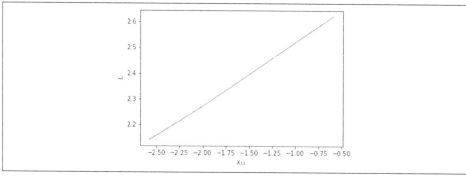

*Figure 1-24. L versus $x_{11}$, holding other values of X and W constant*

---

5 The full function can be found on the book's website (*https://oreil.ly/deep-learning-github*); it is simply a subset of the `matrix function backward sum` function shown on the previous page.

Indeed, eyeballing this relationship in the case of $x_{11}$, it looks like the distance this function increases along the $L$-axis is roughly 0.5 (from just over 2.1 to just over 2.6), and we know that we are showing a change of 2 along the $x_{11}$-axis, which would make the slope roughly $\frac{0.5}{2} = 0.25$—which is exactly what we just calculated!

So our complicated matrix math does in fact seem to have resulted in us correctly computing the partial derivative $L$ with respect to each element of $X$. Furthermore, the gradient of $L$ with respect to $W$ could be computed similarly.

The expression for the gradient of $L$ with respect to $W$ would be $X^T$. However, because of the order in which the $X^T$ expression factors out of the derivative for $L$, $X^T$ would be on the *left* side of the expression for the gradient of $L$ with respect to $W$:

$$\frac{\partial \Lambda}{\partial u}(W) = X^T \times \frac{\partial \Lambda}{\partial u}(S) \times \frac{\partial \sigma}{\partial u}(N)$$

In code, therefore, while we would have dNdW = np.transpose(X, (1, 0)), the next step would be:

```
dLdW = np.dot(dNdW, dSdN)
```

instead of dLdX = np.dot(dSdN, dNdX) as before.

# Conclusion

After this chapter, you should have confidence that you can understand complicated nested mathematical functions and reason out how they work by conceptualizing them as a series of boxes, each one representing a single constituent function, connected by strings. Specifically, you can write code to compute the derivatives of the outputs of such functions with respect to any of the inputs, even when there are matrix multiplications involving two-dimensional ndarrays involved, and understand the math behind *why* these derivative computations are correct. These foundational concepts are exactly what we'll need to start building and training neural networks in the next chapter, and to build and train deep learning models from scratch in the chapters after that. Onward!

## CHAPTER 2

# Fundamentals

In Chapter 1, I described the major conceptual building block for understanding deep learning: nested, continuous, differentiable functions. I showed how to represent these functions as computational graphs, with each node in a graph representing a single, simple function. In particular, I demonstrated that such a representation showed easily how to calculate the derivative of the output of the nested function with respect to its input: we simply take the derivatives of all the constituent functions, evaluate these derivatives at the input that these functions received, and then multiply all of the results together; this will result in a correct derivative for the nested function because of the chain rule. I illustrated that this does in fact work with some simple examples, with functions that took NumPy's ndarrays as inputs and produced ndarrays as outputs.

I showed that this method of computing derivatives works even when the function takes in multiple ndarrays as inputs and combines them via a *matrix multiplication* operation, which, unlike the other operations we saw, changes the shape of its inputs. Specifically, if one input to this operation—call the input $X$—is a B × N ndarray, and another input to this operation, $W$, is an N × M ndarray, then its output $P$ is a B × M ndarray. While it isn't clear what the derivative of such an operation would be, I showed that when a matrix multiplication $v(X, W)$ is included as a "constituent operation" in a nested function, we can still use a simple expression *in place of* its derivative to compute the derivatives of its inputs: specifically, the role of $\frac{\partial v}{\partial u}(W)$ can be filled by $X^T$, and the role of $\frac{\partial v}{\partial u}(X)$ can be played by $W^T$.

In this chapter, we'll start translating these concepts into real-world applications, Specifically, we will:

1. Express linear regression in terms of these building blocks

2. Show that the reasoning around derivatives that we did in Chapter 1 allows us to train this linear regression model

3. Extend this model (still using our building blocks) to a one-layer neural network

Then, in Chapter 3, it will be straightforward to use these same building blocks to build deep learning models.

Before we dive into all this, though, let's give an overview of *supervised learning*, the subset of machine learning that we'll focus on as we see how to use neural networks to solve problems.

# Supervised Learning Overview

At a high level, machine learning can be described as building algorithms that can uncover or "learn" *relationships* in data; supervised learning can be described as the subset of machine learning dedicated to finding relationships *between characteristics of the data that have already been measured.*[1]

In this chapter, we'll deal with a typical supervised learning problem that you might encounter in the real world: finding the relationship between characteristics of a house and the value of the house. Clearly, there is some relationship between characteristics such as the number of rooms, the square footage, or the proximity to schools and how desirable a house is to live in or own. At a high level, the aim of supervised learning is to uncover these relationships, given that we've *already measured* these characteristics.

By "measure," I mean that each characteristic has been defined precisely and represented as a number. Many characteristics of a house, such as the number of bedrooms, the square footage, and so on, naturally lend themselves to being represented as numbers, but if we had other, different kinds of information, such as natural language descriptions of the house's neighborhood from TripAdvisor, this part of the problem would be much less straightforward, and doing the translation of this less-structured data into numbers in a reasonable way could make or break our ability to uncover relationships. In addition, for any concept that is ambiguously defined, such as the value of a house, we simply have to pick a single number to describe it; here, an obvious choice is to use the price of the house.[2]

---

1 The other kind of machine learning, *un*supervised learning, can be thought of as finding relationships between things you have measured and things that have not been measured yet.

2 Though in a real-world problem, even how to choose a price isn't obvious: would it be the price the house last sold for? What about a house that hasn't been on the market for a long time? In this book, we'll focus on examples in which the numeric representation of the data is obvious or has been decided for you, but in many real-world problems, getting this right is critical.

Once we've translated our "characteristics" into numbers, we have to decide what structure to use to represent these numbers. One that is nearly universal across machine learning and turns out to make computations easy is to represent each set of numbers for a single observation—for example, a single house—as a *row* of data, and then stack these rows on top of each other to form "batches" of data that will get fed into our models as two-dimensional `ndarrays`. Our models will then return predictions as output `ndarrays` with each prediction in a row, similarly stacked on top of each other, with one prediction for each observation in the batch.

Now for some definitions: we say that the length of each row in this `ndarray` is the number of *features* of our data. In general, a single characteristic can map to many features, a classic example being a characteristic that describes our data as belonging to one of several *categories*, such as being a red brick house, a tan brick house, or a slate house;[3] in this specific case we might describe this single characteristic with three features. The process of mapping what we informally think of as characteristics of our observations into features is called *feature engineering*. I won't spend much time discussing this process in this book; indeed, in this chapter we'll deal with a problem in which we have 13 characteristics of each observation, and we simply represent each characteristic with a single numeric feature.

I said that the goal of supervised learning is ultimately to uncover relationships between characteristics of data. In practice, we do this by choosing one characteristic that we want to predict from the others; we call this characteristic our *target*. The choice of which characteristic to use as the target is completely arbitrary and depends on the problem you are trying to solve. For example, if your goal is just to *describe* the relationship between the prices of houses and the number of rooms they have, you could do this by training a model with the prices of houses as the target and the number of rooms as a feature, or vice versa; either way, the resulting model will indeed contain a description of the relationship between these two characteristics, allowing you to say, for example, a higher number of rooms in a house is associated with higher prices. On the other hand, if your goal is to *predict* the prices of houses *for which no price information is available*, you have to choose the price as your target, so that you can ultimately feed the other information into your model once it is trained.

Figure 2-1 shows this hierarchy of descriptions of supervised learning, from the highest-level description of finding relationships in data, to the lowest level of quantifying those relationships by training models to uncover numerical representations between the features and the target.

---

3 Most of you probably know that these are called "categorical" features.

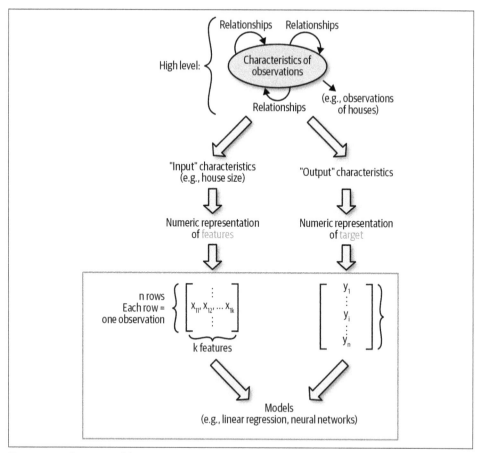

*Figure 2-1. Supervised learning overview*

As mentioned, we'll spend almost all our time on the level highlighted at the bottom of Figure 2-1; nevertheless, in many problems, getting the parts at the top correct—collecting the right data, defining the problem you are trying to solve, and doing feature engineering—is much harder than the actual modeling. Still, since this book is focused on modeling—specifically, on understanding how deep learning models work—let's return to that subject.

## Supervised Learning Models

Now we know at a high level what supervised learning models are trying to do—and as I alluded to earlier in the chapter, such models are just nested, mathematical functions. We spent the last chapter seeing how to represent such functions in terms of diagrams, math, and code, so now I can state the goal of supervised learning more precisely in terms of both math and code (I'll show plenty of diagrams later): the goal is to *find* (a mathematical function) / (a function that takes an `ndarray` as input and produces an `ndarray` as output) that can (map characteristics of observations to the target) / (given an input `ndarray` containing the features we created, produce an output `ndarray` whose values are "close to" the `ndarray` containing the target).

Specifically, our data will be represented in a matrix $X$ with $n$ rows, each of which represents an observation with $k$ features, all of which are numbers. Each row observation will be a vector, as in $x_i = \begin{bmatrix} x_{i1} & x_{i2} & x_{i3} & \cdots & x_{ik} \end{bmatrix}$, and these observations will be stacked on top of one another to form a batch. For example, a batch of size 3 would look like:

$$X_{batch} = \begin{bmatrix} x_{11} & x_{12} & x_{13} & \cdots & x_{1k} \\ x_{21} & x_{22} & x_{23} & \cdots & x_{2k} \\ x_{31} & x_{32} & x_{33} & \cdots & x_{3k} \end{bmatrix}$$

For each batch of observations, we will have a corresponding batch of *targets*, each element of which is the target number for the corresponding observation. We can represent these in a one-dimensional vector:

$$\begin{bmatrix} y_1 \\ y_2 \\ y_3 \end{bmatrix}$$

In terms of these arrays, our goal with supervised learning will be to use the tools I described in the last chapter to build a function that can take as input batches of observations with the structure of $X_{batch}$ and produce vectors of values $p_i$—which we'll interpret as "predictions"—that (for data in our particular dataset $X$, at least) are "close to the target values" $y_i$ for some reasonable measure of closeness.

Finally, we are ready to make all of this concrete and start building our first model for a real-world dataset. We'll start with a straightforward model—*linear regression*—and show how to express it in terms of the building blocks from the prior chapter.

# Linear Regression

Linear regression is often shown as:

$$y_i = \beta_0 + \beta_1 \times x_1 + \dots + \beta_n \times x_k + \epsilon$$

This representation describes mathematically our belief that the numeric value of each target is a linear combination of the $k$ features of $X$, plus the $\beta_0$ term to adjust the "baseline" value of the prediction (specifically, the prediction that will be made when the value of all of the features is 0).

This, of course, doesn't give us much insight into how we would code this up so that we could "train" such a model. To do that, we have to translate this model into the language of the functions we saw in Chapter 1; the best place to start is with a diagram.

## Linear Regression: A Diagram

How can we represent linear regression as a computational graph? We *could* break it down all the way to the individual elements, with each $x_i$ being multiplied by another element $w_i$ and then the results being added together, as in Figure 2-2.

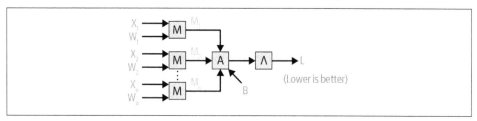

*Figure 2-2. The operations of a linear regression shown at the level of individual multiplications and additions*

But again, as we saw in Chapter 1, if we can represent these operations as just a matrix multiplication, we'll be able to write the function more concisely while still being able to correctly calculate the derivative of the output with respect to the input, which will allow us to train the model.

How can we do this? First, let's handle the simpler scenario in which we don't have an intercept term ($\beta_0$ shown previously). Note that we can represent the output of a linear regression model as the *dot product* of each observation vector $x_i = \begin{bmatrix} x_1 & x_2 & x_3 & \cdots & x_k \end{bmatrix}$ with another vector of parameters that we'll call $W$:

$$W = \begin{bmatrix} w_1 \\ w_2 \\ w_3 \\ \vdots \\ w_k \end{bmatrix}$$

Our prediction would then simply be:

$$p_i = x_i \times W = w_1 \times x_{i1} + w_2 \times x_{i2} + ... + w_k \times x_{ik}$$

So, we can represent "generating the predictions" for a linear regression using a single operation: the dot product.

Furthermore, when we want to make predictions using linear regression with a batch of observations, we can use another, single operation: the matrix multiplication. If we have a batch of size 3, for example:

$$X_{batch} = \begin{bmatrix} x_{11} & x_{12} & x_{13} & \cdots & x_{1k} \\ x_{21} & x_{22} & x_{23} & \cdots & x_{2k} \\ x_{31} & x_{32} & x_{33} & \cdots & x_{3k} \end{bmatrix}$$

then performing the *matrix multiplication* of this batch $X_{batch}$ with $W$ gives a vector of predictions for the batch, as desired:

$$P_{batch} = X_{batch} \times W = \begin{bmatrix} x_{11} & x_{12} & x_{13} & \cdots & x_{1k} \\ x_{21} & x_{22} & x_{23} & \cdots & x_{2k} \\ x_{31} & x_{32} & x_{33} & \cdots & x_{3k} \end{bmatrix} \times \begin{bmatrix} w_1 \\ w_2 \\ w_3 \\ \vdots \\ w_k \end{bmatrix} =$$

$$\begin{bmatrix} x_{11} \times w_1 + x_{12} \times w_2 + x_{13} \times w_3 + ... + x_{1k} \times w_k \\ x_{21} \times w_1 + x_{22} \times w_2 + x_{23} \times w_3 + ... + x_{2k} \times w_k \\ x_{31} \times w_1 + x_{32} \times w_2 + x_{33} \times w_3 + ... + x_{3k} \times w_k \end{bmatrix} = \begin{bmatrix} p_1 \\ p_2 \\ p_3 \end{bmatrix}$$

So generating predictions for a batch of observations in a linear regression can be done with a matrix multiplication. Next, I'll show how to use this fact, along with the reasoning about derivatives from the prior chapter, to train this model.

## "Training" this model

What does it mean to "train" a model? At a high level, models[4] take in data, combine them with *parameters* in some way, and produce predictions. For example, the linear

---

4 At least the ones we'll see in this book.

regression model shown earlier takes in data $X$ and parameters $W$ and produces the predictions $p_{batch}$ using a matrix multiplication:

$$p_{batch} = \begin{bmatrix} p_1 \\ p_2 \\ p_3 \end{bmatrix}$$

To train our model, however, we need another crucial piece of information: whether or not these predictions are good. To learn this, we bring in the vector of *targets* $y_{batch}$ associated with the batch of observations $X_{batch}$ fed into the function, and we compute a *single number* that is a function of $y_{batch}$ and $p_{batch}$ and that represents the model's "penalty" for making the predictions that it did. A reasonable choice is *mean squared error*, which is simply the average squared value that our model's predictions "missed" by:

$$MSE\big(p_{batch}, y_{batch}\big) = MSE\left(\begin{bmatrix} p_1 \\ p_2 \\ p_3 \end{bmatrix}, \begin{bmatrix} y_1 \\ y_2 \\ y_3 \end{bmatrix}\right) = \frac{(y_1 - p_1)^2 + (y_2 - p_2)^2 + (y_3 - p_3)^2}{3}$$

Getting to this number, which we can call $L$, is key: once we have it, we can use all the techniques we saw in Chapter 1 to compute the *gradient* of this number with respect to each element of $W$. Then *we can use these derivatives to update each element of $W$ in the direction that would cause $L$ to decrease*. Repeating this procedure many times, we hope, will "train" our model; in this chapter, we'll see that this can indeed work in practice. To see clearly how to compute these gradients, we'll complete the process of representing linear regression as a computational graph.

## Linear Regression: A More Helpful Diagram (and the Math)

Figure 2-3 shows how to represent linear regression in terms of the diagrams from the last chapter.

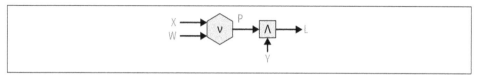

*Figure 2-3. The linear regression equations expressed as a computational graph—the dark blue letters are the data inputs to the function, and the light blue W denotes the weights*

Finally, to reinforce that we're still representing a nested mathematical function with this diagram, we could represent the loss value $L$ that we ultimately compute as:

$$L = \Lambda((\nu(X, W), Y)$$

## Adding in the Intercept

Representing models as diagrams shows us conceptually how we can add an intercept to the model. We simply add an extra step at the end that involves adding a "bias," as shown in Figure 2-4.

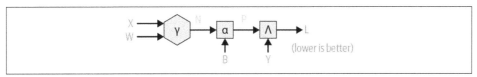

*Figure 2-4. The computational graph of linear regression, with the addition of a bias term at the end*

Here, though, we should reason mathematically about what is going on before moving on to the code; with the bias added, each element of our model's prediction $p_i$ will be the dot product described earlier with the quantity $b$ added to it:

$$P_{batch\_with\_bias} = x_i \text{dot} W + b = \begin{bmatrix} x_{11} \times w_1 + x_{12} \times w_2 + x_{13} \times w_3 + \dots + x_{1k} \times w_k + b \\ x_{21} \times w_1 + x_{22} \times w_2 + x_{23} \times w_3 + \dots + x_{2k} \times w_k + b \\ x_{31} \times w_1 + x_{32} \times w_2 + x_{33} \times w_3 + \dots + x_{3k} \times w_k + b \end{bmatrix} = \begin{bmatrix} p_1 \\ p_2 \\ p_3 \end{bmatrix}$$

Note that because the intercept in linear regression should be just a single number rather than being different for each observation, the *same number* should get added to each observation of the input to the bias operation that is passed in; we'll discuss what this means for computing the derivatives in a later section of this chapter.

## Linear Regression: The Code

We'll now tie things together and code up the function that makes predictions and computes losses given batches of observations $X_{batch}$ and their corresponding targets $y_{batch}$. Recall that computing derivatives for nested functions using the chain rule involves two sets of steps: first, we perform a "forward pass," passing the input successively forward through a series of operations and saving the quantities computed as we go; then we use those quantities to compute the appropriate derivatives during the backward pass.

The following code does this, saving the quantities computed on the forward pass in a dictionary; furthermore, to differentiate between the quantities computed on the forward pass and the parameters themselves (which we'll also need for the backward pass), our function will expect to receive a dictionary containing the parameters:

```
def forward_linear_regression(X_batch: ndarray,
                              y_batch: ndarray,
                              weights: Dict[str, ndarray])
                              -> Tuple[float, Dict[str, ndarray]]:
    '''
    Forward pass for the step-by-step linear regression.
    '''
    # assert batch sizes of X and y are equal
    assert X_batch.shape[0] == y_batch.shape[0]

    # assert that matrix multiplication can work
    assert X_batch.shape[1] == weights['W'].shape[0]

    # assert that B is simply a 1x1 ndarray
    assert weights['B'].shape[0] == weights['B'].shape[1] == 1

    # compute the operations on the forward pass
    N = np.dot(X_batch, weights['W'])

    P = N + weights['B']

    loss = np.mean(np.power(y_batch - P, 2))

    # save the information computed on the forward pass
    forward_info: Dict[str, ndarray] = {}
    forward_info['X'] = X_batch
    forward_info['N'] = N
    forward_info['P'] = P
    forward_info['y'] = y_batch

    return loss, forward_info
```

Now we have all the pieces in place to start "training" this model. Next, we'll cover exactly what this means and how we'll do it.

## Training the Model

We are now going to use all the tools we learned in the last chapter to compute $\frac{\partial L}{\partial w_i}$ for every $w_i$ in $W$, as well as $\frac{\partial L}{\partial b}$. How? Well, since the "forward pass" of this function was passing the input through a series of nested functions, the backward pass will simply involve computing the partial derivatives of each function, evaluating those derivatives at the functions' inputs, and multiplying them together—and even though a matrix multiplication is involved, we'll be able to handle this using the reasoning we covered in the last chapter.

## Calculating the Gradients: A Diagram

Conceptually, we want something like what is depicted in Figure 2-5.

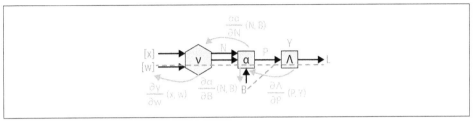

*Figure 2-5. The backward pass through the linear regression computational graph*

We simply step backward, computing the derivative of each constituent function and evaluating those derivatives at the inputs that those functions received on the forward pass, and then multiplying these derivatives together at the end. This is straightforward enough, so let's get into the details.

## Calculating the Gradients: The Math (and Some Code)

From Figure 2-5, we can see that the derivative product that we ultimately want to compute is:

$$\frac{\partial \Lambda}{\partial P}(P, Y) \times \frac{\partial \alpha}{\partial N}(N, B) \times \frac{\partial \nu}{\partial W}(X, W)$$

There are three components here; let's compute each of them in turn.

First up: $\frac{\partial \Lambda}{\partial P}(P, Y)$. Since $\Lambda(P, Y) = (Y - P)^2$ for each element in $Y$ and $P$:

$$\frac{\partial \Lambda}{\partial P}(P, Y) = -1 \times (2 \times (Y - P))$$

We're jumping ahead of ourselves a bit, but note that coding this up would simply be:

```
dLdP = -2 * (Y - P)
```

Next, we have an expression involving matrices: $\frac{\partial \alpha}{\partial N}(N, B)$. But since $\alpha$ is just addition, the same logic that we reasoned through with numbers in the prior chapter applies here: increasing any element of $N$ by one unit will increase $P = \alpha(N, B) = N + B$ by one unit. Thus, $\frac{\partial \alpha}{\partial N}(N, B)$ is just a matrix of +1+s, of the same shape as $N$.

Coding *this* expression, therefore, would simply be:

```
dPdN = np.ones_like(N)
```

Finally, we have $\frac{\partial v}{\partial W}(X, W)$. As we discussed in detail in the last chapter, when computing derivatives of nested functions where one of the constituent functions is a matrix multiplication, we can act *as if*:

$$\frac{\partial v}{\partial W}(X, W) = X^T$$

which in code is simply:

```
dNdW = np.transpose(X, (1, 0))
```

We'll do the same for the intercept term; since we are just adding it, the partial derivative of the intercept term with respect to the output is simply 1:

```
dPdB = np.ones_like(weights['B'])
```

The last step is to simply multiply these together, making sure we use the correct order for the matrix multiplications involving dNdW and dNdX based on what we reasoned through at the end of the last chapter.

## Calculating the Gradients: The (Full) Code

Recall that our goal is to take everything computed on or inputed into the forward pass—which, from the diagram in Figure 2-5, will include X, W, N, B, P, and y—and compute $\frac{\partial \Lambda}{\partial W}$ and $\frac{\partial \Lambda}{\partial B}$. The following code does that, receiving W and B as inputs in a dictionary called `weights` and the rest of the quantities in a dictionary called `for ward_info`:

```
def loss_gradients(forward_info: Dict[str, ndarray],
                   weights: Dict[str, ndarray]) -> Dict[str, ndarray]:
    '''
    Compute dLdW and dLdB for the step-by-step linear regression model.
    '''
    batch_size = forward_info['X'].shape[0]

    dLdP = -2 * (forward_info['y'] - forward_info['P'])

    dPdN = np.ones_like(forward_info['N'])

    dPdB = np.ones_like(weights['B'])

    dLdN = dLdP * dPdN

    dNdW = np.transpose(forward_info['X'], (1, 0))

    # need to use matrix multiplication here,
    # with dNdW on the left (see note at the end of last chapter)
    dLdW = np.dot(dNdW, dLdN)
```

```
# need to sum along dimension representing the batch size
# (see note near the end of this chapter)
dLdB = (dLdP * dPdB).sum(axis=0)

loss_gradients: Dict[str, ndarray] = {}
loss_gradients['W'] = dLdW
loss_gradients['B'] = dLdB

return loss_gradients
```

As you can see, we simply compute the derivatives with respect to each operation and successively multiply them together, taking care that we do the matrix multiplication in the right order.[5] As we'll see shortly, this actually works—and after the intuition we built up around the chain rule in the last chapter, this shouldn't be too surprising.

> An implementation detail about those loss gradients: we're storing them as a dictionary, with the names of the weights as keys and the amounts that increasing the weights affect the losses as values. The weights dictionary is structured the same way. Therefore, we'll iterate through the weights in our model in the following way:
>
> ```
> for key in weights.keys():
>     weights[key] -= learning_rate * loss_grads[key]
> ```
>
> There is nothing special about storing them in this way; if we stored them differently, we would simply iterate through them and refer to them differently.

## Using These Gradients to Train the Model

Now we'll simply run the following procedure over and over again:

1. Select a batch of data.
2. Run the forward pass of the model.
3. Run the backward pass of the model using the info computed on the forward pass.
4. Use the gradients computed on the backward pass to update the weights.

The Jupyter Notebook (*https://oreil.ly/2TDV5q9*) for this chapter of the book includes a train function that codes this up. It isn't too interesting; it simply implements the preceding steps and adds a few sensible things such as shuffling the data to ensure that it is fed through in a random order. The key lines, which get repeated inside of a for loop, are these:

---

5 In addition, we have to sum dLdB along axis 0; we explain this step in more detail later in this chapter.

```
forward_info, loss = forward_loss(X_batch, y_batch, weights)

loss_grads = loss_gradients(forward_info, weights)

for key in weights.keys():  # 'weights' and 'loss_grads' have the same keys
    weights[key] -= learning_rate * loss_grads[key]
```

Then we run the `train` function for a certain number of *epochs*, or cycles through the entire training dataset, as follows:

```
train_info = train(X_train, y_train,
                   learning_rate = 0.001,
                   batch_size=23,
                   return_weights=True,
                   seed=80718)
```

The `train` function returns `train_info`, a `Tuple`, one element of which is the parameters or *weights* that represent what the model has learned.

The terms "parameters" and "weights" are used interchangeably throughout deep learning, so we will use them interchangeably in this book.

# Assessing Our Model: Training Set Versus Testing Set

To understand whether our model uncovered relationships in our data, we have to introduce some terms and ways of thinking from statistics. We think of any dataset received as being a *sample* from a *population*. Our goal is always to find a model that uncovers relationships in the population, despite us seeing only a sample.

There is always a danger that we build a model that picks up relationships that exist in the sample but not in the population. For example, it might be the case in our sample that yellow slate houses with three bathrooms are relatively inexpensive, and a complicated neural network model we build could pick up on this relationship even though it may not exist in the population. This is a problem known as *overfitting*. How can we detect whether a model structure we use is likely to have this problem?

The solution is to split our sample into a *training set* and a *testing set*. We use the training data to train the model (that is, to iteratively update the weights), and then we evaluate the model on the testing set to estimate its performance.

The full logic here is that if our model was able to successfully pick up on relationships that generalize from the *training set* to *the rest of the sample* (our whole dataset), then it is likely that the same "model structure" will generalize from our *sample*— which, again, is our entire dataset—to the *population*, which is what we want.

# Assessing Our Model: The Code

With that understanding, let's evaluate our model on the testing set. First, we'll write a function to generate predictions by truncating the `forward_pass` function we saw previously:

```
def predict(X: ndarray,
            weights: Dict[str, ndarray]):
    '''
    Generate predictions from the step-by-step linear regression model.
    '''
    N = np.dot(X, weights['W'])

    return N + weights['B']
```

Then we simply use the weights returned earlier from the `train` function and write:

```
preds = predict(X_test, weights)  # weights = train_info[0]
```

How good are these predictions? Keep in mind that at this point we haven't validated our seemingly strange approach of defining models as a series of operations, and training them by iteratively adjusting the parameters involved using the partial derivatives of the loss calculated with respect to the parameters using the chain rule; thus, we should be pleased if this approach works at all.

The first thing we can do to see whether our model worked is to make a plot with the model's predictions on the x-axis and the actual values on the y-axis. If every point fell exactly on the 45-degree line, the model would be perfect. Figure 2-6 shows a plot of our model's predicted and actual values.

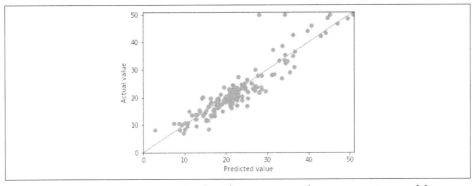

*Figure 2-6. Predicted versus actual values for our custom linear regression model*

Our plot looks pretty good, but let's quantify how good the model is. There are a couple of common ways to do that:

- Calculate the mean distance, in absolute value, between our model's predictions and the actual values, a metric called *mean absolute error*:

```
def mae(preds: ndarray, actuals: ndarray):
    '''
    Compute mean absolute error.
    '''
    return np.mean(np.abs(preds - actuals))
```

- Calculate the mean squared distance between our model's predictions and the actual values, a metric known as *root mean squared error*:

```
def rmse(preds: ndarray, actuals: ndarray):
    '''
    Compute root mean squared error.
    '''
    return np.sqrt(np.mean(np.power(preds - actuals, 2)))
```

The values for this particular model are:

```
Mean absolute error: 3.5643
Root mean squared error: 5.0508
```

Root mean squared error is a particularly common metric since it is on the same scale as the target. If we divide this number by the mean value of the target, we can get a measure of how far off a prediction is, on average, from its actual value. Since the mean value of y_test is 22.0776, we see that this model's predictions of house prices are off by 5.0508 / 22.0776 $\cong$ 22.9% on average.

So are these numbers any good? In the Jupyter Notebook (*https://oreil.ly/2TDV5q9*) containing the code for this chapter, I show that performing a linear regression on this dataset using the most popular Python library for machine learning, Sci-Kit Learn, results in a mean absolute error and root mean squared error of 3.5666 and 5.0482, respectively, which are virtually identical to what we calculated in our "first-principles-based" linear regression previously. This should give you confidence that the approach we've been taking so far in this book is in fact a valid approach for reasoning about and training models! Both later in this chapter, and in the next chapter we'll extend this approach to neural networks and deep learning models.

## Analyzing the Most Important Feature

Before beginning modeling, we scaled each feature of our data to have mean 0 and standard deviation 1; this has computational advantages that we'll discuss in more detail in Chapter 4. A benefit of doing this that is specific to linear regression is that we can interpret the absolute values of the coefficients as corresponding to the importance of the different features to the model; a larger coefficient means that the feature is more important. Here are the coefficients:

```
np.round(weights['W'].reshape(-1), 4)

array([-1.0084,  0.7097,  0.2731,  0.7161, -2.2163,  2.3737,  0.7156,
       -2.6609,  2.629 , -1.8113, -2.3347,  0.8541, -4.2003])
```

The fact that the last coefficient is largest means that the last feature in the dataset is the most important one.

In Figure 2-7, we plot this feature against our target.

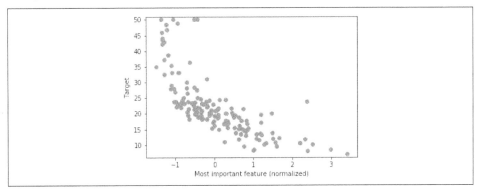

*Figure 2-7. Most important feature versus target in custom linear regression*

We see that this feature is indeed strongly correlated with the target: as this feature increases, the value of the target decreases, and vice versa. However, this relationship is *not* linear. The expected amount that the target changes as the feature changes from −2 to −1 is *not* the same amount that it changes as the feature changes from 1 to 2. We'll come back to this later.

In Figure 2-8, we overlay onto this plot the relationship between this feature and the *model predictions*. We'll generate this by feeding the following data through our trained model:

- The values of all features set equal to their mean
- The values of the most important feature linearly interpolated over 40 steps from −1.5 to 3.5, which is roughly the range of this scaled feature in our data

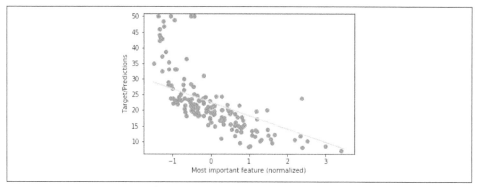

*Figure 2-8. Most important feature versus target and predictions in custom linear regression*

This figure shows (literally) a limitation of linear regression: despite the fact that there is a visually clear and "model-able" *non*linear relationship between this feature and the target, our model is only able to "learn" a linear relationship because of its intrinsic structure.

To have our model learn a more complex, nonlinear relationship between our features and our target, we're going to have to build a more complicated model than linear regression. But how? The answer will lead us, in a principles-based way, to building a neural network.

# Neural Networks from Scratch

We've just seen how to build and train a linear regression model from first principles. How can we extend this chain of reasoning to design a more complex model that can learn nonlinear relationships? The central idea is that we'll first do *many* linear regressions, then feed the results through a nonlinear function, and finally do one last linear regression that ultimately makes the predictions. As it will turn out, we can reason through how to compute the gradients for this more complicated model in the same way we did for the linear regression model.

## Step 1: A Bunch of Linear Regressions

What does it mean to do "a bunch of linear regressions"? Well, doing one linear regression involved doing a matrix multiplication with a set of parameters: if our data $X$ had dimensions [`batch_size, num_features`], then we multiplied it by a weight matrix $W$ with dimensions [`num_features, 1`] to get an output of dimension [`batch_size, 1`]; this output is, for each observation in the batch, simply a *weighted sum* of the original features. To do multiple linear regressions, we'll simply multiply our input by a weight matrix with dimensions [`num_features, num_outputs`], resulting in an output of dimensions [batch_size, num_outputs]; now, *for each observation*, we have num_outputs different weighted sums of the original features.

What are these weighted sums? We should think of each of them as a "learned feature"—a combination of the original features that, once the network is trained, will represent its attempt to learn combinations of features that help it accurately predict house prices. How many learned features should we create? Let's create 13 of them, since we created 13 original features.

## Step 2: A Nonlinear Function

Next, we'll feed each of these weighted sums through a *non*linear function; the first function we'll try is the sigmoid function that was mentioned in Chapter 1. As a refresher, Figure 2-9 plots the sigmoid function.

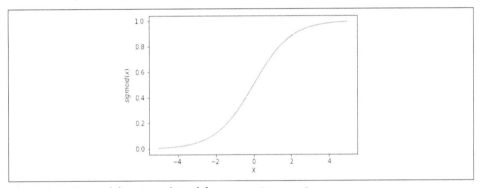

*Figure 2-9. Sigmoid function plotted from x = −5 to x = 5*

Why is using this nonlinear function a good idea? Why not the square function $f(x) = x^2$, for example? There are a couple of reasons. First, we want the function we use here to be *monotonic* so that it "preserves" information about the numbers that were fed in. Let's say that, given the date that was fed in, two of our linear regressions produced values of −3 and 3, respectively. Feeding these through the square function would then produce a value of 9 for each, so that any function that receives these numbers as inputs after they were fed through the square function would "lose" the information that one of them was originally −3 and the other was 3.

The second reason, of course, is that the function is nonlinear; this nonlinearity will enable our neural network to model the inherently nonlinear relationship between the features and the target.

Finally, the sigmoid function has the nice property that its derivative can be expressed in terms of the function itself:

$$\frac{\partial \sigma}{\partial u}(x) = \sigma(x) \times (1 - \sigma(x))$$

We'll make use of this shortly when we use the `sigmoid` function in the backward pass of our neural network.

## Step 3: Another Linear Regression

Finally, we'll take the resulting 13 elements—each of which is a combination of the original features, fed through the `sigmoid` function so that they all have values between 0 and 1—and feed them into a regular linear regression, using them the same way we used our original features previously.

Then, we'll try training the *entire* resulting function in the same way we trained the standard linear regression earlier in this chapter: we'll feed data through the model, use the chain rule to figure out how much increasing the weights would increase (or decrease) the loss, and then update the weights in the direction that decreases the loss at each iteration. Over time (we hope) we'll end up with a more accurate model than before, one that has "learned" the inherent nonlinearity of the relationship between our features and our target.

It might be tough to wrap your mind around what's going on based on this description, so let's look at an illustration.

## Diagrams

Figure 2-10 is a diagram of what our more complicated model now looks like.

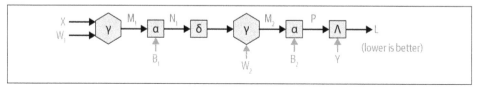

*Figure 2-10. Steps 1–3 translated into a computational graph of the kind we saw in Chapter 1*

You'll see that we start with matrix multiplication and matrix addition, as before. Now let's formalize some terminology that was mentioned previously: when we apply these operations in the course of a nested function, we'll call the first matrix that we use to transform the input features the *weight* matrix, and we'll call the second matrix, the one that is added to each resulting set of features, the *bias*. That's why we'll denote these as $W_1$ and $B_1$.

After applying these operations, we'll feed the results through a sigmoid function and then repeat the process again with *another* set of weights and biases—now called $W_2$ and $B_2$—to get our final prediction, $P$.

## Another diagram?

Does representing things in terms of these individual steps give you intuition for what is going on? This question gets at a key theme of this book: to fully understand neural networks, we have to see multiple representations, each one of which highlights a different aspect of how neural networks work. The representation in Figure 2-10 doesn't give much intuition about the "structure" of the network, but it does indicate clearly how to train such a model: on the backward pass, we'll compute the partial derivative of each constituent function, evaluated at the input to that function, and then calculate the gradients of the loss with respect to each of the weights by simply multiplying all of these derivatives together—just as we saw in the simple chain rule examples from Chapter 1.

Nevertheless, there is another, more standard way to represent a neural network like this: we could represent each of our original features as circles. Since we have 13 features, we need 13 circles. Then we need 13 more circles to represent the 13 outputs of the "linear regression-sigmoid" operation we're doing. In addition, each of these circles is a function of all 13 of our original features, so we'll need lines connecting all of the first set of 13 circles to all of the second set.[6]

Finally, all of these 13 outputs are used to make a single final prediction, so we'll draw one more circle to represent the final prediction and 13 lines showing that these "intermediate outputs" are "connected" to this final prediction.

Figure 2-11 shows the final diagram.[7]

---

6 This highlights an interesting idea: we *could* have outputs that are connected to only *some* of our original features; this is in fact what convolutional neural networks do.

7 Well, not quite: we haven't drawn *all* of the 169 lines we would need to show all the connections between the first two "layers" of features, but we have drawn enough of them so that you get the idea.

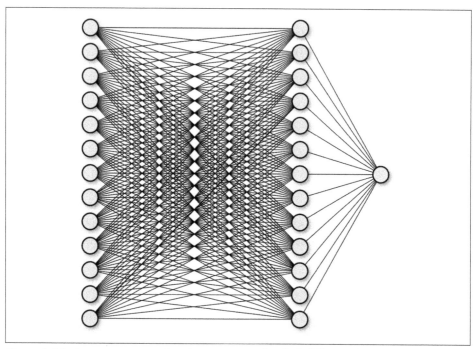

*Figure 2-11. A more common (but in many ways less helpful) visual representation of a neural network*

If you've read anything about neural networks before, you may have seen them represented like the diagram in Figure 2-11: as circles with lines connecting them. While this representation does have some advantages—it lets you see "at a glance" what kind of neural network this is, how many layers it has, and so on—it doesn't give any indication of the actual calculations involved, or of how such a network might be trained. Therefore, while this diagram is extremely important for you to see because you'll see it in other places, it's included here primarily so you can see the *connection* between it and the primary way we are representing neural networks: as boxes with lines connecting them, where each box represents a function that defines both what should happen on the forward pass for the model to make predictions and what should happen on the backward pass for the model to learn. We'll see in the next chapter how to translate even more directly between these diagrams and code by coding each function as a Python class inheriting from a base `Operation` class—and speaking of code, let's cover that next.

## Code

In coding this up, we follow the same function structure as in the simpler linear regression function from earlier in the chapter—taking in `weights` as a dictionary and returning both the loss value and the `forward_info` dictionary, while replacing the internals with the operations specified in Figure 2-10:

```python
def forward_loss(X: ndarray,
                 y: ndarray,
                 weights: Dict[str, ndarray]
                 ) -> Tuple[Dict[str, ndarray], float]:
    '''
    Compute the forward pass and the loss for the step-by-step
    neural network model.
    '''
    M1 = np.dot(X, weights['W1'])

    N1 = M1 + weights['B1']

    O1 = sigmoid(N1)

    M2 = np.dot(O1, weights['W2'])

    P = M2 + weights['B2']

    loss = np.mean(np.power(y - P, 2))

    forward_info: Dict[str, ndarray] = {}
    forward_info['X'] = X
    forward_info['M1'] = M1
    forward_info['N1'] = N1
    forward_info['O1'] = O1
    forward_info['M2'] = M2
    forward_info['P'] = P
    forward_info['y'] = y

    return forward_info, loss
```

Even though we're now dealing with a more complicated diagram, we're still just going step by step through each operation, doing the appropriate computation, and saving the results in `forward_info` as we go.

# Neural Networks: The Backward Pass

The backward pass works the same way as in the simpler linear regression model from earlier in the chapter, just with more steps.

### Diagram

The steps, as a reminder, are:

1. Compute the derivative of each operation and evaluate it at its input.

2. Multiply the results together.

As we'll see yet again, this will work because of the chain rule. Figure 2-12 shows all the partial derivatives we have to compute.

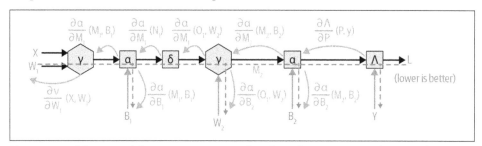

*Figure 2-12. The partial derivatives associated with each operation in the neural network that will be multiplied together on the backward pass*

Conceptually, we want to compute all these partial derivatives, tracing backward through our function, and then multiply them together to get the gradients of the loss with respect to each of the weights, just as we did for the linear regression model.

### Math (and code)

Table 2-1 lists these partial derivatives and the lines in the code that correspond to each one.

*Table 2-1. Derivative table for neural network*

| Derivative | Code |
| --- | --- |
| $\frac{\partial \Lambda}{\partial P}(P, y)$ | dLdP = -(forward_info[y] - forward_info[P]) |
| $\frac{\partial \alpha}{\partial M_2}(M_2, B_2)$ | np.ones_like(forward_info[M2]) |
| $\frac{\partial \alpha}{\partial B_2}(M_2, B_2)$ | np.ones_like(weights[B2]) |
| $\frac{\partial v}{\partial W_2}(O_1, W_2)$ | dM2dW2 = np.transpose(forward_info[O1], (1, 0)) |
| $\frac{\partial v}{\partial O_1}(O_1, W_2)$ | dM2dO1 = np.transpose(weights[W2], (1, 0)) |
| $\frac{\partial \sigma}{\partial u}(N_1)$ | dO1dN1 = sigmoid(forward_info[N1] × (1 - sigmoid(forward_info[N1]) |
| $\frac{\partial \alpha}{\partial M_1}(M_1, B_1)$ | dN1dM1 = np.ones_like(forward_info[M1]) |
| $\frac{\partial \alpha}{\partial B_1}(M_1, B_1)$ | dN1dB1 = np.ones_like(weights[B1]) |
| $\frac{\partial v}{\partial W_1}(X, W_1)$ | dM1dW1 = np.transpose(forward_info[X], (1, 0)) |

The expressions we compute for the gradient of the loss with respect to the bias terms, dLdB1 and dLdB2, will have to be summed along the rows to account for the fact that the same bias element is added to each row in the batch of data passed through. See "Gradient of the Loss with Respect to the Bias Terms" on page 225 for details.

### The overall loss gradient

You can see the full `loss_gradients` function in the Jupyter Notebook (*https://oreil.ly/2TDV5q9*) for this chapter on the book's GitHub page. This function computes each of the partial derivatives in Table 2-1 and multiplies them together to get the gradients of the loss with respect to each of the `ndarrays` containing the weights:

- dLdW2
- dLdB2
- dLdW1
- dLdB1

The only caveat is that we sum the expressions we compute for dLdB1 and dLdB2 along `axis = 0`, as described in "Gradient of the Loss with Respect to the Bias Terms" on page 225.

We've finally built our first neural network from scratch! Let's see if it is in fact any better than our linear regression model.

# Training and Assessing Our First Neural Network

Just as the forward and backward passes worked the same for our neural network as for the linear regression model from earlier in the chapter, so too are training and evaluation the same: for each iteration of data, we pass the input forward through the function on the forward pass, compute the gradients of loss with respect to the weights on the backward pass, and then use these gradients to update the weights. In fact, we can use the following identical code inside the training loop:

```
forward_info, loss = forward_loss(X_batch, y_batch, weights)

loss_grads = loss_gradients(forward_info, weights)

for key in weights.keys():
    weights[key] -= learning_rate * loss_grads[key]
```

The difference simply lies in the internals of the `forward_loss` and `loss_gradients` functions, and in the `weights` dictionary, which now has four keys (W1, B1, W2, and B2) instead of two. Indeed, this is a major takeaway from this book: even for very complex architectures, the mathematical principles and high-level training procedures are the same as for simple models.

We also get predictions from this model in the same way:

```
preds = predict(X_test, weights)
```

The difference again is simply in the internals of the predict function:

```
def predict(X: ndarray,
            weights: Dict[str, ndarray]) -> ndarray:
    '''
    Generate predictions from the step-by-step neural network model.
    '''
    M1 = np.dot(X, weights['W1'])

    N1 = M1 + weights['B1']

    O1 = sigmoid(N1)

    M2 = np.dot(O1, weights['W2'])

    P = M2 + weights['B2']

    return P
```

Using these predictions, we can calculate the mean absolute error and root mean squared error on the validation set, as before:

```
Mean absolute error: 2.5289
Root mean squared error: 3.6775
```

Both values are significantly lower than the prior model! Looking at the plot of predictions versus actuals in Figure 2-13 shows similar improvements.

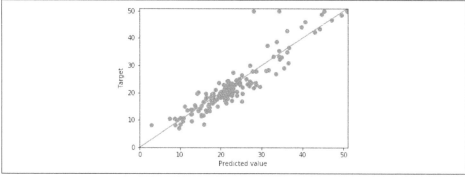

*Figure 2-13. Predicted value versus target, in neural network regression*

Visually, the points look closer to the 45-degree line than in Figure 2-6. I encourage you to step through the Jupyter Notebook (*https://oreil.ly/2TDV5q9*) on the book's GitHub page and run the code yourself!

## Two Reasons Why This Is Happening

Why does this model appear to be performing better than the model before? Recall that there was a *nonlinear* relationship between the most important feature of our earlier model and our target; nevertheless, our model was constrained to learn only *linear* relationships between individual features and our target. I claim that, by adding a nonlinear function into the mix, we have allowed our model to learn the proper, nonlinear relationship between our features and our target.

Let's visualize this. Figure 2-14 shows the same plot we showed in the linear regression section, plotting the normalized values of the most important feature from our model along with both the values of the target and the *predictions* that would result from feeding the mean values of the other features while varying the values of the most important feature from –3.5 to 1.5, as before.

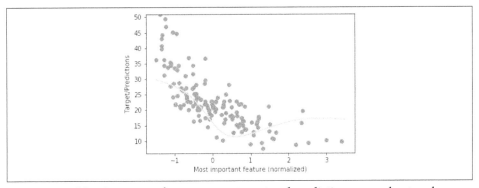

*Figure 2-14. Most important feature versus target and predictions, neural network regression*

We can see that the relationship shown (a) is now nonlinear and (b) more closely matches the relationship between this feature and the target (represented by the points), as desired. So adding the nonlinear function to our model allowed it to learn, via iteratively updating the weights using the training, the nonlinear relationship that existed between the inputs and the outputs.

That's the first reason why our neural network performed better than a straightforward linear regression. The second reason is that our neural network can learn relationships between *combinations* of our original features and our target, as opposed to just individual features. This is because the neural network uses a matrix multiplication to create 13 "learned features," each of which is a combination of all the original features, and then essentially applies another linear regression on top of these learned features. For example, doing some exploratory analysis that is shared on the book's website, we can see that the most important combinations of the 13 original features that the model has learned are:

$$-4.44 \times \text{feature}_6 - 2.77 \times \text{feature}_1 - 2.07 \times \text{feature}_7 + \ldots$$

and:

$$4.43 \times \text{feature}_2 - 3.39 \times \text{feature}_4 - 2.39 \times \text{feature}_1 + \ldots$$

These will then be included, along with 11 other learned features, in a linear regression in the last two layers of the neural network.

These two things—learning *nonlinear* relationships between individual features and our target, and learning relationships between *combinations* of features and our target—are what allow neural networks to often work better than straightforward regressions on real-world problems.

## Conclusion

In this chapter, you learned how to use the building blocks and mental models from Chapter 1 to understand, build, and train two standard machine learning models to solve real problems. I started by showing how to represent a simple machine learning model from classical statistics—linear regression—using a computational graph. This representation allowed us to compute the gradients of the loss from this model with respect to the model's parameters and thus train the model by continually feeding in data from the training set and updating the model's parameters in the direction that would decrease the loss.

Then we saw a limitation of this model: it can only learn *linear* relationships between the features and target; this motivated us to try building a model that could learn *nonlinear* relationships between the features and target, which led us to build our first neural network. You learned how neural networks work by building one from scratch, and you also learned how to train them using the same high-level procedure we used to train our linear regression models. You then saw empirically that the neural network performed better than the simple linear regression model and learned two key reasons why: the neural network was able to learn *nonlinear* relationships between the features and the target and also to learn relationships between *combinations* of features and the target.

Of course, there's a reason we ended this chapter still covering a relatively simple model: defining neural networks in this way is an extremely manual process. Defining the forward pass involved 6 individually coded operations, and the backward pass involved 17. However, discerning readers will have noticed that there is a lot of repetition in these steps, and by properly defining abstractions, we can move from defining models in terms of individual operations (as in this chapter) to defining models in terms of these abstractions. This will allow us to build more complex models, including deep learning models, while deepening our understanding of how these models work. That is what we'll begin to do in the next chapter. Onward!

## CHAPTER 3

# Deep Learning from Scratch

You may not realize it, but you now have all the mathematical and conceptual foundations to answer the key questions about deep learning models that I posed at the beginning of the book: you understand *how* neural networks work—the computations involved with the matrix multiplications, the loss, and the partial derivatives with respect to that loss—as well as *why* those computations work (namely, the chain rule from calculus). We achieved this understanding by building neural networks from first principles, representing them as a series of "building blocks" where each building block was a single mathematical function. In this chapter, you'll learn to represent these building blocks themselves as abstract Python classes and then use these classes to build deep learning models; by the end of this chapter, you will indeed have done "deep learning from scratch"!

We'll also map the descriptions of neural networks in terms of these building blocks to more conventional descriptions of deep learning models that you may have heard before. For example, by the end of this chapter, you'll know what it means for a deep learning model to have "multiple hidden layers." This is really the essence of understanding a concept: being able to translate between high-level descriptions and low-level details of what is actually going on. Let's begin building toward this translation. So far, we've described models just in terms of the operations that happen at a low level. In the first part of this chapter, we'll map this description of models to common higher-level concepts such as "layers" that will ultimately allow us to more easily describe more complex models.

# Deep Learning Definition: A First Pass

What *is* a "deep learning" model? In the previous chapter, we defined a model as a mathematical function represented by a computational graph. The purpose of such a model was to try to map inputs, each drawn from some dataset with common characteristics (such as separate inputs representing different features of houses) to outputs drawn from a related distribution (such as the prices of those houses). We found that if we defined the model as a function that included *parameters* as inputs to some of its operations, we could "fit" it to optimally describe the data using the following procedure:

1. Repeatedly feed observations through the model, keeping track of the quantities computed along the way during this "forward pass."

2. Calculate a *loss* representing how far off our model's predictions were from the desired outputs or *target*.

3. Using the quantities computed on the forward pass and the chain rule math worked out in Chapter 1, compute how much each of the input *parameters* ultimately affects this loss.

4. Update the values of the parameters so that the loss will hopefully be reduced when the next set of observations is passed through the model.

We started out with a model containing just a series of linear operations transforming our features into the target (which turned out to be equivalent to a traditional linear regression model). This had the expected limitation that, even when fit "optimally," the model could nevertheless represent only linear relationships between our features and our target.

We then defined a function structure that applied these linear operations first, then a *non*linear operation (the `sigmoid` function), and then a final set of linear operations. We showed that with this modification, our model *could* learn something closer to the true, nonlinear relationship between input and output, while having the additional benefit that it could learn relationships between *combinations* of our input features and the target.

What is the connection between models like these and deep learning models? We'll start with a somewhat clumsy attempt at a definition: deep learning models are represented by series of operations that have *at least two, nonconsecutive* nonlinear functions involved.

I'll show where this definition comes from shortly, but first note that since deep learning models are just a series of operations, the process of training them is in fact *identical* to the process we've been using for the simpler models we've already seen. After all, what allows this training process to work is the differentiability of the model with respect to its inputs; and as mentioned in Chapter 1, the composition of differentiable functions is differentiable, so as long as the individual operations making up the function are differentiable, the whole function will be differentiable, and we'll be able to train it using the same four-step training procedure just described.

However, so far our approach to actually training these models has been to compute these derivatives by manually coding the forward and backward passes and then multiplying the appropriate quantities together to get the derivatives. For the simple neural network model in Chapter 2, this required 17 steps. Because we're describing the model at such a low level, it isn't immediately clear how we could add more complexity to this model (or what exactly what that would mean) or even make a simple change such as swapping out a different nonlinear function for the sigmoid function. To transition to being able to build arbitrarily "deep" and otherwise "complex" deep learning models, we'll have to think about where in these 17 steps we can create reusable components, at a higher level than individual operations, that we can swap in and out to build different models. To guide us in the right direction as far as which abstractions to create, we'll try to map the operations we've been using to traditional descriptions of neural networks as being made up of "layers," "neurons," and so on.

As our first step, we'll have to create an abstraction to represent the individual operations we've been working with so far, instead of continuing to code the same matrix multiplication and bias addition over and over again.

# The Building Blocks of Neural Networks: Operations

The Operation class will represent one of the constituent functions in our neural networks. We know that at a high level, based on the way we've used such functions in our models, it should have forward and backward methods, each of which receives an ndarray as an input and outputs an ndarray. Some operations, such as matrix multiplication, seem to have *another* special kind of input, also an ndarray: the parameters. In our Operation class—or perhaps in another class that inherits from it—we should allow for params as another instance variable.

Another insight is that there seem to be two types of Operations: some, such as the matrix multiplication, return an ndarray as output that is a different shape than the ndarray they received as input; by contrast, some Operations, such as the sigmoid function, simply apply some function to each element of the input ndarray. What, then, is the "general rule" about the shapes of the ndarrays that get passed between our operations? Let's consider the ndarrays passed through our Operations: each Operation will send outputs forward on the forward pass and will receive an "output gradient" on the backward pass, which will represent the partial derivative of the loss with respect to every element of the Operation's output (computed by the other Operations that make up the network). Also on the backward pass, each Operation will send an "input gradient" backward, representing the partial derivative of the loss with respect to each element of the input.

These facts place a few important restrictions on the workings of our Operations that will help us ensure we're computing the gradients correctly:

- The shape of the *output gradient* ndarray must match the shape of the *output*.

- The shape of the *input gradient* that the Operation sends backward during the backward pass must match the shape of the Operation's *input*.

This will all be clearer once you see it in a diagram; let's look at that next.

## Diagram

This is all summarized in Figure 3-1, for an operation O that is receiving inputs from an operation N and passing outputs on to another operation P.

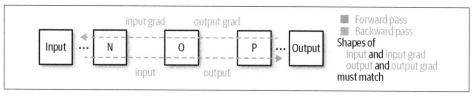

*Figure 3-1. An Operation, with input and output*

Figure 3-2 covers the case of an Operation with parameters.

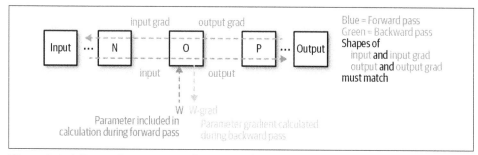

*Figure 3-2. A ParamOperation, with input and output and parameters*

## Code

With all this, we can write the fundamental building block for our neural network, an Operation, as:

```
class Operation(object):
    '''
    Base class for an "operation" in a neural network.
    '''
    def __init__(self):
        pass

    def forward(self, input_: ndarray):
        '''
        Stores input in the self._input instance variable
        Calls the self._output() function.
        '''
        self.input_ = input_

        self.output = self._output()

        return self.output


    def backward(self, output_grad: ndarray) -> ndarray:
        '''
        Calls the self._input_grad() function.
        Checks that the appropriate shapes match.
        '''
        assert_same_shape(self.output, output_grad)

        self.input_grad = self._input_grad(output_grad)

        assert_same_shape(self.input_, self.input_grad)
        return self.input_grad


    def _output(self) -> ndarray:
        '''
        The _output method must be defined for each Operation.
        '''
        raise NotImplementedError()


    def _input_grad(self, output_grad: ndarray) -> ndarray:
        '''
        The _input_grad method must be defined for each Operation.
        '''
        raise NotImplementedError()
```

For any individual Operation that we define, we'll have to implement the _output
and _input_grad functions, so named because of the quantities they compute.

We're defining base classes like this primarily for pedagogical reasons: it is important to have the mental model that *all* Operations you'll encounter throughout deep learning fit this blueprint of sending inputs forward and gradients backward, with the shapes of what they receive on the forward pass matching the shapes of what they send backward on the backward pass, and vice versa.

We'll define the specific Operations we've used thus far—matrix multiplication and so on—later in this chapter. First we'll define another class that inherits from Operation that we'll use specifically for Operations that involve parameters:

```
class ParamOperation(Operation):
    '''
    An Operation with parameters.
    '''

    def __init__(self, param: ndarray) -> ndarray:
        '''
        The ParamOperation method
        '''
        super().__init__()
        self.param = param

    def backward(self, output_grad: ndarray) -> ndarray:
        '''
        Calls self._input_grad and self._param_grad.
        Checks appropriate shapes.
        '''

        assert_same_shape(self.output, output_grad)

        self.input_grad = self._input_grad(output_grad)
        self.param_grad = self._param_grad(output_grad)

        assert_same_shape(self.input_, self.input_grad)
        assert_same_shape(self.param, self.param_grad)

        return self.input_grad

    def _param_grad(self, output_grad: ndarray) -> ndarray:
        '''
        Every subclass of ParamOperation must implement _param_grad.
        '''
        raise NotImplementedError()
```

Similar to the base Operation, an individual ParamOperation would have to define the _param_grad function in addition to the _output and _input_grad functions.

We have now formalized the neural network building blocks we've been using in our models so far. We could skip ahead and define neural networks directly in terms of these `Operations`, but there is an intermediate class we've been dancing around for a chapter and a half that we'll define first: the `Layer`.

# The Building Blocks of Neural Networks: Layers

In terms of `Operations`, layers are a series of linear operations followed by a nonlinear operation. For example, our neural network from the last chapter could be said to have had five total operations: two linear operations—a weight multiplication and the addition of a bias term—followed the `sigmoid` function and then two more linear operations. In this case, we would say that the first three operations, up to and including the nonlinear one, would constitute the first layer, and the last two operations would constitute the second layer. In addition, we say that the input itself represents a special kind of layer called the *input* layer (in terms of numbering the layers, this layer doesn't count, so that we can think of it as the "zeroth" layer). The last layer, similarly, is called the *output* layer. The middle layer—the "first one," according to our numbering—also has an important name: it is called a *hidden* layer, since it is the only layer whose values we don't typically see explicitly during the course of training.

The output layer is an important exception to this definition of layers, in that it does not *have* to have a nonlinear operation applied to it; this is simply because we often want the values that come out of this layer to have values between negative infinity and infinity (or at least between 0 and infinity), whereas nonlinear functions typically "squash down" their input to some subset of that range relevant to the particular problem we're trying to solve (for example, the `sigmoid` function squashes down its input to between 0 and 1).

## Diagrams

To make the connection explicit, Figure 3-3 shows the diagram of the neural network from the prior chapter with the individual operations grouped into layers.

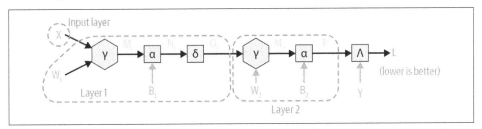

*Figure 3-3. The neural network from the prior chapter with the operations grouped into layers*

You can see that the input represents an "input" layer, the next three operations (ending with the sigmoid function) represent the next layer, and the last two operations represent the last layer.

This is, of course, rather cumbersome. And that's the point: representing neural networks as a series of individual operations, while showing clearly how neural networks work and how to train them, is too "low level" for anything more complicated than a two-layer neural network. That's why the more common way to represent neural networks is in terms of layers, as shown in Figure 3-4.

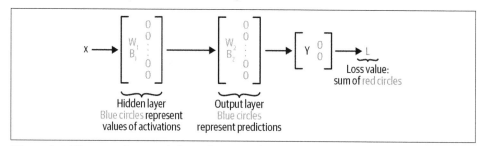

*Figure 3-4. The neural network from the prior chapter in terms of layers*

### Connection to the brain

Finally, let's make one last connection between what we've seen so far and a notion you've likely heard before: each layer can be said to have a certain number of *neurons* equal to *the dimensionality of the vector that represents each observation in the layer's output*. The neural network from the prior example can thus be thought of as having 13 neurons in the input layer, then 13 neurons (again) in the hidden layer, and one neuron in the output layer.

Neurons in the brain have the property that they can receive inputs from many other neurons and will "fire" and send a signal forward only if the signals they receive cumulatively reach a certain "activation energy." Neurons in the context of neural networks have a loosely analogous property: they do indeed send signals forward based on their inputs, but the inputs are transformed into outputs simply via a nonlinear function. Thus, this nonlinear function is called the *activation function*, and the values that come out of it are called the *activations* for that layer.[1]

Now that we've defined layers, we can state the more conventional definition of deep learning: *deep learning models are neural networks with more than one hidden layer.*

---

[1] Among all activation functions, the sigmoid function, which maps inputs to between 0 and 1, most closely mimics the actual activation of neurons in the brain, but in general activation functions can be any monotonic, nonlinear function.

We can see that this is equivalent to the earlier definition that was purely in terms of Operations, since a layer is just a series of Operations with a nonlinear operation at the end.

Now that we've defined a base class for our Operations, let's show how it can serve as the fundamental building block of the models we saw in the prior chapter.

# Building Blocks on Building Blocks

What specific Operations do we need to implement for the models in the prior chapter to work? Based on our experience of implementing that neural network step by step, we know there are three kinds:

- The matrix multiplication of the input with the matrix of parameters
- The addition of a bias term
- The sigmoid activation function

Let's start with the WeightMultiply Operation:

```
class WeightMultiply(ParamOperation):
    '''
    Weight multiplication operation for a neural network.
    '''

    def __init__(self, W: ndarray):
        '''
        Initialize Operation with self.param = W.
        '''
        super().__init__(W)

    def _output(self) -> ndarray:
        '''
        Compute output.
        '''
        return np.dot(self.input_, self.param)

    def _input_grad(self, output_grad: ndarray) -> ndarray:
        '''
        Compute input gradient.
        '''
        return np.dot(output_grad, np.transpose(self.param, (1, 0)))

    def _param_grad(self, output_grad: ndarray)  -> ndarray:
        '''
        Compute parameter gradient.
        '''
        return np.dot(np.transpose(self.input_, (1, 0)), output_grad)
```

Here we simply code up the matrix multiplication on the forward pass, as well as the rules for "sending gradients backward" to both the inputs and the parameters on the backward pass (using the rules for doing so that we reasoned through at the end of Chapter 1). As you'll see shortly, we can now use this as a *building block* that we can simply plug into our Layers.

Next up is the addition operation, which we'll call BiasAdd:

```python
class BiasAdd(ParamOperation):
    '''
    Compute bias addition.
    '''

    def __init__(self,
                 B: ndarray):
        '''
        Initialize Operation with self.param = B.
        Check appropriate shape.
        '''
        assert B.shape[0] == 1

        super().__init__(B)

    def _output(self) -> ndarray:
        '''
        Compute output.
        '''
        return self.input_ + self.param

    def _input_grad(self, output_grad: ndarray) -> ndarray:
        '''
        Compute input gradient.
        '''
        return np.ones_like(self.input_) * output_grad

    def _param_grad(self, output_grad: ndarray) -> ndarray:
        '''
        Compute parameter gradient.
        '''
        param_grad = np.ones_like(self.param) * output_grad
        return np.sum(param_grad, axis=0).reshape(1, param_grad.shape[1])
```

Finally, let's do sigmoid:

```python
class Sigmoid(Operation):
    '''
    Sigmoid activation function.
    '''

    def __init__(self) -> None:
        '''Pass'''
        super().__init__()
```

```
def _output(self) -> ndarray:
    '''
    Compute output.
    '''
    return 1.0/(1.0+np.exp(-1.0 * self.input_))

def _input_grad(self, output_grad: ndarray) -> ndarray:
    '''
    Compute input gradient.
    '''
    sigmoid_backward = self.output * (1.0 - self.output)
    input_grad = sigmoid_backward * output_grad
    return input_grad
```

This simply implements the math described in the previous chapter.

For both `sigmoid` and the `ParamOperation`, the step during the backward pass where we compute:

```
input_grad = <something> * output_grad
```

is the step where we are applying the chain rule, and the corresponding rule for `WeightMultiply`:

```
np.dot(output_grad, np.transpose(self.param, (1, 0)))
```

is, as I argued in Chapter 1, the analogue of the chain rule when the function in question is a matrix multiplication.

Now that we've defined these `Operations` precisely, we can use *them* as building blocks to define a `Layer`.

## The Layer Blueprint

Because of the way we've written the `Operations`, writing the `Layer` class is easy:

- The `forward` and `backward` methods simply involve sending the input successively forward through a series of `Operations`—exactly as we've been doing in the diagrams all along! This is the most important fact about the working of `Layers`; the rest of the code is a wrapper around this and mostly involves bookkeeping:

  — Defining the correct series of `Operations` in the `_setup_layer` function and initializing and storing the parameters in these `Operations` (which will also take place in the `_setup_layer` function)

  — Storing the correct values in `self.input_` and `self.output` on the `forward` method

  — Performing the correct assertion checking in the `backward` method

- Finally, the _params and _param_grads functions simply extract the parameters and their gradients (with respect to the loss) from the ParamOperations within the layer.

Here's what all that looks like:

```python
class Layer(object):
    '''
    A "layer" of neurons in a neural network.
    '''

    def __init__(self,
                 neurons: int):
        '''
        The number of "neurons" roughly corresponds to the "breadth" of the
        layer
        '''
        self.neurons = neurons
        self.first = True
        self.params: List[ndarray] = []
        self.param_grads: List[ndarray] = []
        self.operations: List[Operation] = []

    def _setup_layer(self, num_in: int) -> None:
        '''
        The _setup_layer function must be implemented for each layer.
        '''
        raise NotImplementedError()

    def forward(self, input_: ndarray) -> ndarray:
        '''
        Passes input forward through a series of operations.
        '''
        if self.first:
            self._setup_layer(input_)
            self.first = False

        self.input_ = input_

        for operation in self.operations:

            input_ = operation.forward(input_)

        self.output = input_

        return self.output

    def backward(self, output_grad: ndarray) -> ndarray:
        '''
        Passes output_grad backward through a series of operations.
        Checks appropriate shapes.
        '''
```

```
        assert_same_shape(self.output, output_grad)

        for operation in reversed(self.operations):
            output_grad = operation.backward(output_grad)

        input_grad = output_grad

        self._param_grads()

        return input_grad

    def _param_grads(self) -> ndarray:
        '''
        Extracts the _param_grads from a layer's operations.
        '''

        self.param_grads = []
        for operation in self.operations:
            if issubclass(operation.__class__, ParamOperation):
                self.param_grads.append(operation.param_grad)

    def _params(self) -> ndarray:
        '''
        Extracts the _params from a layer's operations.
        '''

        self.params = []
        for operation in self.operations:
            if issubclass(operation.__class__, ParamOperation):
                self.params.append(operation.param)
```

Just as we moved from an abstract definition of an Operation to the implementation of specific Operations needed for the neural network from Chapter 2, let's now implement the Layer from that network as well.

## The Dense Layer

We called the Operations we've been dealing with WeightMultiply, BiasAdd, and so on. What should we call the layer we've been using so far? A LinearNonLinear layer?

A defining characteristic of this layer is that *each output neuron is a function of all of the input neurons*. That is what the matrix multiplication is really doing: if the matrix is $n_{in}$ rows by $n_{out}$ columns, the multiplication itself is computing $n_{out}$ new features, each of which is a weighted linear combination of *all* of the $n_{in}$ input features.[2] Thus

---

[2] As we'll see in Chapter 5, this is not true of all layers: in *convolutional* layers, for example, each output feature is a combination of *only a small subset* of the input features.

these layers are often called *fully connected* layers; recently, in the popular Keras library, they are also often called Dense layers, a more concise term that gets across the same idea.

Now that we know what to call it and why, let's define the Dense layer in terms of the operations we've already defined—as you'll see, because of how we defined our Layer base class, all we need to do is to put the Operations defined in the previous section in as a list in the _setup_layer function.

```python
class Dense(Layer):
    '''
    A fully connected layer that inherits from "Layer."
    '''
    def __init__(self,
                 neurons: int,
                 activation: Operation = Sigmoid()) -> None:
        '''
        Requires an activation function upon initialization.
        '''
        super().__init__(neurons)
        self.activation = activation

    def _setup_layer(self, input_: ndarray) -> None:
        '''
        Defines the operations of a fully connected layer.
        '''
        if self.seed:
            np.random.seed(self.seed)

        self.params = []

        # weights
        self.params.append(np.random.randn(input_.shape[1], self.neurons))

        # bias
        self.params.append(np.random.randn(1, self.neurons))

        self.operations = [WeightMultiply(self.params[0]),
                           BiasAdd(self.params[1]),
                           self.activation]

        return None
```

Note that we'll make the default activation a Linear activation, which really means we apply no activation, and simply apply the identity function to the output of the layer.

What building blocks should we now add on top of Operation and Layer? To train our model, we know we'll need a NeuralNetwork class to wrap around Layers, just as Layers wrapped around Operations. It isn't obvious what other classes will be needed, so we'll just dive in and build NeuralNetwork and figure out the other classes we'll need as we go.

# The NeuralNetwork Class, and Maybe Others

What should our NeuralNetwork class be able to do? At a high level, it should be able to *learn from data*: more precisely, it should be able to take in batches of data representing "observations" (X) and "correct answers" (y) and learn the relationship between X and y, which means learning a function that can transform X into predictions p that are very close to y.

How exactly will this learning take place, given the Layer and Operation classes just defined? Recalling how the model from the last chapter worked, we'll implement the following:

1. The neural network should take X and pass it successively forward through each Layer (which is really a convenient wrapper around feeding it through many Operations), at which point the result will represent the prediction.

2. Next, prediction should be compared with the value y to calculate the loss and generate the "loss gradient," which is the partial derivative of the loss with respect to each element in the last layer in the network (namely, the one that generated the prediction).

3. Finally, we'll send this loss gradient successively backward through each layer, along the way computing the "parameter gradients"—the partial derivative of the loss with respect to each of the parameters—and storing them in the corresponding Operations.

## Diagram

Figure 3-5 captures this description of a neural network in terms of Layers.

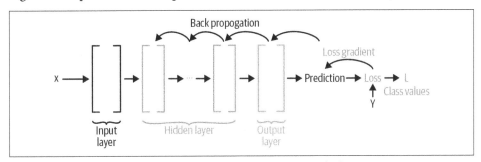

*Figure 3-5. Backpropagation, now in terms of Layers instead of Operations*

# Code

How should we implement this? First, we'll want our neural network to ultimately deal with Layers the same way our Layers dealt with Operations. For example, we want the forward method to receive X as input and simply do something like:

```
for layer in self.layers:
    X = layer.forward(X)

return X
```

Similarly, we'll want our backward method to take in an argument—let's initially call it grad—and do something like:

```
for layer in reversed(self.layers):
    grad = layer.backward(grad)
```

Where will grad come from? It has to come from the *loss*, a special function that takes in the prediction along with y and:

- Computes a single number representing the "penalty" for the network making that prediction.
- Sends backward a gradient for every element of the prediction with respect to the loss. This gradient is what the last Layer in the network will receive as the input to its backward function.

In the example from the prior chapter, the loss function was the squared difference between the prediction and the target, and the gradient of the prediction with respect to the loss was computed accordingly.

How should we implement this? It seems like this concept is important enough to deserve its own class. Furthermore, this class can be implemented similarly to the Layer class, except the forward method will produce an actual number (a float) as the loss, instead of an ndarray to be sent forward to the next Layer. Let's formalize this.

## Loss Class

The Loss base class will be similar to Layer—the forward and backward methods will check that the shapes of the appropriate ndarrays are identical and define two methods, _output and _input_grad, that any subclass of Loss will have to define:

```
class Loss(object):
    '''
    The "loss" of a neural network.
    '''

    def __init__(self):
```

```python
        '''Pass'''
        pass

    def forward(self, prediction: ndarray, target: ndarray) -> float:
        '''
        Computes the actual loss value.
        '''
        assert_same_shape(prediction, target)

        self.prediction = prediction
        self.target = target

        loss_value = self._output()

        return loss_value

    def backward(self) -> ndarray:
        '''
        Computes gradient of the loss value with respect to the input to the
        loss function.
        '''
        self.input_grad = self._input_grad()

        assert_same_shape(self.prediction, self.input_grad)

        return self.input_grad

    def _output(self) -> float:
        '''
        Every subclass of "Loss" must implement the _output function.
        '''
        raise NotImplementedError()

    def _input_grad(self) -> ndarray:
        '''
        Every subclass of "Loss" must implement the _input_grad function.
        '''
        raise NotImplementedError()
```

As in the Operation class, we check that the gradient that the loss sends backward is
the same shape as the prediction received as input from the last layer of the
network:

```python
class MeanSquaredError(Loss):

    def __init__(self)
        '''Pass'''
        super().__init__()

    def _output(self) -> float:
        '''
        Computes the per-observation squared error loss.
```

```
        '''
        loss =
            np.sum(np.power(self.prediction - self.target, 2)) /
            self.prediction.shape[0]

        return loss

    def _input_grad(self) -> ndarray:
        '''
        Computes the loss gradient with respect to the input for MSE loss.
        '''

        return 2.0 * (self.prediction - self.target) / self.prediction.shape[0]
```

Here, we simply code the forward and backward rules of the mean squared error loss formula.

This is the last key building block we need to build deep learning from scratch. Let's review how these pieces fit together and then proceed with building a model!

# Deep Learning from Scratch

We ultimately want to build a NeuralNetwork class, using Figure 3-5 as a guide, that we can use to define and train deep learning models. Before we dive in and start coding, let's describe precisely what such a class would be and how it would interact with the Operation, Layer, and Loss classes we just defined:

1. A NeuralNetwork will have a list of Layers as an attribute. The Layers would be as defined previously, with forward and backward methods. These methods take in ndarray objects and return ndarray objects.

2. Each Layer will have a list of Operations saved in the operations attribute of the layer during the _setup_layer function.

3. These Operations, just like the Layer itself, have forward and backward methods that take in ndarray objects as arguments and return ndarray objects as outputs.

4. In each operation, the shape of the output_grad received in the backward method must be the same as the shape of the output attribute of the Layer. The same is true for the shapes of the input_grad passed backward during the back ward method and the input_ attribute.

5. Some operations have parameters (stored in the param attribute); these operations inherit from the ParamOperation class. The same constraints on input and output shapes apply to Layers and their forward and backward methods as well —they take in ndarray objects and output ndarray objects, and the shapes of the input and output attributes and their corresponding gradients must match.

6. A `NeuralNetwork` will also have a `Loss`. This class will take the output of the last operation from the `NeuralNetwork` and the target, check that their shapes are the same, and calculate both a loss value (a number) and an `ndarray` `loss_grad` that will be fed into the output layer, starting backpropagation.

## Implementing Batch Training

We've covered several times the high-level steps for training a model one batch at a time. They are important and worth repeating:

1. Feed input through the model function (the "forward pass") to get a prediction.
2. Calculate the number representing the loss.
3. Calculate the gradient of the loss with respect to the parameters, using the chain rule and the quantities computed during the forward pass.
4. Update the parameters using these gradients.

We would then feed a new batch of data through and repeat these steps.

Translating these steps into the `NeuralNetwork` framework just described is straight-forward:

1. Receive X and y as inputs, both `ndarrays`.
2. Feed X successively forward through each `Layer`.
3. Use the `Loss` to produce loss value and the loss gradient to be sent backward.
4. Use the loss gradient as input to the `backward` method for the network, which will calculate the `param_grads` for each layer in the network.
5. Call the `update_params` function on each layer, which will use the overall learning rate for the `NeuralNetwork` as well as the newly calculated `param_grads`.

We finally have our full definition of a neural network that can accommodate batch training. Now let's code it up.

## NeuralNetwork: Code

Coding all of this up is pretty straightforward:

```
class NeuralNetwork(object):
    '''
    The class for a neural network.
    '''
    def __init__(self, layers: List[Layer],
                 loss: Loss,
                 seed: float = 1)
```

```
        '''
        Neural networks need layers, and a loss.
        '''
        self.layers = layers
        self.loss = loss
        self.seed = seed
        if seed:
            for layer in self.layers:
                setattr(layer, "seed", self.seed)

    def forward(self, x_batch: ndarray) -> ndarray:
        '''
        Passes data forward through a series of layers.
        '''
        x_out = x_batch
        for layer in self.layers:
            x_out = layer.forward(x_out)

        return x_out

    def backward(self, loss_grad: ndarray) -> None:
        '''
        Passes data backward through a series of layers.
        '''

        grad = loss_grad
        for layer in reversed(self.layers):
            grad = layer.backward(grad)

        return None

    def train_batch(self,
                    x_batch: ndarray,
                    y_batch: ndarray) -> float:
        '''
        Passes data forward through the layers.
        Computes the loss.
        Passes data backward through the layers.
        '''

        predictions = self.forward(x_batch)

        loss = self.loss.forward(predictions, y_batch)

        self.backward(self.loss.backward())

        return loss

    def params(self):
        '''
        Gets the parameters for the network.
        '''
```

```
    for layer in self.layers:
        yield from layer.params

def param_grads(self):
    '''
    Gets the gradient of the loss with respect to the parameters for the
    network.
    '''
    for layer in self.layers:
        yield from layer.param_grads
```

With this NeuralNetwork class, we can implement the models from the prior chapter in a more modular, flexible way and define other models to represent complex non-linear relationships between input and output. For example, here's how to easily instantiate the two models we covered in the last chapter—the linear regression and the neural network:[3]

```
linear_regression = NeuralNetwork(
    layers=[Dense(neurons = 1)],
            loss = MeanSquaredError(),
            learning_rate = 0.01
            )

neural_network = NeuralNetwork(
    layers=[Dense(neurons=13,
                  activation=Sigmoid()),
            Dense(neurons=1,
                  activation=Linear())],
            loss = MeanSquaredError(),
            learning_rate = 0.01
            )
```

We're basically done; now we just feed data repeatedly through the network in order for it to learn. To make this process cleaner and easier to extend to the more compli-cated deep learning scenarios we'll see in the following chapter, however, it will help us to define another class that carries out the training, as well as an additional class that carries out the "learning," or the actual updating of the NeuralNetwork parame-ters given the gradients computed on the backward pass. Let's quickly define these two classes.

# Trainer and Optimizer

First, let's note the similarities between these classes and the code we used to train the network in Chapter 2. There, we used the following code to implement the four steps described earlier for training the model:

---

3 The learning rate of 0.01 isn't special; we simply found it to be optimal in the course of experimenting while writing the prior chapter.

```
# pass X_batch forward and compute the loss
forward_info, loss = forward_loss(X_batch, y_batch, weights)

# compute the gradient of the loss with respect to each of the weights
loss_grads = loss_gradients(forward_info, weights)

# update the weights
for key in weights.keys():
    weights[key] -= learning_rate * loss_grads[key]
```

This code was within a for loop that repeatedly fed data through the function defining and updated our network.

With the classes we have now, we'll ultimately do this inside a fit function within the Trainer class that will mostly be a wrapper around the train function used in the prior chapter. (The full code for it is in this chapter's Jupyter Notebook (*https://oreil.ly/2MV0aZI*) on the book's GitHub page.) The main difference is that inside this new function, the first two lines from the preceding code block will be replaced with this line:

```
neural_network.train_batch(X_batch, y_batch)
```

Updating the parameters, which happens in the following two lines, will take place in a separate Optimizer class. And finally, the for loop that previously wrapped around all of this will take place in the Trainer class that wraps around the NeuralNetwork and the Optimizer.

Next, let's discuss why we need an Optimizer class and what it should look like.

# Optimizer

In the model we described in the last chapter, each Layer contains a simple rule for updating the weights based on the parameters and their gradients. As we'll touch on in the next chapter, there are many other update rules we can use, such as ones involving the *history* of gradient updates rather than just the gradient updates from the specific batch that was fed in at that iteration. Creating a separate Optimizer class will give us the flexibility to swap in one update rule for another, something that we'll explore in more detail in the next chapter.

## Description and code

The base Optimizer class will take in a NeuralNetwork and, every time the step function is called, will update the parameters of the network based on their current values, their gradients, and any other information stored in the Optimizer:

```
class Optimizer(object):
    '''
    Base class for a neural network optimizer.
    '''
```

```
def __init__(self,
             lr: float = 0.01):
    '''
    Every optimizer must have an initial learning rate.
    '''
    self.lr = lr

def step(self) -> None:
    '''
    Every optimizer must implement the "step" function.
    '''
    pass
```

And here's how this looks with the straightforward update rule we've seen so far, known as *stochastic gradient descent*:

```
class SGD(Optimizer):
    '''
    Stochastic gradient descent optimizer.
    '''
    def __init__(self,
                 lr: float = 0.01) -> None:
        '''Pass'''
        super().__init__(lr)

    def step(self):
        '''
        For each parameter, adjust in the appropriate direction, with the
        magnitude of the adjustment based on the learning rate.
        '''
        for (param, param_grad) in zip(self.net.params(),
                                       self.net.param_grads()):

            param -= self.lr * param_grad
```

 Note that while our NeuralNetwork class does not have an _update_params method, we do rely on the params() and param_grads() methods to extract the correct ndarrays for optimization.

That's the basic Optimizer class; let's cover the Trainer class next.

# Trainer

In addition to training the model as described previously, the Trainer class also links together the NeuralNetwork with the Optimizer, ensuring the latter trains the former properly. You may have noticed in the previous section that we didn't pass in a Neural Network when initializing our Optimizer; instead, we'll assign the NeuralNetwork to be an attribute of the Optimizer when we initialize the Trainer class shortly, with this line:

```
setattr(self.optim, 'net', self.net)
```

In the following subsection, I show a simplified but working version of the Trainer class that for now contains just the fit method. This method trains our model for a number of *epochs* and prints out the loss value after each set number of epochs. In each epoch, we:

1. Shuffle the data at the beginning of the epoch

2. Feed the data through the network in batches, updating the parameters after each batch has been fed through

The epoch ends when we have fed the entire training set through the Trainer.

## Trainer code

In the following is the code for a simple version of the Trainer class, we hide two self-explanatory helper methods used during the fit function: generate_batches, which generates batches of data from X_train and y_train for training, and per mute_data, which shuffles X_train and y_train at the beginning of each epoch. We also include a restart argument in the train function: if True (default), it will reini-tialize the model's parameters to random values upon calling the train function:

```
class Trainer(object):
    '''
    Trains a neural network.
    '''
    def __init__(self,
                 net: NeuralNetwork,
                 optim: Optimizer)
        '''
        Requires a neural network and an optimizer in order for training to
        occur. Assign the neural network as an instance variable to the optimizer.
        '''
        self.net = net
        setattr(self.optim, 'net', self.net)

    def fit(self, X_train: ndarray, y_train: ndarray,
            X_test: ndarray, y_test: ndarray,
```

```
    epochs: int=100,
    eval_every: int=10,
    batch_size: int=32,
    seed: int = 1,
    restart: bool = True) -> None:
'''
Fits the neural network on the training data for a certain number of
epochs. Every "eval_every" epochs, it evaluates the neural network on
the testing data.
'''
np.random.seed(seed)

if restart:
    for layer in self.net.layers:
        layer.first = True

for e in range(epochs):

    X_train, y_train = permute_data(X_train, y_train)

    batch_generator = self.generate_batches(X_train, y_train,
                                             batch_size)

    for ii, (X_batch, y_batch) in enumerate(batch_generator):

        self.net.train_batch(X_batch, y_batch)

        self.optim.step()

    if (e+1) % eval_every == 0:

        test_preds = self.net.forward(X_test)

        loss = self.net.loss.forward(test_preds, y_test)

        print(f"Validation loss after {e+1} epochs is {loss:.3f}")
```

In the full version of this function in the book's GitHub repository (*https://oreil.ly/2MV0aZI*), we also implement *early stopping*, which does the following:

1. It saves the loss value every eval_every epochs.

2. It checks whether the validation loss is lower than the last time it was calculated.

3. If the validation loss is *not* lower, it uses the model from eval_every epochs ago.

Finally, we have everything we need to train these models!

# Putting Everything Together

Here is the full code to train our network using all the `Trainer` and `Optimizer` classes and the two models defined before—`linear_regression` and `neural_network`. We'll set the learning rate to `0.01` and the maximum number of epochs to `50` and evaluate our models every 10 epochs:

```
optimizer = SGD(lr=0.01)
trainer = Trainer(linear_regression, optimizer)

trainer.fit(X_train, y_train, X_test, y_test,
       epochs = 50,
       eval_every = 10,
       seed=20190501);

Validation loss after 10 epochs is 30.295
Validation loss after 20 epochs is 28.462
Validation loss after 30 epochs is 26.299
Validation loss after 40 epochs is 25.548
Validation loss after 50 epochs is 25.092
```

Using the same model-scoring functions from Chapter 2, and wrapping them inside an `eval_regression_model` function, gives us these results:

```
eval_regression_model(linear_regression, X_test, y_test)

Mean absolute error: 3.52

Root mean squared error 5.01
```

These are similar to the results of the linear regression we ran in the last chapter, confirming that our framework is working.

Running the same code with the `neural_network` model with a hidden layer with 13 neurons, we get the following:

```
Validation loss after 10 epochs is 27.434
Validation loss after 20 epochs is 21.834
Validation loss after 30 epochs is 18.915
Validation loss after 40 epochs is 17.193
Validation loss after 50 epochs is 16.214

eval_regression_model(neural_network, X_test, y_test)

Mean absolute error: 2.60

Root mean squared error 4.03
```

Again, these results are similar to what we saw in the prior chapter, and they're significantly better than our straightforward linear regression.

# Our First Deep Learning Model (from Scratch)

Now that all of that setup is out of the way, defining our first deep learning model is trivial:

```
deep_neural_network = NeuralNetwork(
    layers=[Dense(neurons=13,
                  activation=Sigmoid()),
            Dense(neurons=13,
                  activation=Sigmoid()),
            Dense(neurons=1,
                  activation=LinearAct())],
    loss=MeanSquaredError(),
    learning_rate=0.01
)
```

We won't even try to be clever with this (yet). We'll just add a hidden layer with the same dimensionality as the first layer, so that our network now has two hidden layers, each with 13 neurons.

Training this using the same learning rate and evaluation schedule as the prior models yields the following result:

```
Validation loss after 10 epochs is 44.134
Validation loss after 20 epochs is 25.271
Validation loss after 30 epochs is 22.341
Validation loss after 40 epochs is 16.464
Validation loss after 50 epochs is 14.604

eval_regression_model(deep_neural_network, X_test, y_test)

Mean absolute error: 2.45

Root mean squared error 3.82
```

We finally worked up to doing deep learning from scratch—and indeed, on this real-world problem, without the use of any tricks (just a bit of learning rate tuning), our deep learning model does perform slightly better than a neural network with just one hidden layer.

More importantly, we did so by building a framework that is easily extensible. We could easily implement other kinds of Operations, wrap them in new Layers, and drop them right in, assuming that they have defined _output and _input_grad methods and that the dimensions of their inputs, outputs, and parameters match those of their respective gradients. Similarly, we could easily drop different activation functions into our existing layers and see if it decreases our error metrics; I encourage you to clone the book's GitHub repo (*https://oreil.ly/deep-learning-github*) and try this!

# Conclusion and Next Steps

In the next chapter, I'll cover several tricks that will be essential to getting our models to train properly once we get to more challenging problems than this simple one[4]—in particular, defining other Losses and Optimizers. I'll also cover additional tricks for tuning our learning rates and modifying them throughout training, and I'll show how to incorporate this into the Optimizer and Trainer classes. Finally, we'll see Dropout, a new kind of Operation that has proven essential for increasing the training stability of deep learning models. Onward!

---

[4] Even on this simple problem, changing the hyperparameters slightly can cause the deep learning model to fail to beat the two-layer neural network. Clone the GitHub repo (*https://oreil.ly/deep-learning-github*) and try it yourself!

## CHAPTER 4

# Extensions

In the last chapter, after having spent two chapters reasoning from first principles about what deep learning models are and how they should work, we finally built our first deep learning model and trained it to solve the relatively simple problem of predicting house prices given numeric features about houses. On most real-world problems, however, successfully training deep learning models isn't so easy: while these models can conceivably find an optimal solution to any problem that can be framed as a supervised learning problem, in practice they often fail, and indeed there are few theoretical guarantees that a given model architecture will in fact find a good solution to a given problem. Still, there are some well-understood techniques that make neural network training more likely to succeed; these will be the focus of this chapter.

We'll start out by reviewing what neural networks are "trying to do" mathematically: find the minimum of a function. Then I'll show a series of techniques that can help the networks achieve this, demonstrating their effectiveness on the classic MNIST dataset of handwritten digits. We'll start with a loss function that is used throughout classification problems in deep learning, showing that it significantly accelerates learning (we've only covered regression problems thus far in this book because we hadn't yet introduced this loss function and thus haven't been able to do classification problems justice). On a similar note, we'll cover activation functions other than sigmoid and show why *they* might also accelerate learning, while discussing the tradeoffs involved with activation functions in general. Next, we'll cover momentum, the most important (and straightforward) extension of the stochastic gradient descent optimization technique we've been using thus far, as well as briefly discussing what more advanced optimizers can do. We'll end by covering three techniques that are unrelated to each other but that are all essential: learning rate decay, weight initialization, and dropout. As we'll see, each of these techniques will help our neural network find successively more optimal solutions.

In the first chapter, we followed the "diagram-math-code" model for introducing each concept. Here, there isn't an obvious diagram for each technique, so we'll instead begin with the "intuition" for each technique, then follow up with the math (which will typically be much simpler than in the first chapter), and end with the code, which will really entail incorporating the technique into the framework we've built and thus describing precisely how it interacts with the building blocks we formalized in the last chapter. In this spirit, we'll start the chapter with some "overall" intuition on what neural networks are trying to do: find the minimum of a function.

## Some Intuition About Neural Networks

As we've seen, neural networks contain a bunch of weights; given these weights, along with some input data X and y, we can compute a resulting "loss." Figure 4-1 shows this extremely high-level (but still correct) view of neural networks.

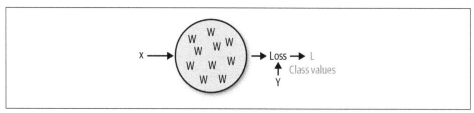

*Figure 4-1. A simple way to think of a neural network with weights*

In reality, each individual weight has some complex, nonlinear relationship with the features X, the target y, the other weights, and ultimately the loss L. If we plotted this out, varying the value of the weight while holding constant the values of the other weights, X, and y, and plotted the resulting value of the loss L, we could see something like what is shown in Figure 4-2.

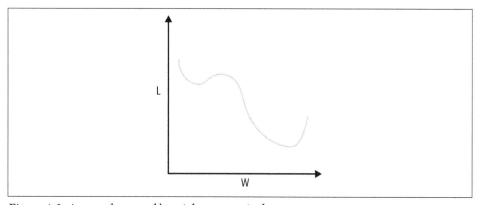

*Figure 4-2. A neural network's weights versus its loss*

When we start to train neural networks, we initialize each weight to have a value somewhere along the x-axis in Figure 4-2. Then, using the gradients we calculate during backpropagation, we iteratively update the weight, with our first update based on the slope of this curve at the initial value we happened to choose.[1] Figure 4-3 shows this geometric interpretation of what it means to update the weights in a neural network based on the gradients and the learning rate. The blue arrows on the left represent repeatedly applying this update rule with a smaller learning rate than the red arrows on the right; note that in both cases, the updates in the horizontal direction are proportional to the slope of the curve at the value of the weight (steeper slope means a larger update).

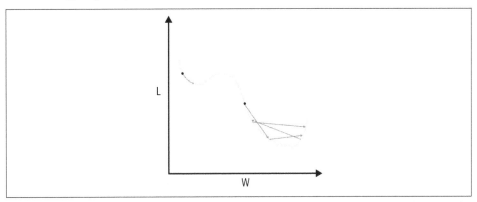

*Figure 4-3. Updating the weights of a neural network as a function of the gradients and the learning rate, depicted geometrically*

The goal of training a deep learning model is to move each weight to the "global" value for which the loss is minimized. As we can see from Figure 4-3, if the steps we take are too small, we risk ending up in a "local" minimum, which is less optimal than the global one (the path of a weight that follows that scenario is illustrated by the blue arrows). If the steps are too large, we risk "repeatedly hopping over" the global minimum, even if we are near it (this scenario is represented by the red arrows). This is the fundamental trade-off of tuning learning rates: if they are too small, we can get stuck in a local minimum; if they are too large, they can skip over the global minimum.

In reality, the picture is far more complicated than this. One reason is that there are thousands, if not millions, of weights in a neural network, so we are searching for a global minimum in a space that has thousands or millions of dimensions. Moreover, since we update the weights on each iteration as well as passing in a different X and y,

---

1 In addition, as we saw in Chapter 3, we multiply these gradients by a learning rate to give us more fine-grained control over how much the weights change.

*the curve we are trying to find the minimum of is constantly changing!* The latter is one of the main reasons neural networks were met with skepticism for so many years; it didn't seem like iteratively updating the weights in this way could actually find a globally desirable solution. Yann LeCun et al. say it best in a 2015 *Nature* article (*https://www.nature.com/articles/nature14539*):

> *In particular, it was commonly thought that simple gradient descent would get trapped in poor local minima—weight configurations for which no small change would reduce the average error. In practice, poor local minima are rarely a problem with large networks. Regardless of the initial conditions, the system nearly always reaches solutions of very similar quality. Recent theoretical and empirical results strongly suggest that local minima are not a serious issue in general.*

So *in practice*, Figure 4-3 provides both a good mental model for why learning rates should not be too large or too small and adequate intuition for why many of the tricks we're going to learn in this chapter actually work. Equipped with this intuition of what neural networks are trying to do, let's start examining these tricks. We'll start with a loss function, the *softmax cross entropy* loss function, that works in large part because of its ability to provide steeper gradients to the weights than the mean squared error loss function we saw in the prior chapter.

# The Softmax Cross Entropy Loss Function

In Chapter 3, we used mean squared error (MSE) as our loss function. This function had the nice property that it was convex, meaning the further the prediction was from the target, the steeper would be the initial gradient that the Loss sent backward to the network Layers and thus the greater would be all the gradients received by the parameters. It turns out that in classification problems, however, we can do better than this, since in such problems *we know that the values our network outputs should be interpreted as probabilities*; thus, not only should each value be between 0 and 1, but the vector of probabilities should sum to 1 for each observation we have fed through our network. The softmax cross entropy loss function exploits this to produce steeper gradients than the mean squared error loss for the same inputs. This function has two components: the first is the *softmax* function, and the second component is the "cross entropy" loss; we'll cover each of these in turn.

## Component #1: The Softmax Function

For a classification problem with N possible classes, we'll have our neural network output a vector of N values for each observation. For a problem with three classes, these values could, for example, be:

```
[5, 3, 2]
```

## Math

Again, since this is a classification problem, we know that this *should* be interpreted as a vector of probabilities (the probability of this observation belonging to class 1, 2, or 3, respectively). One way to transform these values into a vector of probabilities would be to simply normalize them, summing and dividing by the sum:

$$\text{Normalize}\left(\begin{bmatrix} x_1 \\ x_2 \\ x_3 \end{bmatrix}\right) = \begin{bmatrix} \dfrac{x_1}{x_1 + x_2 + x_3} \\ \dfrac{x_2}{x_1 + x_2 + x_3} \\ \dfrac{x_3}{x_1 + x_2 + x_3} \end{bmatrix}$$

However, there turns out to be a way that both produces steeper gradients and has some elegant mathematical properties: the softmax function. This function, for a vector of length 3, would be defined as:

$$\text{Softmax}\left(\begin{bmatrix} x_1 \\ x_2 \\ x_3 \end{bmatrix}\right) = \begin{bmatrix} \dfrac{e^{x_1}}{e^{x_1} + e^{x_2} + e^{x_3}} \\ \dfrac{e^{x_2}}{e^{x_1} + e^{x_2} + e^{x_3}} \\ \dfrac{e^{x_3}}{e^{x_1} + e^{x_2} + e^{x_3}} \end{bmatrix}$$

## Intuition

The intuition behind the softmax function is that it more strongly amplifies the maximum value relative to the other values, forcing the neural network to be "less neutral" toward which prediction it thinks is the correct one in the context of a classification problem. Let's compare what both of these functions, normalize and softmax, would do to our preceding vector of probabilities:

```
normalize(np.array([5,3,2]))

array([0.5, 0.3, 0.2])

softmax(np.array([5,3,2]))

array([0.84, 0.11, 0.04])
```

We can see that the original maximum value—5—has a significantly higher value than it would have upon simply normalizing the data, and the other two values are lower than they were coming out of the normalize function. Thus, the softmax function is partway between normalizing the values and actually applying the max function (which in this case would result in an output of array([1.0, 0.0, 0.0])— hence the name "softmax."

## Component #2: The Cross Entropy Loss

Recall that any loss function will take in a vector of probabilities $\begin{bmatrix} p_1 \\ \vdots \\ p_n \end{bmatrix}$ and a vector of

actual values $\begin{bmatrix} y_1 \\ \vdots \\ y_n \end{bmatrix}$.

### Math

The cross entropy loss function, for each index $i$ in these vectors, is:

$$CE(p_i, y_i) = -y_i \times \log(p_i) - (1 - y_i) \times \log(1 - p_i)$$

### Intuition

To see why this makes sense as a loss function, consider that since every element of $y$ is either 0 or 1, the preceding equation reduces to:

$$CE(p_i, y_i) = \begin{cases} -\log(1 - p_i) & \text{if } y_i = 0 \\ -\log(p_i) & \text{if } y_i = 1 \end{cases}$$

Now we can break this down more easily. If $y = 0$, then the plot of the value of this loss versus the value of the mean squared error loss over the interval 0 to 1 is as depicted in Figure 4-4.

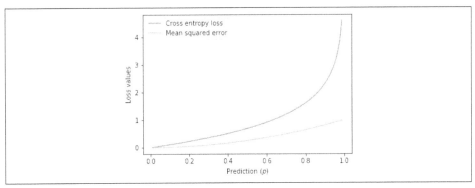

*Figure 4-4. Cross entropy loss versus MSE when y = 0*

Not only are the penalties for the cross entropy loss much higher over this interval,[2] but they get steeper at a higher rate; indeed, the value of the cross entropy loss approaches infinity as the difference between our prediction and the target approaches 1! The plot for when $y = 1$ is similar, just "flipped" (that is, it's rotated 180 degrees around the line $x = 0.5$).

So, for problems where we know the output will be between 0 and 1, the cross entropy loss produces steeper gradients than MSE. The real magic happens when we combine this loss with the softmax function—first feeding the neural network output through the softmax function to normalize it so the values add to 1, and then feeding the resulting probabilities into the cross entropy loss function.

Let's see what this looks like with the three-class scenario we've been using so far; the expression for the component of the loss vector from $i = 1$—that is, the first component of the loss for a given observation, which we'll denote as $SCE_1$—is:

$$SCE_1 = -y_1 \times log\left(\frac{e^{x_1}}{e^{x_1} + e^{x_2} + e^{x_3}}\right) - (1 - y_1) \times log\left(1 - \frac{e^{x_1}}{e^{x_1} + e^{x_2} + e^{x_3}}\right)$$

Based on this expression, the gradient would seem to be a bit trickier for this loss. Nevertheless, there's an elegant expression that is both easy to write mathematically and easy to implement:

---

2 We can be more specific: the average value of $-log(1 - x)$ over the interval 0 to 1 turns out to be 1, while the average value of $x^2$ over the same interval is just $\frac{1}{3}$.

$$\frac{\partial SCE_1}{\partial x_1} = \frac{e^{x_1}}{e^{x_1} + e^{x_2} + e^{x_3}} - y_1$$

That means that the *total* gradient to the softmax cross entropy is:

$$\text{softmax}\left(\begin{bmatrix} x_1 \\ x_2 \\ x_3 \end{bmatrix}\right) - \begin{bmatrix} y_1 \\ y_2 \\ y_3 \end{bmatrix}$$

That's it! As promised, the resulting implementation is simple as well:

```
softmax_x = softmax(x, axis = 1)
loss_grad = softmax_x - y
```

Let's code this up.

## Code

To recap Chapter 3, any Loss class is expected to receive two 2D arrays, one with the network's predictions and the other with the targets. The number of rows in each array is the batch size, and the number of columns is the number of classes n in the classification problem; a row in each represents an observation in the dataset, with the n values in the row representing the neural network's best guess for the probabilities of that observation belonging to each of the n classes. Thus, we'll have to apply the softmax to *each row* in the prediction array. This leads to a first potential issue: we'll next feed the resulting numbers into the log function to compute the loss. This should worry you, since $log(x)$ goes to negative infinity as $x$ goes to 0, and similarly, 1 − $x$ goes to infinity as $x$ goes to 1. To prevent extremely large loss values that could lead to numeric instability, we'll clip the output of the softmax function to be no less than $10^{-7}$ and no greater than $10^7$.

Finally, we can put everything together!

```
class SoftmaxCrossEntropyLoss(Loss):
    def __init__(self, eps: float=1e-9)
        super().__init__()
        self.eps = eps
        self.single_output = False

    def _output(self) -> float:

        # applying the softmax function to each row (observation)
        softmax_preds = softmax(self.prediction, axis=1)

        # clipping the softmax output to prevent numeric instability
```

```
        self.softmax_preds = np.clip(softmax_preds, self.eps, 1 - self.eps)

        # actual loss computation
softmax_cross_entropy_loss = (
    -1.0 * self.target * np.log(self.softmax_preds) - \
        (1.0 - self.target) * np.log(1 - self.softmax_preds)
)

        return np.sum(softmax_cross_entropy_loss)

    def _input_grad(self) -> ndarray:

        return self.softmax_preds - self.target
```

Soon I'll show via some experiments on the MNIST dataset how this loss is an improvement on the mean squared error loss. But first let's discuss the trade-offs involved with choosing an activation function and see if there's a better choice than sigmoid.

## A Note on Activation Functions

We argued in Chapter 2 that sigmoid was a good activation function because it:

- Was a nonlinear and monotonic function
- Provided a "regularizing" effect on the model, forcing the intermediate features down to a finite range, specifically between 0 and 1

Nevertheless, sigmoid has a downside, similar to the downside of the mean squared error loss: *it produces relatively flat gradients* during the backward pass. The gradient that gets passed to the sigmoid function (or any function) on the backward pass represents how much the function's *output* ultimately affects the loss; because the maximum slope of the sigmoid function is 0.25, these gradients will *at best* be divided by 4 when sent backward to the previous operation in the model. Worse still, when the input to the sigmoid function is less than –2 or greater than 2, the gradient those inputs receive will be almost 0, since *sigmoid*($x$) is almost flat at $x = -2$ or $x = 2$. What this means is that any parameters influencing these inputs will receive small gradients, and our network could learn slowly as a result.[3] Furthermore, if multiple sigmoid activation functions are used in successive layers of a neural network, this problem will compound, further diminishing the gradients that weights earlier in the neural network could receive.

---

3 To get an intuition for why this can happen: imagine a weight $w$ is contributing to a feature $f$ (so that $f = w \times x_1 + ...$), and during the forward pass of our neural network, $f = -10$ for some observation. Because *sigmoid*($x$) is so flat at $x = -10$, changing the value of $w$ will have almost no effect on the model prediction and thus the loss.

What would an activation "at the other extreme"—one with the opposite strengths and weaknesses—look like?

### The other extreme: the Rectified Linear Unit

The Rectified Linear Unit, or ReLU, activation is a commonly used activation with the opposite strengths and weaknesses of sigmoid. ReLU is simply defined to be 0 if $x$ is less than 0, and $x$ otherwise. A plot of this is shown in Figure 4-5.

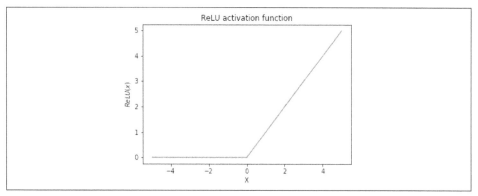

*Figure 4-5. ReLU activation*

This is a "valid" activation function in the sense that it is monotonic and nonlinear. It produces much larger gradients than sigmoid—1 if the input to the function is greater than 0, and 0 otherwise, for an average of 0.5—whereas the *maximum* gradient sigmoid can produce is 0.25. ReLU activation is a very popular choice in deep neural network architectures, because its downside (that it draws a sharp, somewhat arbitrary distinction between values less than or greater than 0) can be addressed by other techniques, including some that will be covered in this chapter, and its benefits (of producing large gradients) are critical to training the weights in the architectures of deep neural networks.

Nevertheless, there's an activation function that is a happy medium between these two, and that we'll use in the demos in this chapter: Tanh.

### A happy medium: Tanh

The Tanh function is shaped similarly to the sigmoid function but maps inputs to values between –1 and 1. Figure 4-6 shows this function.

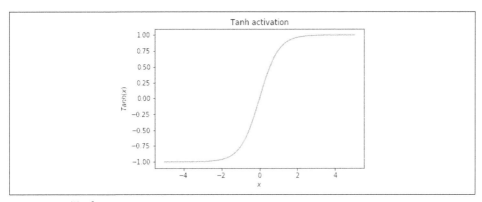

*Figure 4-6. Tanh activation*

This function produces significantly steeper gradients than sigmoid; specifically, the maximum gradient of Tanh turns out to be 1, in contrast to sigmoid's 0.25. Figure 4-7 shows the gradients of these two functions.

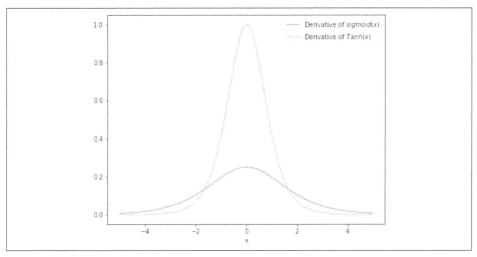

*Figure 4-7. Sigmoid derivative versus Tanh derivative*

In addition, just as $f(x) = sigmoid(x)$ has the easy-to-express derivative $f'(x) = sigmoid(x) \times (1 - sigmoid(x))$, so too does $f(x) = tanh(x)$ have the easy-to-express derivative $f'(x) = (1 - tanh(x)^2$.

The point here is that there are trade-offs involved with choosing an activation function regardless of the architecture: we want an activation function that will allow our network to learn nonlinear relationships between input and output, while not adding unnecessary complexity that will make it harder for the network to find a good solution. For example, the "Leaky ReLU" activation function allows a slight negative slope when the input to the ReLU function is less than 0, enhancing ReLU's ability to send gradients backward, and the "ReLU6" activation function caps the positive end of ReLU at 6, introducing even more nonlinearity into the network. Still, both of these activation functions are more complex than ReLU; and if the problem we are dealing with is relatively simple, those more sophisticated activation functions could make it even harder for the network to learn. Thus, in the models we demo in the rest of this book, we'll simply use the Tanh activation function, which balances these considerations well.

Now that we've chosen an activation function, let's use it to run some experiments.

# Experiments

We've justified using Tanh throughout our experiments, so let's get back to the original point of this section: showing why the softmax cross entropy loss is so pervasive throughout deep learning.[4] We'll use the MNIST dataset, which consists of black-and-white images of handwritten digits that are 28 × 28 pixels, with the value of each pixel ranging from 0 (white) to 255 (black). Furthermore, the dataset is predivided into a training set of 60,000 images and a testing set of 10,000 additional images. In the book's GitHub repo (*https://oreil.ly/2H7rJvf*), we show a helper function to read both the images and their corresponding labels into training and testing sets using the following line of code:

```
X_train, y_train, X_test, y_test = mnist.load()
```

Our goal will be to train a neural network to learn which of the 10 digits from 0 to 9 the image contains.

## Data Preprocessing

For classification, we have to perform *one-hot encoding* to transform our vectors representing the labels into an ndarray of the same shape as the predictions: specifically, we'll map the label "0" to a vector with a 1 in the first position (at index 0) and 0s in all the other positions, "1" to a vector with a 1 in the second position (at index 1), and so on (*https://oreil.ly/2KTRm3z*):

$$[0, 2, 1] \Rightarrow \begin{bmatrix} 1 & 0 & 0 & \dots & 0 \\ 0 & 0 & 1 & \dots & 0 \\ 0 & 1 & 0 & \dots & 0 \end{bmatrix}$$

---

4 For example, TensorFlow's MNIST classification tutorial uses the softmax_cross_entropy_with_logits function, and PyTorch's nn.CrossEntropyLoss actually computes the softmax function inside it.

---

Finally, it is always helpful to scale our data to mean 0 and variance 1, just as we did with the "real-world" datasets in the prior chapters. Here, however, since each data point is an image, we won't scale each *feature* to have mean 0 and variance 1, since that would result in the values of adjacent pixels being changed by different amounts, which could distort the image! Instead, we'll simply provide a global scaling to our dataset that subtracts off the overall mean and divides by the overall variance (note that we use the statistics from the training set to scale the testing set):

```
X_train, X_test = X_train - np.mean(X_train), X_test - np.mean(X_train)
X_train, X_test = X_train / np.std(X_train), X_test / np.std(X_train)
```

## Model

We'll have to define our model to have 10 outputs for each input: one for each of the probabilities of our model belonging to each of the 10 classes. Since we know each of our outputs will be a probability, we'll give our model a sigmoid activation on the last layer. Throughout this chapter, to illustrate whether the "training tricks" we're describing actually enhance our models' ability to learn, we'll use a consistent model architecture of a two-layer neural network with the number of neurons in the hidden layer close to the geometric mean of our number of inputs (784) and our number of outputs (10): $89 \approx \sqrt{784 \times 10}$.

Let's now turn to our first experiment, comparing a neural network trained with simple mean squared error loss to one trained with softmax cross entropy loss. The loss values you see displayed are per observation (recall that on average cross entropy loss will have absolute loss values three times as large as mean squared error loss). If we run:

```
model = NeuralNetwork(
    layers=[Dense(neurons=89,
                  activation=Tanh()),
            Dense(neurons=10,
                  activation=Sigmoid())],
            loss = MeanSquaredError(),
seed=20190119)

optimizer = SGD(0.1)

trainer = Trainer(model, optimizer)
trainer.fit(X_train, train_labels, X_test, test_labels,
            epochs = 50,
            eval_every = 10,
            seed=20190119,
            batch_size=60);

calc_accuracy_model(model, X_test)
```

it gives us:

```
Validation loss after 10 epochs is 0.611
Validation loss after 20 epochs is 0.428
Validation loss after 30 epochs is 0.389
Validation loss after 40 epochs is 0.374
Validation loss after 50 epochs is 0.366

The model validation accuracy is: 72.58%
```

Now let's test the claim we made earlier in the chapter: that the softmax cross entropy loss function would help our model learn faster.

## Experiment: Softmax Cross Entropy Loss

First let's change the preceding model to:

```
model = NeuralNetwork(
    layers=[Dense(neurons=89,
                  activation=Tanh()),
            Dense(neurons=10,
                  activation=Linear())],
            loss = SoftmaxCrossEntropy(),
seed=20190119)
```

 Since we are now feeding the model outputs through the softmax function as part of the loss, we no longer need to feed them through a sigmoid activation function.

Then we run it for model for 50 epochs, which gives us these results:

```
Validation loss after 10 epochs is 0.630
Validation loss after 20 epochs is 0.574
Validation loss after 30 epochs is 0.549
Validation loss after 40 epochs is 0.546
Loss increased after epoch 50, final loss was 0.546, using the model from
epoch 40

The model validation accuracy is: 91.01%
```

Indeed, changing our loss function to one that gives much steeper gradients alone gives a huge boost to the accuracy of our model![5]

---

[5] You may argue that the softmax cross entropy loss is getting an "unfair advantage" here, since the softmax function normalizes the values it receives so that they add to 1, whereas the mean squared error loss simply gets 10 inputs that have been fed through the sigmoid function and have not been normalized to add to 1. However, on the book's website (*https://oreil.ly/2H7rJvf*) I show that MSE still performs worse than the softmax cross entropy loss even after normalizing the inputs to the mean squared error loss so that they sum to 1 for each observation.

Of course, we can do significantly better than this, even without changing our architecture. In the next section, we'll cover momentum, the most important and straightforward extension to the stochastic gradient descent optimization technique we've been using up until now.

# Momentum

So far, we've been using only one "update rule" for our weights at each time step. Simply take the derivative of the loss with respect to the weights and move the weights in the resulting correct direction. This means that our `_update_rule` function in the `Optimizer` looked like:

```
update = self.lr*kwargs['grad']
kwargs['param'] -= update
```

Let's first cover the intuition for why we might want to extend this update rule to incorporate momentum.

## Intuition for Momentum

Recall Figure 4-3, which plotted an individual parameter's value against the loss value from the network. Imagine a scenario in which the parameter's value is continually updated in the same direction because the loss continues to decrease with each iteration. This would be analogous to the parameter "rolling down a hill," and the value of the update at each time step would be analogous to the parameter's "velocity." In the real world, however, objects don't instantaneously stop and change directions; that's because they have *momentum*, which is just a concise way of saying their velocity at a given instant is a function not just of the forces acting on them in that instant but also of their accumulated past velocities, with more recent velocities weighted more heavily. This physical interpretation is the motivation for applying momentum to our weight updates. In the next section we'll make this precise.

## Implementing Momentum in the Optimizer Class

Basing our parameter updates on momentum means that *the parameter update at each time step will be a weighted average of the parameter updates at past time steps, with the weights decayed exponentially*. There will thus be a second parameter we have to choose, the momentum parameter, which will determine the degree of this decay; the higher it is, the more the weight update at each time step will be based on the parameter's accumulated momentum as opposed to its current velocity.

### Math

Mathematically, if our momentum parameter is $\mu$, and the gradient at each time step is $\nabla_t$, our weight update is:

$$\text{update} = \nabla_t + \mu \times \nabla_{t-1} + \mu^2 \times \nabla_{t-2} + \dots$$

If our momentum parameter was 0.9, for example, we would multiply the gradient from one time step ago by 0.9, the one from two time steps ago by $0.9^2 = 0.81$, the one from three time steps ago by $0.9^3 = 0.729$, and so on, and then finally add all of these to the gradient from the current time step to get the overall weight update for the current time step.

### Code

How do we implement this? Do we have to compute an infinite sum every time we want to update our weights?

It turns out there is a cleverer way. Our `Optimizer` will keep track of a separate quantity representing the *history* of parameter updates in addition to just receiving a gradient at each time step. Then, at each time step, we'll use the current gradient to update this history and compute the actual parameter update as a function of this history. Since momentum is loosely based on an analogy with physics, we'll call this quantity "velocity."

How should we update velocity? It turns out we can use the following steps:

1. Multiply it by the momentum parameter.
2. Add the gradient.

This results in the velocity taking on the following values at each time step, starting at $t = 1$:

1. $\nabla_1$
2. $\nabla_2 + \mu \times \nabla_1$
3. $\nabla_3 + \mu \times (\nabla_2 + \mu \times \nabla_1) = \mu \times \nabla_2 + \mu^2 \times \nabla_1)$

With this, we can use the velocity as the parameter update! We can then incorporate this into a new subclass of `Optimizer` that we'll call `SGDMomentum`; this class will have `step` and `_update_rule` functions that look as follows:

```
def step(self) -> None:
    '''
    If first iteration: intialize "velocities" for each param.
    Otherwise, simply apply _update_rule.
    '''
    if self.first:
        # now we will set up velocities on the first iteration
        self.velocities = [np.zeros_like(param)
                           for param in self.net.params()]
```

```
        self.first = False

    for (param, param_grad, velocity) in zip(self.net.params(),
                                             self.net.param_grads(),
                                             self.velocities):
        # pass in velocity into the "_update_rule" function
        self._update_rule(param=param,
                          grad=param_grad,
                          velocity=velocity)

def _update_rule(self, **kwargs) -> None:
    '''
    Update rule for SGD with momentum.
    '''
    # Update velocity
    kwargs['velocity'] *= self.momentum
    kwargs['velocity'] += self.lr * kwargs['grad']

    # Use this to update parameters
    kwargs['param'] -= kwargs['velocity']
```

Let's see if this new optimizer can improve our network's training.

## Experiment: Stochastic Gradient Descent with Momentum

Let's train the same neural network with one hidden layer on the MNIST dataset, changing nothing except using optimizer = SGDMomentum(lr=0.1, momentum=0.9) as the optimizer instead of optimizer = SGD(lr=0.1):

```
Validation loss after 10 epochs is 0.441
Validation loss after 20 epochs is 0.351
Validation loss after 30 epochs is 0.345
Validation loss after 40 epochs is 0.338
Loss increased after epoch 50, final loss was 0.338, using the model from epoch 40

The model validation accuracy is: 95.51%
```

You can see that the loss is significantly lower and the accuracy significantly higher, which is simply a result of adding momentum into our parameter update rule![6]

Of course, another way to modify our parameter update at each iteration would be to modify our learning rate; while we can manually change our initial learning rate, we can also automatically decay the learning rate as training proceeds using some rule. The most common such rules are covered next.

---

6 Moreover, momentum is just one way we can use information beyond the gradient from the current batch of data to update the parameters; we briefly cover other update rules in Appendix A, and you can see these update rules implemented in the Lincoln library included on the book's GitHub repo (*https://oreil.ly/2MhdQ1B*).

# Learning Rate Decay

*[The learning rate] is often the single most important hyper-parameter and one should always make sure that it has been tuned.*

—Yoshua Bengio, *Practical Recommendations for Gradient-Based Training of Deep Architectures*, 2012

The motivation for decaying the learning rate as training progresses comes, yet again, from Figure 4-3 in the previous section: while we want to "take big steps" toward the beginning of training, it is likely that as we continue to iteratively update the weights, we will reach a point where we start to "skip over" the minimum. Note that this won't *necessarily* be a problem, since if the relationship between our weights and the loss "smoothly declines" as we approach the minimum, as in Figure 4-3, the magnitude of the gradients will automatically decrease as the slope decreases. Still, this may not happen, and even if it does, learning rate decay can give us more fine-grained control over this process.

## Types of Learning Rate Decay

There are different ways of decaying the learning rate. The simplest is linear decay, where the learning rate declines linearly from its initial value to some terminal value, with the actual decline being implemented at the end of each epoch. More precisely, at time step $t$, if the learning rate we want to start with is $\alpha_{start}$, and our final learning rate is $\alpha_{end}$, then our learning rate at each time step is:

$$\alpha_t = \alpha_{start} - \left(\alpha_{start} - \alpha_{end}\right) \times \frac{t}{N}$$

where $N$ is the total number of epochs.

Another simple method that works about as well is exponential decay, in which the learning rate declines by a constant *proportion* each epoch. The formula here would simply be:

$$\alpha_t = \alpha \times \delta^t$$

where:

$$\delta = \frac{\alpha_{end}}{\alpha_{start}}^{\frac{1}{N-1}}$$

Implementing these is straightforward: we'll initialize our Optimizers to have a "final learning rate" final_lr that the initial learning rate will decay toward throughout the epochs of training:

```
def __init__(self,
             lr: float = 0.01,
             final_lr: float = 0,
             decay_type: str = 'exponential')
    self.lr = lr
    self.final_lr = final_lr
    self.decay_type = decay_type
```

Then, at the beginning of training, we can call a _setup_decay function that calculates how much the learning rate will decay at each epoch:

```
self.optim._setup_decay()
```

These calculations will implement the linear and exponential learning rate decay formulas we just saw:

```
def _setup_decay(self) -> None:

    if not self.decay_type:
        return
    elif self.decay_type == 'exponential':
        self.decay_per_epoch = np.power(self.final_lr / self.lr,
                                1.0 / (self.max_epochs-1))
    elif self.decay_type == 'linear':
        self.decay_per_epoch = (self.lr - self.final_lr) / (self.max_epochs-1)
```

Then, at the end of each epoch, we'll actually decay the learning rate:

```
def _decay_lr(self) -> None:

    if not self.decay_type:
        return

    if self.decay_type == 'exponential':
        self.lr *= self.decay_per_epoch

    elif self.decay_type == 'linear':
        self.lr -= self.decay_per_epoch
```

Finally, we'll call the _decay_lr function from the Trainer during the fit function, at the end of each epoch:

```
if self.optim.final_lr:
    self.optim._decay_lr()
```

Let's run some experiments to see if this improves training.

## Experiments: Learning Rate Decay

Next we try training the same model architecture with learning rate decay. We initialize the learning rates so that the "average learning rate" over the run is equal to the previous learning rate of 0.1: for the run with linear learning rate decay, we initialize the learning rate to 0.15 and decay it down to 0.05, and for the run with exponential decay, we initialize the learning rate to 0.2 and decay it down to 0.05. For the linear decay run with:

```
optimizer = SGDMomentum(0.15, momentum=0.9, final_lr=0.05, decay_type='linear')
```

we have:

```
Validation loss after 10 epochs is 0.403
Validation loss after 20 epochs is 0.343
Validation loss after 30 epochs is 0.282
Loss increased after epoch 40, final loss was 0.282, using the model from epoch 30
The model validation accuracy is: 95.91%
```

For the run with exponential decay, with:

```
optimizer = SGDMomentum(0.2, momentum=0.9, final_lr=0.05, decay_type='exponential')
```

we have:

```
Validation loss after 10 epochs is 0.461
Validation loss after 20 epochs is 0.323
Validation loss after 30 epochs is 0.284
Loss increased after epoch 40, final loss was 0.284, using the model from epoch 30
The model validation accuracy is: 96.06%
```

The losses in the "best models" from these runs were 0.282 and 0.284, significantly lower than the 0.338 that we had before!

Next up: how and why to more intelligently initialize the weights of our model.

# Weight Initialization

As we mentioned in the section on activation functions, several activation functions, such as sigmoid and Tanh, have their steepest gradients when their inputs are 0, with the functions quickly flattening out as the inputs move away from 0. This can potentially limit the effectiveness of these functions, because if many of the inputs have values far from 0, the weights attached to those inputs will receive very small gradients on the backward pass.

This turns out to be a major problem in the neural networks we are now dealing with. Consider the hidden layer in the MNIST network we've been looking at. This layer will receive 784 inputs and then multiply them by a weight matrix, ending up with some number n of neurons (and then optionally add a bias to each neuron). Figure 4-8 shows the distribution of these n values in the hidden layer of our neural network (with 784 inputs) before and after feeding them through the Tanh activation function.

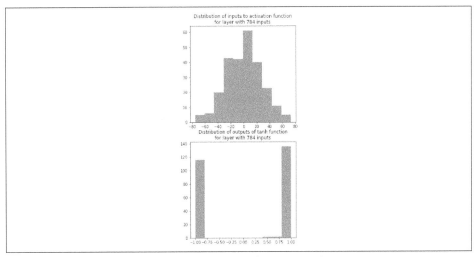

*Figure 4-8. Distribution of inputs to activation function and activations*

After being fed through the activation function, most of the activations are either −1 or 1! This is because each feature is mathematically defined to be:

$$f_n = w_{1,n} \times x_1 + ... + w_{784,n} \times x_{784} + b_n$$

Since we initialized each weight to have variance 1 ($\text{Var}(w_{i,j}) = 1$—and $\text{Var}(b_n) = 1$) and $\text{Var}(X_1 + X_2) = \text{Var}(X_1) + \text{Var}(X_2)$ for independent random variables $X_1$ and $X_2$, we have:

$$\text{Var}(f_n) = 785$$

That gives it a standard deviation ($\sqrt{785}$) of just over 28, which reflects the spread of the values we see in the top half of Figure 4-8.

This tells us we have a problem. But is the problem simply that the features that we feed into the activation functions can't be "too spread out"? If that were the problem, we could simply divide the features by some value to reduce their variance. However, that invites an obvious question: how do we know what to divide the values by? The answer is that the values should be scaled *based on the number of neurons being fed into the layer*. If we had a multilayer neural network, and one layer had 200 neurons and the next layer had 100, the 200-neuron layer would pass values forward that had a wider distribution than the 100-neuron layer. This is undesirable—we don't want the *scale* of the features our neural network learns during training to depend on the number of features passed forward, for the same reason that we don't want our network's predictions to depend on the scale of our input features. Our model's predictions shouldn't be affected, for example, if we multiplied or divided all the values in a feature by 2.

There are several ways to correct for this; here we'll cover the single most prevalent one, suggested by the prior paragraph: we can *adjust the initial variance of the weights based on the number of neurons in the layers they connect so that the values passed forward to the following layer during the forward pass* and *backward to the prior layer during the backward pass* have roughly the same scale. Yes, we have to think about the backward pass too, since the same problem exists there: the variance of the gradients the layer receives during backpropagation will depend directly on the number of features in the *following* layer since that is the one that sends gradients backward to the layer in question.

## Math and Code

How, specifically, do we balance these concerns? If each layer has $n_{in}$ neurons feeding in and $n_{out}$ neurons coming out, the variance for each weight that would keep the variance of the resulting features constant *just on the forward pass* would be:

$$\frac{1}{n_{in}}$$

Similarly, the weight variance that would keep the variance of the features constant on the backward pass would be:

$$\frac{1}{n_{out}}$$

As a compromise between these, what is most often called *Glorot initialization*[7] involves initializing the variance of the weights in each layer to be:

$$\frac{2}{n_{in} + n_{out}}$$

---

7 This is so known because it was proposed by Glorot and Bengio in a 2010 paper: "Understanding the difficulty of training deep feedforward neural networks" (*http://proceedings.mlr.press/v9/glorot10a/glorot10a.pdf*).

Coding this up is simple—we add a `weight_init` argument to each layer, and we add the following to our `_setup_layer` function:

```
if self.weight_init == "glorot":
    scale = 2/(num_in + self.neurons)
else:
    scale = 1.0
```

Now our models will look like:

```
model = NeuralNetwork(
    layers=[Dense(neurons=89,
                  activation=Tanh(),
                  weight_init="glorot"),
            Dense(neurons=10,
                  activation=Linear(),
                  weight_init="glorot")],
            loss = SoftmaxCrossEntropy(),
    seed=20190119)
```

with `weight_init="glorot"` specified for each layer.

## Experiments: Weight Initialization

Running the same models from the prior section but with the weights initialized using Glorot initialization gives:

```
Validation loss after 10 epochs is 0.352
Validation loss after 20 epochs is 0.280
Validation loss after 30 epochs is 0.244
Loss increased after epoch 40, final loss was 0.244, using the model from epoch 30
The model validation accuracy is: 96.71%
```

for the model with linear learning rate decay, and:

```
Validation loss after 10 epochs is 0.305
Validation loss after 20 epochs is 0.264
Validation loss after 30 epochs is 0.245
Loss increased after epoch 40, final loss was 0.245, using the model from epoch 30
The model validation accuracy is: 96.71%
```

for the model with exponential learning rate decay. We see another significant drop in the loss here, from the 0.282 and 0.284 we achieved earlier down to 0.244 and 0.245! Note that with all of these changes, *we haven't been increasing the size or training time of our model*; we've simply tweaked the training process based on our intuition about what neural networks are trying to do that I showed at the beginning of this chapter.

There is one last technique we'll cover in this chapter. As motivation, you may have noticed that *none of the models we've used throughout this chapter were deep learning models*; rather, they were simply neural networks with one hidden layer. That is because without *dropout*, the technique we will now learn, deep learning models are very challenging to train effectively without overfitting.

# Dropout

In this chapter, I've shown several modifications to our neural network's training procedure that got it closer and closer to its global minimum. You may have noticed that we haven't tried the seemingly most obvious thing: adding more layers to our network or more neurons per layer. The reason is that simply adding more "firepower" to most neural network architectures can make it *more* difficult for the network to find a solution that generalizes well. The intuition here is that, while adding more capacity to a neural network allows it to model more complex relationships between input and output, it also risks leading the network to a solution that is overfit to the training data. *Dropout allows us to add capacity to our neural networks while in most cases making it less likely that the network will overfit.*

What specifically *is* dropout?

## Definition

Dropout simply involves randomly choosing some proportion $p$ of the neurons in a layer and setting them equal to 0 during each forward pass of training. This odd trick reduces the capacity of the network, but empirically in many cases it can indeed prevent the network from overfitting. This is especially true in deeper networks, where the features being learned are, by construction, multiple layers of abstraction removed from the original features.

Though dropout can help our network avoid overfitting during training, we still want to give our network its "best shot" of making correct predictions when it comes time to predict. So, the Dropout operation will have two "modes": a "training" mode in which dropout is applied, and an "inference" mode, in which it is not. This causes another problem, however: applying dropout to a layer reduces the overall magnitude of the values being passed forward by a factor of $1 - p$ on average, meaning that if the weights in the following layers would normally expect values with magnitude $M$, they are instead getting magnitude $M \times (1 - p)$. We want to mimic this magnitude shift when running the network in inference mode, so, in addition to removing dropout, we'll multiply *all* the values by $1 - p$.

To make this more clear, let's code it up.

## Implementation

We can implement dropout as an Operation that we'll tack onto the end of each layer. It will look as follows:

```
class Dropout(Operation):

    def __init__(self,
                 keep_prob: float = 0.8):
```

```
            super().__init__()
            self.keep_prob = keep_prob

        def _output(self, inference: bool) -> ndarray:
            if inference:
                return self.inputs * self.keep_prob
            else:
                self.mask = np.random.binomial(1, self.keep_prob,
                                               size=self.inputs.shape)
                return self.inputs * self.mask

        def _input_grad(self, output_grad: ndarray) -> ndarray:
            return output_grad * self.mask
```

On the forward pass, when applying dropout, we save a "mask" representing the individual neurons that got set to 0. Then, on the backward pass, we multiply the gradient the operation receives by this mask. This is because dropout makes the gradient 0 for the input values that are zeroed out (since changing their values will now have no effect on the loss) and leaves the other gradients unchanged.

## Adjusting the rest of our framework to accommodate dropout

You may have noticed that we included an `inference` flag in the _output method that affects whether dropout is applied or not. For this flag to be called properly, we actually have to add it in several other places throughout training:

1. The `Layer` and `NeuralNetwork` forward methods will take in `inference` as an argument (`False` by default) and pass the flag into each `Operation`, so that every `Operation` will behave differently in training mode than in inference mode.

2. Recall that in the `Trainer`, we evaluate the trained model on the testing set every `eval_every` epochs. Now, every time we do that, we'll evaluate with the `infer ence` flag equal to `True`:

   ```
   test_preds = self.net.forward(X_test, inference=True)
   ```

3. Finally, we add a dropout keyword to the Layer class; the full signature of the __init__ function for the Layer class now looks like:

   ```
   def __init__(self,
                neurons: int,
                activation: Operation = Linear(),
                dropout: float = 1.0,
                weight_init: str = "standard")
   ```

   and we append the dropout operation by adding the following to the class's _setup_layer function:

   ```
   if self.dropout < 1.0:
       self.operations.append(Dropout(self.dropout))
   ```

That's it! Let's see if dropout works.

## Experiments: Dropout

First, we see that adding dropout to our existing model does indeed decrease the loss. Adding dropout of 0.8 (so that 20% of the neurons get set to 0) to the first layer, so that our model looks like:

```
mnist_soft = NeuralNetwork(
    layers=[Dense(neurons=89,
                  activation=Tanh(),
                  weight_init="glorot",
                  dropout=0.8),
            Dense(neurons=10,
                  activation=Linear(),
                  weight_init="glorot")],
            loss = SoftmaxCrossEntropy(),
    seed=20190119)
```

and training the model with the same hyperparameters as before (exponential weight decay from an initial learning rate of 0.2 to a final learning rate of 0.05) results in:

```
Validation loss after 10 epochs is 0.285
Validation loss after 20 epochs is 0.232
Validation loss after 30 epochs is 0.199
Validation loss after 40 epochs is 0.196
Loss increased after epoch 50, final loss was 0.196, using the model from epoch 40
The model validation accuracy is: 96.95%
```

This is another significant decrease in loss over what we saw previously: the model achieves a minimum loss of 0.196, compared to 0.244 before.

The real power of dropout comes when we add more layers. Let's change the model we've been using throughout this chapter to be a deep learning model, defining the first hidden layer to have twice as many neurons as did our hidden layer before (178) and our second hidden layer to have half as many (46). Our model looks like:

```
model = NeuralNetwork(
    layers=[Dense(neurons=178,
                  activation=Tanh(),
                  weight_init="glorot",
                  dropout=0.8),
            Dense(neurons=46,
                  activation=Tanh(),
                  weight_init="glorot",
                  dropout=0.8),
            Dense(neurons=10,
                  activation=Linear(),
                  weight_init="glorot")],
            loss = SoftmaxCrossEntropy(),
    seed=20190119)
```

Note the inclusion of dropout in the first two layers.

Training this model with the same optimizer as before yields another significant decrease in the minimum loss achieved—and an increase in accuracy!

```
Validation loss after 10 epochs is 0.321
Validation loss after 20 epochs is 0.268
Validation loss after 30 epochs is 0.248
Validation loss after 40 epochs is 0.222
Validation loss after 50 epochs is 0.217
Validation loss after 60 epochs is 0.194
Validation loss after 70 epochs is 0.191
Validation loss after 80 epochs is 0.190
Validation loss after 90 epochs is 0.182
Loss increased after epoch 100, final loss was 0.182, using the model from epoch 90
The model validation accuracy is: 97.15%
```

More importantly, however, this improvement isn't possible without dropout. Here are the results of training the same model with no dropout:

```
Validation loss after 10 epochs is 0.375
Validation loss after 20 epochs is 0.305
Validation loss after 30 epochs is 0.262
Validation loss after 40 epochs is 0.246
Loss increased after epoch 50, final loss was 0.246, using the model from epoch 40
The model validation accuracy is: 96.52%
```

Without dropout, the deep learning model performs *worse* than the model with just one hidden layer—despite having more than twice as many parameters and taking more than twice as long to train! This illustrates how essential dropout is for training deep learning models effectively; indeed, dropout was an essential component of the ImageNet-winning model from 2012 that kicked off the modern deep learning era.[8] Without dropout, you might not be reading this book!

## Conclusion

In this chapter, you have learned some of the most common techniques for improving neural network training, learning both the intuition for why they work as well as the low-level details of how they work. To summarize these, we'll leave you with a checklist of things you can try to squeeze some extra performance out of your neural network, regardless of the domain:

- Add momentum—or one of many similarly effective advanced optimization techniques—to your weight update rule.

---

8 For more on this, see G. E. Hinton et al., "Improving neural networks by preventing co-adaptation of feature detectors" (*https://arxiv.org/pdf/1207.0580.pdf*).

- Decay your learning rate over time using either linear or exponential decay as shown in this chapter or a more modern technique such as cosine decay. In fact, more effective learning rate schedules vary the learning rate based not just on each epoch but also *on the loss on the testing set*, decreasing the learning rate only when this loss fails to decrease. You should try implementing this as an exercise!

- Ensure the scale of your weight initialization is a function of the number of neurons in your layer (this is done by default in most neural network libraries).

- Add dropout, especially if your network contains multiple fully connected layers in succession.

Next, we'll shift to discussing advanced architectures specialized for specific domains, starting with convolutional neural networks, which are specialized to understand image data. Onward!

## CHAPTER 5

# Convolutional Neural Networks

In this chapter, we'll cover convolutional neural networks (CNNs). CNNs are the standard neural network architecture used for prediction when the input observations are images, which is the case in a wide range of neural network applications. So far in the book, we've focused exclusively on fully connected neural networks, which we implemented as a series of Dense layers. Thus, we'll start this chapter by reviewing some key elements of these networks and use this to motivate why we might want to use a different architecture for images. We'll then cover CNNs in a manner similar to that in which we introduced other concepts in this book: we'll first discuss how they work at a high level, then move to discussing them at a lower level, and finally show in detail how they work by coding up the convolution operation from scratch.[1] By the end of this chapter, you'll have a thorough enough understanding of how CNNs work to be able to use them both to solve problems and to learn about advanced CNN variants, such as ResNets, DenseNets, and Octave Convolutions on your own.

## Neural Networks and Representation Learning

Neural networks initially receive data on observations, with each observation represented by some number $n$ features. So far we've seen two examples of this in two very different domains: the first was the house prices dataset, where each observation was made up of 13 features, each of which represented a numeric characteristic about that house. The second was the MNIST dataset of handwritten digits; since the images were represented with 784 pixels (28 pixels wide by 28 pixels high), each observation was represented by 784 values indicating the lightness or darkness of each pixel.

---

1 The code we'll write, while clearly expressing how convolutions work, will be extremely inefficient. In "Gradient of the Loss with Respect to the Bias Terms" on page 225, I provide a more efficient implementation of the batch, multichannel convolution operation we'll describe in this chapter using NumPy.

In each case, after appropriately scaling the data, we were able to build a model that predicted the appropriate outcome for that dataset with high accuracy. Also in each case, a simple neural network model with one hidden layer performed better than a model without that hidden layer. Why is that? One reason, as I showed in the case of the house prices data, is that the neural network could learn *nonlinear* relationships between input and output. However, a more general reason is that in machine learning, we often need *linear combinations* of our original features in order to effectively predict our target. Let's say that the pixel values for an MNIST digit are $x_1$ through $x_{784}$. It could be the case, for example, that a combination of $x_1$ being higher than average, $x_{139}$ being lower than average, *and* $x_{237}$ also being lower than average strongly predicts that an image will be of digit 9. There may be many other such combinations, all of which contribute positively or negatively to the probability that an image is of a particular digit. Neural networks can automatically *discover* combinations of the original features that are important through their training process. That process starts by creating initially random combinations of the original features via multiplication by a random weight matrix; through training, the neural network learns to refine combinations that are helpful and discard those that aren't. This process of learning which combinations of features are important is known as *representation learning*, and it's the main reason why neural networks are successful across different domains. This is summarized in Figure 5-1.

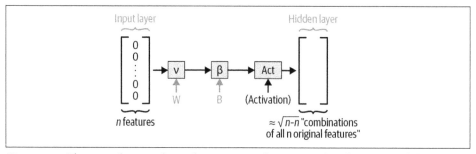

*Figure 5-1. The neural networks we have seen so far start with n features and then learn somewhere between √n and n "combinations" of these features to make predictions*

Is there any reason to modify this process for image data? The fundamental insight that suggests the answer is "yes" is that *in images, the interesting "combinations of features" (pixels) tend to come from pixels that are close together in the image*. In an image, it is simply much less likely that an interesting feature will result from a combination of 9 randomly selected pixels throughout the image than from a 3 × 3 patch of adjacent pixels. We want to exploit this fundamental fact about image data: that the order of the features matters since it tells us which pixels are near each other spatially, whereas in the house prices data the order of the features doesn't matter. But how do we do it?

## A Different Architecture for Image Data

The solution, at a high level, will be to create combinations of features, as before, but an order of magnitude more of them, and have each one be only a combination of the pixels from a small rectangular patch in the input image. Figure 5-2 describes this.

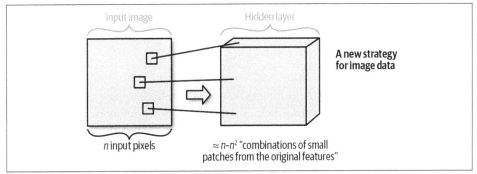

Figure 5-2. With image data, we can define each learned feature to be a function of a small patch of data, and thus define somewhere between n and $n^2$ output neurons

Having our neural network learn combinations of *all* of the input features—that is, combinations of *all* of the pixels in the input image—turns out to be very inefficient, since it ignores the insight described in the prior section: that most of the interesting combinations of features in images occur in these small patches. Nevertheless, previously it was at least extremely easy to compute new features that were combinations of all the input features: if we had $f$ input features and wanted to compute $n$ new features, we could simply multiply the ndarray containing our input features by an $f \times n$ matrix. What operation can we use to compute many combinations of the pixels from local patches of the input image? The answer is the convolution operation.

## The Convolution Operation

Before we describe the convolution operation, let's make clear what we mean by "a feature that is a combination of pixels from a local patch of an image." Let's say we have a $5 \times 5$ input image $I$:

$$I = \begin{bmatrix} i_{11} & i_{12} & i_{13} & i_{14} & i_{15} \\ i_{21} & i_{22} & i_{23} & i_{24} & i_{25} \\ i_{31} & i_{32} & i_{33} & i_{34} & i_{35} \\ i_{41} & i_{42} & i_{43} & i_{44} & i_{45} \\ i_{51} & i_{52} & i_{53} & i_{54} & i_{55} \end{bmatrix}$$

And let's say we want to calculate a new feature that is a function of the $3 \times 3$ patch of pixels in the middle. Well, just as we've defined new features as linear combinations of old features in the neural networks we've seen so far, we'll define a new feature that is a function of this $3 \times 3$ patch, which we'll do by defining a $3 \times 3$ set of weights, $W$:

$$W = \begin{bmatrix} w_{11} & w_{12} & w_{13} \\ w_{21} & w_{22} & w_{23} \\ w_{31} & w_{32} & w_{33} \end{bmatrix}$$

Then we'll simply take the dot product of $W$ with the relevant patch from $I$ to get the value of the feature in the output, which, since the section of the input image involved was centered at (3,3), we'll denote as $o_{33}$ (the $o$ stands for "output"):

$$o_{33} = w_{11} \times i_{22} + w_{12} \times i_{23} + w_{13} \times i_{24} + w_{21} \times i_{32} + w_{22} \times i_{33} + w_{23} \times i_{34} + w_{31} \times i_{42} + w_{32} \times i_{43} + w_{33} \times i_{44}$$

This value will then be treated like the other computed features we've seen in neural networks: it may have a bias added to it and then will probably be fed through an activation function, and then it will represent a "neuron" or "learned feature" that will get passed along to subsequent layers of the network. Thus we *can* define features that are functions of small patches of an input image.

How should we interpret such features? It turns out that features computed in this way have a special interpretation: they represent whether a *visual pattern defined by the weights* is present at that location of the image. The fact that $3 \times 3$ or $5 \times 5$ arrays of numbers can represent "pattern detectors" when their dot product is taken with the pixel values at each location of an image has been well known in the field of computer vision for a long time. For example, taking the dot product of the following $3 \times 3$ array of numbers:

$$\begin{bmatrix} 0 & 1 & 0 \\ 1 & -4 & 1 \\ 0 & 1 & 0 \end{bmatrix}$$

with a given section of an input image detects whether there is an edge at that location of the image. There are similar matrices known to be able to detect whether corners exist, whether vertical or horizontal lines exist, and so on.[2]

---

2 See the Wikipedia page for "Kernel (image processing)" (*https://oreil.ly/2KOwfzs*) for more examples.

Now suppose that we used the *same set of weights* $W$ to detect whether the visual pattern defined by $W$ existed at each location in the input image. We could imagine "sliding $W$ over the input image," taking the dot product of $W$ with the pixels at each location of the image, and ending up with a new image $O$ of almost identical size to the original image (it may be slightly different, depending on how we handle the edges). This image $O$ would be a kind of "feature map" showing the locations in the input image where the pattern defined by $W$ was present. This operation is in fact what happens in convolutional neural networks; it is called a *convolution*, and its output is indeed called a *feature map*.

This operation is at the core of how CNNs work. Before we can incorporate it into a full-fledged Operation, of the kind we've seen in the prior chapters, we have to add another dimension to it—literally.

## The Multichannel Convolution Operation

To review: convolutional neural networks differ from regular neural networks in that they create an order of magnitude more features, and in that each feature is a function of just a small patch from the input image. Now we can get more specific: starting with $n$ input pixels, the convolution operation just described will create $n$ output features, one for each location in the input image. What actually happens in a convolutional Layer in a neural network goes one step further: there, we'll create $f$ *sets* of $n$ features, *each* with a corresponding (initially random) set of weights defining a visual pattern whose detection at each location in the input image will be captured in the feature map. These $f$ feature maps will be created via $f$ convolution operations. This is captured in Figure 5-3.

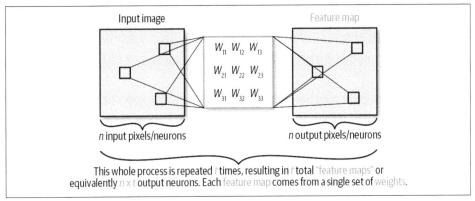

*Figure 5-3. More specifically than before, for an input image with n pixels, we define an output with f feature maps, each of which has about the same size as the original image, for a total of n × f total output neurons for the image, each of which is a function of only a small patch of the original image*

Now that we've introduced a bunch of concepts, let's define them for clarity. While each "set of features" detected by a particular set of weights is called a feature map, in the context of a convolutional Layer, the number of feature maps is referred to as the number of *channels* of the Layer—this is why the operation involved with the Layer is called the multichannel convolution. In addition, the $f$ sets of weights $W_i$ are called the convolutional *filters*.[3]

# Convolutional Layers

Now that we understand the multichannel convolution operation, we can think about how to incorporate this operation into a neural network layer. Previously, our neural network layers were relatively straightforward: they received two-dimensional ndarrays as input and produced two-dimensional ndarrays as output. Based on the description in the prior section, however, convolutional layers will have a 3D ndarray as output *for a single image*, with dimensions *number of channels* (same as "feature maps") × *image height* × *image width*.

This raises a question: how can we feed this ndarray forward into another convolutional layer to create a "deep convolutional" neural network? We've seen how to perform the convolution operation on an image with a single channel and our filters; how can we perform the multichannel convolution on an *input* with *multiple* channels, as we'll have to do when two convolutional layers are strung together? Understanding this is the key to understanding *deep* convolutional neural networks.

Consider what happens in a neural network with fully connected layers: in the first hidden layer, we have, let's say, $h_1$ features that are combinations of all of the original features from the input layer. In the layer that follows, the features are combinations of all of the features from the prior layer, so that we might have $h_2$ "features of features" of the original features. To create this next layer of $h_2$ features, we use $h_1 \times h_2$ weights to represent that each of the $h_2$ features is a function of each of the $h_1$ features in the prior layer.

As described in the prior section, an analogous process happens in the first layer of a convolutional neural network: we first transform the input image into $m_1$ *feature maps*, using $m_1$ convolutional *filters*. We should think of the output of this layer as representing whether each of the $m_1$ different visual patterns represented by the weights of the $m_1$ filters is present at each location in the input image. Just as different layers of a fully connected neural network can contain different numbers of neurons, the next layer of the convolutional neural network could contain $m_2$ filters. In order for the network to learn complex patterns, the interpretation of each of these should

---

3 These are also referred to as *kernels*.

be whether each of the *"patterns of patterns"* or higher-order visual features represented by *combinations of the $m_1$ visual patterns from the prior layer* was present at that location of the image. This implies that if the output of the convolutional layer is a 3D `ndarray` of shape $m_2$ channels × image height × image width, then a given location in the image on one of the $m_2$ feature maps is *a linear combination of convolving $m_1$ different filters over that same location in each of the corresponding $m_1$ feature maps from the prior layer*. This will allow each location in each of the $m_2$ filter maps to represent a *combination* of the $m_1$ visual features already learned in the prior convolutional layer.

## Implementation Implications

This understanding of how two multichannel convolutional layers are connected tells us how to implement the operation: just as we need $h_1 \times h_2$ weights to connect a fully connected layer with $h_1$ neurons to one with $h_2$, we need $m_1 \times m_2$ *convolutional filters* to connect a convolutional layer with $m_1$ channels to one with $m_2$. With this last detail in place, we can now specify the dimensions of the `ndarray`s that will make up the input, output, and parameters of the full, multichannel convolution operation:

1. The input will have shape:

   - Batch size
   - Input channels
   - Image height
   - Image width

2. The output will have shape:

   - Batch size
   - Output channels
   - Image height
   - Image width

3. The convolutional filters themselves will have shape:

   - Input channels
   - Output channels
   - Filter height
   - Filter width

The order of the dimensions may vary from library to library, but these four dimensions will always be present.

We'll keep all of this in mind when we implement this convolution operation later in the chapter.

## The Differences Between Convolutional and Fully Connected Layers

At the beginning of the chapter, we discussed the differences between convolutional and fully connected layers at a high level; Figure 5-4 revisits that comparison, now that we've described convolutional layers in more detail.

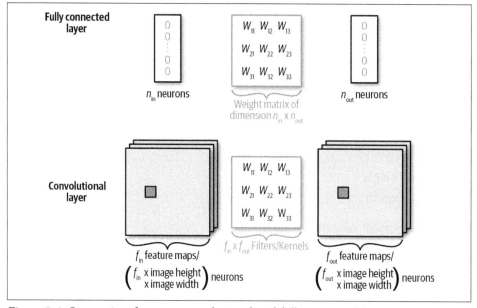

*Figure 5-4. Comparison between convolutional and fully connected layers*

In addition, one last difference between the two kinds of layers is the way in which the individual neurons themselves are interpreted:

- The interpretation of each neuron of a fully connected layer is that it detects whether or not *a particular combination of the features learned by the prior layer* is present in the current observation.

- The interpretation of a neuron of a convolutional layer is that it detects whether or not *a particular combination of visual patterns* learned by the prior layer is present *at the given location* of the input image.

There's one more problem we need to solve before we can incorporate such a layer into a neural network: how to use the dimensional ndarrays we obtain as output to make predictions.

## Making Predictions with Convolutional Layers: The Flatten Layer

We've covered how convolutional layers learn features that represent whether visual patterns exist in images and store those features in layers of feature maps; how do we use these layers of feature maps to make predictions? When using fully connected neural networks to predict which of 10 classes an image belonged to in the prior chapter, we just had to ensure that the last layer had dimension 10; we could then feed these 10 numbers into the softmax cross entropy loss function to ensure they were interpreted as probabilities. Now we need to figure out what we can do in the case of our convolutional layer, where we have a three-dimensional ndarray per observation of shape $m$ channels × image height × image width.

To see the answer, recall that each neuron simply represents whether a particular combination of visual features (which, if this is a deep convolutional neural network, could be a feature of features or a feature of features of features) is present at a given location in the image. This is no different from the features that would be learned if we applied a fully connected neural network to this image: the first fully connected layer would represent features of the individual pixels, the second would represent features of these features, and so on. And in a fully connected architecture, we would simply treat each "feature of features" that the network had learned as a single neuron that would be used as input to a prediction of which class the image belonged to.

It turns out that we can do the same thing with convolutional neural networks—we treat the $m$ feature maps as $m \times image_{height} \times image_{width}$ neurons and use a Flatten operation to squash these three dimensions (the number of channels, the image height, and the image width) down into a one-dimensional vector, after which we can use a simple matrix multiplication to make our final predictions. The intuition for why this works is that each individual neuron *fundamentally represents the same "kind of thing"* as the neurons in a fully connected layer—specifically, whether a given visual feature (or combination of features) is present at a given location in an image)—and thus we can treat them the same way in the final layer of the neural network.[4]

We'll see how to implement the `Flatten` layer later in the chapter. But before we dive into the implementation, let's discuss another kind of layer that is important in many CNN architectures, though we won't cover it in great detail in this book.

## Pooling Layers

*Pooling* layers are another kind of layer commonly used in convolutional neural networks. They simply *downsample* each of the feature maps created by a convolution operation; for the most typically used pooling size of 2, this involves mapping each 2 × 2 section of each feature map either to the maximum value of that section, in the case of *max-pooling*, or to the average value of that section, in the case of *average-pooling*. For an $n \times n$ image, then, this would map the entire image to one of size $\frac{n}{2} \times \frac{n}{2}$. Figure 5-5 illustrates this.

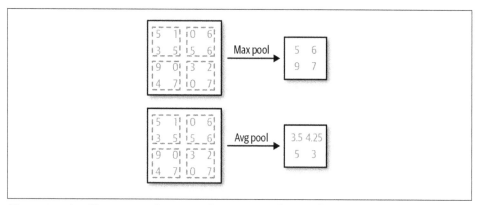

*Figure 5-5. An illustration of max- and average-pooling with a 4 × 4 input; each 2 × 2 patch is mapped to either the average or the max values for that patch*

The main advantage of pooling is computational: by downsampling the image to contain one-fourth as many pixels as the prior layer, pooling decreases both the number of weights and the number of computations needed to train the network by a factor of 4; this can be further compounded if multiple pooling layers are used in the network, as they were in many architectures in the early days of CNNs. The downside of pooling, of course, is that only one-fourth as much information can be extracted from

---

4 This is why it is important to understand the output of convolution operations both as creating a number of filter maps—say, $m$—as well as creating $m \times image_{height} \times image_{width}$ individual neurons. As is the case throughout neural networks, holding multiple levels of interpretation in one's mind all at one time, and seeing the connection between them, is key.

the downsampled image. However, the fact that architectures showed very strong performance on benchmarks in image recognition despite the use of pooling suggested that, even though pooling was causing the networks to "lose information" about the images by decreasing the images' resolution, the trade-offs in terms of increased computational speed were worth it. Nevertheless, pooling was considered by many to be a trick that just happened to work but should probably be done away with; as Geoffrey Hinton wrote on a Reddit AMA (*https://oreil.ly/2YZU0Kc*) in 2014, "The pooling operation used in convolutional neural networks is a big mistake and the fact that it works so well is a disaster." And indeed, most recent CNN architectures (such as Residual Networks, or "ResNets"[5]) use pooling minimally or not at all. Thus, in this book, we're not going to implement pooling layers, but given their importance for "putting CNNs on the map" via their use in famous architectures such as AlexNet, we mention them here for completeness.

## Applying CNNs beyond images

Everything we have described so far is extremely standard for dealing with images using neural networks: the images are typically represented as a set of $m_1$ channels of pixels, where $m_1 = 1$ for black-and-white images, and $m_1 = 3$ for color images—and then some number $m_2$ of convolution operations are applied to each channel (using the $m_1 \times m_2$ filter maps as explained previously), with this pattern continuing on for several layers. This has all been covered in other treatments of convolutional neural networks; what is less commonly covered is that the idea of organizing data into "channels" and then processing that data using a CNN goes beyond just images. For example, this data representation was a key to DeepMind's series of AlphaGo programs showing that neural networks could learn to play Go. To quote the paper:[6]

> The input to the neural network is a 19 × 19 × 17 image stack comprising 17 binary feature planes. 8 feature planes $X_t$ consist of binary values indicating the presence of the current player's stones ($X_{t_i} = 1$ if intersection $i$ contains a stone of the player's color at time-step t; 0 if the intersection is empty, contains an opponent stone, or if t < 0). A further 8 feature planes, $Y_t$, represent the corresponding features for the opponent's stones. The final feature plane, C, represents the color to play, and has a constant value of either 1 if black is to play or 0 if white is to play. These planes are concatenated together to give input features $s_t = X_t, Y_t, X_{t-1}, Y_{t-1}, ..., X_{t-7}, Y_{t-7}, C$. History features $X_t, Y_t$ are necessary because Go is not fully observable solely from the current stones, as repetitions are forbidden; similarly, the color feature C is necessary because the *komi* is not observable.

---

5 See the original ResNet paper (*http://tiny.cc/dlfs_resnet_paper*), "Deep Residual Learning for Image Recognition," by Kaiming He et al.

6 DeepMind (David Silver et al.), *Mastering the Game of Go Without Human Knowledge* (*https://oreil.ly/wUpMW*), 2017.

In other words, they essentially represented the board as a 19 × 19 pixel "image" with 17 channels! They used 16 of these channels to encode what had happened on the 8 prior moves that each player had taken; this was necessary so that they could encode rules that prevented repetition of earlier moves. The 17th channel was actually a 19 × 19 grid of either all 1s or all 0s, depending on whose turn it was to move.[7] CNNs and their multichannel convolution operations are mostly commonly applied to images, but the even more general idea of representing data that is arranged along some spatial dimension with multiple "channels" is applicable even beyond images.

In keeping with the theme of this book, however, to truly understand the multichannel convolution operation, you have to implement it from scratch; the next several sections will describe this process in detail.

# Implementing the Multichannel Convolution Operation

It turns out that implementing this daunting operation—which involves a four-dimensional input `ndarray` and a four-dimensional parameter `ndarray`—is much clearer if we first examine the *one*-dimensional case. Building up to the full operation from that starting point will turn out mostly to be a matter of adding a bunch of `for` loops. Throughout, we'll take the same approach we took in Chapter 1, alternating between diagrams, math, and working Python code.

## The Forward Pass

The convolution in one dimension is conceptually identical to the convolution in two dimensions: we take in a one-dimensional input and a one-dimensional convolutional filter as inputs and then create the output by sliding the filter along the input.

Let's suppose our input is of length 5:

$$\text{Input: } [t_1, t_2, t_3, t_4, t_5]$$

And let's say the size of the "patterns" we want to detect is length 3:

$$\text{Filter: } [w_1, w_2, w_3]$$

---

7 A year later, DeepMind published results using a similar representation with chess—only this time, to encode the more complex ruleset of chess, the input had 119 channels! See DeepMind (David Silver et al.), "A General Reinforcement Learning Algorithm That Masters Chess, Shogi, and Go Through Self-Play" (*https://oreil.ly/E6ydw*).

---

## Diagrams and math

The first element of the output would be created by convolving the first element of the input with the filter:

$$\text{Output Feature 1: } t_1 w_1 + t_2 w_2 + t_3 w_3$$

The second element of the output would be created by sliding the filter one unit to the right and convolving it with the next set values of the series:

$$\text{Output Feature 2: } t_2 w_1 + t_3 w_2 + t_4 w_3$$

Fair enough. However, when we compute the next output value, we realize that we have run out of room:

$$\text{Output Feature 3: } O_3 = t_3 w_1 + t_4 w_2 + t_5 w_3$$

We have hit the end of our input, and the resulting output has just three elements, when we started with five! How can we address this?

## Padding

To avoid the output shrinking as a result of the convolution operation, we'll introduce a trick used throughout convolutional neural networks: we "pad" the input with zeros around the edges, enough so that the output remains the same size as the input. Otherwise, every time we convolve a filter over the input, we'll end up with an output that is slightly smaller than the input, as seen previously.

As you can reason from the preceding convolution example: for a filter of size 3, there should be one unit of padding around the edges to keep the output the same size as the input. More generally, since we almost always use odd-numbered filter sizes, we add padding equal to the filter size divided by 2 and rounded down to the nearest integer.

Let's say we add this padding, so that instead of the input ranging from $i_1$ to $i_5$, it ranges from $i_0$ to $i_6$, where both $i_0$ and $i_6$ are 0. Then we can compute the output of the convolution as:

$$o_1 = i_0 \times w_1 + i_1 \times w_2 + i_2 \times w_3$$

And so on, up until:

$$o_5 = i_4 \times w_1 + i_5 \times w_2 + i_6 \times w_3$$

And now the output is the same size as the input. How might we code this up?

## Code

Coding up this part turns out to be pretty straightforward. Before we do, let's summarize the steps we just discussed:

1. We ultimately want to produce an output that is the same size as the input.
2. To do this without "shrinking" the output, we'll first need to pad the input.
3. Then we'll have to write some sort of loop that goes through the input and convolves each position of it with the filter.

We'll start with our input and our filter:

```
input_1d = np.array([1,2,3,4,5])
param_1d = np.array([1,1,1])
```

Here's a helper function that can pad our one-dimensional input on each end:

```
def _pad_1d(inp: ndarray,
            num: int) -> ndarray:
    z = np.array([0])
    z = np.repeat(z, num)
    return np.concatenate([z, inp, z])

_pad_1d(input_1d, 1)

array([0., 1., 2., 3., 4., 5., 0.])
```

What about the convolution itself? Observe that for each element in the output that we want to produce, we have a corresponding element in the *padded* input where we "start" the convolution operation; once we figure out where to start, we simply loop through all the elements in the filter, doing a multiplication at each element and adding the result to the total.

How do we find this "corresponding element"? Note that, simply, the value at the first element in the output gets its value starting at the first element of the padded input! This makes the for loop quite easy to write:

```
def conv_1d(inp: ndarray,
            param: ndarray) -> ndarray:

    # assert correct dimensions
    assert_dim(inp, 1)
    assert_dim(param, 1)

    # pad the input
    param_len = param.shape[0]
```

```
    param_mid = param_len // 2
    input_pad = _pad_1d(inp, param_mid)

    # initialize the output
    out = np.zeros(inp.shape)

    # perform the 1d convolution
    for o in range(out.shape[0]):
        for p in range(param_len):
            out[o] += param[p] * input_pad[o+p]

    # ensure shapes didn't change
    assert_same_shape(inp, out)

    return out

conv_1d_sum(input_1d, param_1d)

array([ 3.,  6.,  9., 12.,  9.])
```

That's simple enough. Before we move on to the backward pass of this operation—the tricky part—let's briefly discuss a hyperparameter of convolutions that we're glossing over: stride.

### A note on stride

We noted earlier that pooling operations were one way to downsample images from feature maps. In many early convolutional architectures, these did indeed significantly reduce the amount of computation needed without any significant hit to accuracy; nevertheless, they've fallen out of favor because of their downside: they effectively downsample the image so that an image with just half the resolution is passed forward into the next layer.

A much more widely accepted way to do this is to modify the *stride* of the convolution operation. The stride is the amount that the filter is incrementally slid over the image—in the previous case, we are using a stride of 1, and as a result each filter is convolved with every element of the input, which is why the output ends up being the same size as the input. With a stride of 2, the filter would be convolved with *every other* element of the input image, so that the output would be half the size of the input; with a stride of 3, the filter would be convolved with *every third* element of the input image, and so on. This means that, for example, using a stride of 2 would result in the same output size and thus much the same reduction in computation we would get from pooling with size 2, but without as much *loss of information*: with pooling of size 2, only one-fourth of the elements in the input have *any* effect on the output, whereas with a stride of 2, *every* element of the input has *some* effect on the output. The use of a stride of greater than 1 is thus significantly more prevalent than pooling for downsampling even in the most advanced CNN architectures of today.

Nevertheless, in this book I'll just show examples with a stride of 1—modifying these operations to allow a stride of greater than 1 is left as an exercise for the reader. Using a stride equal to 1 also makes writing the backward pass easier.

# Convolutions: The Backward Pass

The backward pass is where convolutions get a bit trickier. Let's recall what we're trying to do: before, we produced the output of a convolution operation using the input and the parameters. We now want to compute:

- The partial derivative of the loss with respect to each element of the *input* to the convolution operation—inp previously
- The partial derivative of the loss with respect to each element of the *filter*— param_1d previously

Think of how the ParamOperations we saw in Chapter 4 work: in the backward method, they receive an output gradient representing how much each element of the output ultimately affects the loss and then use this output gradient to compute the gradients for the input and the parameters. So we need to write a function that takes in an output_grad with the same shape as the input and produces an input_grad and a param_grad.

How can we test whether the computed gradients are correct? We'll bring back an idea from the first chapter: we know that the partial derivative of a sum with respect to any one of its inputs is 1 (if the sum $s = a + b + c$, then $\frac{\partial s}{\partial a} = \frac{\partial s}{\partial b} = \frac{\partial s}{\partial c} = 1$). So we can compute the input_grad and param_grad quantities using our _input_grad and _param_grad functions (which we'll reason through and write shortly) and an out put_grad equal to all 1s. Then we'll check whether these gradients are correct by changing elements of the input by some quantity $\alpha$ and seeing whether the resulting sum changes by the gradient times $\alpha$.

## What "should" the gradient be?

Using the logic just described, let's calculate what an element of the gradient vector for the input *should* be:

```
def conv_1d_sum(inp: ndarray,
                param: ndarray) -> ndarray:
    out = conv_1d(inp, param)
    return np.sum(out)

# randomly choose to increase 5th element by 1
input_1d_2 = np.array([1,2,3,4,6])
param_1d = np.array([1,1,1])
```

```
print(conv_1d_sum(input_1d, param_1d))
print(conv_1d_sum(input_1d_2, param_1d))
```

```
39.0
41.0
```

So, the gradient of the fifth element of the input *should* be 41 − 39 = 2.

Now let's try to reason through how we should compute such a gradient without simply computing the difference between these two sums. Here is where things get interesting.

### Computing the gradient of a 1D convolution

We see that increasing this element of the input increased the output by 2. Taking a close look at the output shows exactly how it does this:

$$\text{Output:}[\ t_0w_1+t_1w_2+t_2w_3,=o_1$$
$$t_1w_1+t_2w_2+t_3w_3,=o_2$$
$$t_2w_1+t_3w_2+t_4w_3,=o_3$$
$$t_3w_1+t_4w_2+t_5w_3,=o_4$$
$$t_4w_1+t_5w_2+t_6w_3]=o_5$$

This particular element of the input is denoted $t_5$. It appears in the output in two places:

- As part of $o_4$, it is multiplied by $w_3$.
- As part of $o_5$, it is multiplied by $w_2$.

To help see the general pattern of how inputs map to the sum of outputs, note that if there was an $o_6$ present, $t_5$ would also contribute to the output through being multiplied by $w_1$.

Therefore, the amount that $t_5$ ultimately affects the loss, which we can denote as $\frac{\partial L}{\partial t_5}$, will be:

$$\frac{\partial L}{\partial t_5} = \frac{\partial L}{\partial o_4} \times w_3 + \frac{\partial L}{\partial o_5} \times w_2 + \frac{\partial L}{\partial o_6} \times w_1$$

Of course, in this simple example, when the loss is just the sum, $\frac{\partial L}{\partial o_i} = 1$ for all elements, in the output (except for the "padding" elements for which this quantity is 0). This sum is very easy to compute: it is simply $w_2 + w_3$, which is indeed 2 since $w_2 = w_3 = 1$.

## What's the general pattern?

Now let's look for the general pattern for a generic input element. This turns out to be an exercise in keeping track of indices. Since we're translating math into code here, let's use $o_i^{grad}$ to denote the $i$th element of the output gradient (since we'll ultimately be accessing it via `output_grad[i]`). Then:

$$\frac{\partial L}{\partial t_5} = o_4^{grad} \times w_3 + o_5^{grad} \times w_2 + o_6^{grad} \times w_1$$

Looking closely at this output, we can reason similarly that:

$$\frac{\partial L}{\partial t_3} = o_2^{grad} \times w_3 + o_3^{grad} \times w_2 + o_4^{grad} \times w_1$$

and:

$$\frac{\partial L}{\partial t_4} = o_3^{grad} \times w_3 + o_4^{grad} \times w_2 + o_5^{grad} \times w_1$$

There's clearly a pattern here, and translating it into code is a bit tricky, especially since the indices on the output increase at the same time the indices on the weights decrease. Nevertheless, the way to express this turns out to be via the following double for loop:

```
# param: in our case an ndarray of shape (1,3)
# param_len: the integer 3
# inp: in our case an ndarray of shape (1,5)
# input_grad: always an ndarray the same shape as "inp"
# output_pad: in our case an ndarray of shape (1,7)
for o in range(inp.shape[0]):
    for p in range(param.shape[0]):
        input_grad[o] += output_pad[o+param_len-p-1] * param[p]
```

This does the appropriate incrementing of the indices of the weights, while decreasing the weights on the output at the same time.

Though it may not be obvious now, reasoning through this and getting it is out to be the trickiest part of calculating the gradients for convolution operations. Adding more complexity to this, such as batch sizes, convolutions with two-dimensional inputs, or inputs with multiple channels, is simply a matter of adding more for loops to the preceding lines, as we'll see in the next few sections.

## Computing the parameter gradient

We can reason similarly about how increasing an element of the filter should increase the output. First, let's increase (arbitrarily) the first element of the filter by one unit and observe the resulting impact on the sum:

```
input_1d = np.array([1,2,3,4,5])
# randomly choose to increase first element by 1
param_1d_2 = np.array([2,1,1])

print(conv_1d_sum(input_1d, param_1d))
print(conv_1d_sum(input_1d, param_1d_2))

39.0
49.0
```

So we should find that $\frac{\partial L}{\partial w_1} = 10$.

Just as we did for the input, by closely examining the output and seeing which elements of the filter affect it, as well as padding the input to more clearly see the pattern, we see that:

$$w_1^{grad} = t_0 \times o_1^{grad} + t_1 \times o_2^{grad} + t_2 \times o_3^{grad} + t_3 \times o_4^{grad} + t_4 \times o_5^{grad}$$

And since, for the sum, all of the $o_i^{grad}$ elements are just 1, and $t_0$ is 0, we have:

$$w_1^{grad} = t_1 + t_2 + t_3 + t_4 = 1 + 2 + 3 + 4 = 10$$

This confirms the calculation from earlier.

## Coding this up

Coding this up turns out to be easier than writing the code for the input gradient, since this time "the indices are moving in the same direction." Within the same nested for loop, the code is:

```
# param: in our case an ndarray of shape (1,3)
# param_grad: an ndarray the same shape as param
# inp: in our case an ndarray of shape (1,5)
# input_pad: an ndarray the same shape as (1,7)
# output_grad: in our case an ndarray of shape (1,5)
for o in range(inp.shape[0]):
    for p in range(param.shape[0]):
        param_grad[p] += input_pad[o+p] * output_grad[o]
```

Finally, we can combine these two computations and write a function to compute both the input gradient and the filter gradient with the following steps:

1. Take the input and filter as arguments.

2. Compute the output.

3. Pad the input and the output gradient (to get, say, `input_pad` and `output_pad`).

4. As shown earlier, use the padded output gradient and the filter to compute the gradient.

5. Similarly, use the output gradient (not padded) and the padded input to compute the filter gradient.

I show the full function that wraps around the preceding code blocks in the book's GitHub repo (*https://oreil.ly/2H99xkJ*).

That concludes our explanation of how to implement convolutions in 1D! As we'll see in the next several sections, extending this reasoning to work on two-dimensional inputs, batches of two-dimensional inputs, or even multichannel batches of two-dimensional inputs is (perhaps surprisingly) straightforward.

## Batches, 2D Convolutions, and Multiple Channels

First, let's add the capability for these convolution functions to work with *batches* of inputs—2D inputs whose first dimension represents the batch size of the input and whose second dimension represents the length of the 1D sequence:

```
input_1d_batch = np.array([[0,1,2,3,4,5,6],
                           [1,2,3,4,5,6,7]])
```

We can follow the same general steps defined before: we'll first pad the input, use this to compute the output, and then pad the output gradient to compute both the input and filter gradients.

### 1D convolutions with batches: forward pass

The only difference in implementing the forward pass when the input has a second dimension representing the batch size is that we have to pad and compute the output for each observation individually (as we did previously) and then `stack` the results to get a batch of outputs. For example, `conv_1d` becomes:

```
def conv_1d_batch(inp: ndarray,
                  param: ndarray) -> ndarray:

    outs = [conv_1d(obs, param) for obs in inp]
    return np.stack(outs)
```

### 1D convolutions with batches: backward pass

The backward pass is similar: computing the input gradient now simply takes the `for` loop for computing the input gradient from the prior section, computes it for each observation, and `stacks` the results:

```
# "_input_grad" is the function containing the for loop from earlier:
# it takes in a 1d input, a 1d filter, and a 1d output_gradient and computes
# the input grad
grads = [_input_grad(inp[i], param, out_grad[i])[1] for i in range(batch_size)]
np.stack(grads)
```

The gradient for the filter when dealing with a batch of observations is a bit different. This is because the filter is convolved with every observation in the input and is thus connected to every observation in the output. So, to compute the parameter gradient, we have to loop through all of the observations and increment the appropriate values of the parameter gradient as we do so. Still, this just involves adding an outer `for` loop to the code to compute the parameter gradient that we saw earlier:

```
# param: in our case an ndarray of shape (1,3)
# param_grad: an ndarray the same shape as param
# inp: in our case an ndarray of shape (1,5)
# input_pad: an ndarray the same shape as (1,7)
# output_grad: in our case an ndarray of shape (1,5)
for i in range(inp.shape[0]): # inp.shape[0] = 2
    for o in range(inp.shape[1]): # inp.shape[0] = 5
        for p in range(param.shape[0]): # param.shape[0] = 3
            param_grad[p] += input_pad[i][o+p] * output_grad[i][o]
```

Adding this dimension on top of the original 1D convolution was indeed simple; extending this from one- to two-dimensional inputs is similarly straightforward.

# 2D Convolutions

The 2D convolution is a straightforward extension of the 1D case because, fundamentally, the way the input is connected to the output via the filters in each dimension of the 2D case is identical to the 1D case. As a result, the high-level steps on both the forward and backward passes remain the same:

1. On the forward pass, we:

   - Appropriately pad the input.
   - Use the padded input and the parameters to compute the output.

2. On the backward pass, to compute the input gradient we:

   - Appropriately pad the output gradient.

- Use this padded output gradient, along with the input and the parameters, to compute both the input gradient and the parameter gradient.

3. Also on the backward pass, to compute the parameter gradient we:

- Appropriately pad the input.
- Loop through the elements of the padded input and increment the parameter gradient appropriately as we go along.

## 2D convolutions: coding the forward pass

To make this concrete, recall that for 1D convolutions the code for computing the output given the input and the parameters on the forward pass looked as follows:

```
# input_pad: a version of the input that has been padded appropriately based on
# the size of param

out = np.zeros_like(inp)

for o in range(out.shape[0]):
    for p in range(param_len):
        out[o] += param[p] * input_pad[o+p]
```

For 2D convolutions, we simply modify this to be:

```
# input_pad: a version of the input that has been padded appropriately based on
# the size of param

out = np.zeros_like(inp)

for o_w in range(img_size): # loop through the image height
    for o_h in range(img_size): # loop through the image width
        for p_w in range(param_size): # loop through the parameter width
            for p_h in range(param_size): # loop through the parameter height
                out[o_w][o_h] += param[p_w][p_h] * input_pad[o_w+p_w][o_h+p_h]
```

You can see that we've simply "blown each for loop out" into two for loops.

The extension to two dimensions when we have a batch of images is also similar to the 1D case: just as we did there, we simply add a for loop to the outside of the loops shown here.

## 2D convolutions: coding the backward pass

Sure enough, just as in the forward pass, we can use the same indexing for the backward pass as in the 1D case. Recall that in the 1D case, the code was:

```
input_grad = np.zeros_like(inp)

for o in range(inp.shape[0]):
```

```
        for p in range(param_len):
            input_grad[o] += output_pad[o+param_len-p-1] * param[p]
```

In the 2D case, the code is simply:

```
# output_pad: a version of the output that has been padded appropriately based
# on the size of param
input_grad = np.zeros_like(inp)

for i_w in range(img_width):
    for i_h in range(img_height):
        for p_w in range(param_size):
            for p_h in range(param_size):
                input_grad[i_w][i_h] +=
                output_pad[i_w+param_size-p_w-1][i_h+param_size-p_h-1] \
                * param[p_w][p_h]
```

Note that the indexing on the output is the same as in the 1D case but is simply taking place in two dimensions; in the 1D case, we had:

```
output_pad[i+param_size-p-1] * param[p]
```

and in the 2D case, we have:

```
output_pad[i_w+param_size-p_w-1][i_h+param_size-p_h-1] * param[p_w][p_h]
```

The other facts from the 1D case also apply:

- For a batch of input images, we simply perform the preceding operation for each observation and then stack the results.

- For the parameter gradient, we have to loop through all the images in the batch and add components from each one to the appropriate places in the parameter gradient:[8]

```
# input_pad: a version of the input that has been padded appropriately based on
# the size of param

param_grad = np.zeros_like(param)

for i in range(batch_size): # equal to inp.shape[0]
    for o_w in range(img_size):
        for o_h in range(img_size):
            for p_w in range(param_size):
                for p_h in range(param_size):
                    param_grad[p_w][p_h] += input_pad[i][o_w+p_w][o_h+p_h] \
                    * output_grad[i][o_w][o_h]
```

At this point, we've almost written the code for the complete multichannel convolution operation; currently, our code convolves filters over a two-dimensional input and

---

8 See the full implementations of these on the book's website (*https://oreil.ly/2H99xkJ*).

produces a two-dimensional output. Of course, as we described earlier, each convolutional layer not only has neurons arranged along these two dimensions but also has some number of "channels" equal to the number of feature maps that the layer creates. Addressing this last challenge is what we'll cover next.

## The Last Element: Adding "Channels"

How can we modify what we've written thus far to account for cases where both the input and the output are multichannel? The answer, as it was when we added batches earlier, is simple: we add two outer for loops to the code we've already seen—one loop for the input channels and another for the output channels. By looping through all combinations of the input channel and the output channel, we make each output feature map a combination of all of the input feature maps, as desired.

For this to work, we will have to *always* represent our images as three-dimensional ndarrays, as opposed to the two-dimensional arrays we've been using; we'll represent black-and-white images with one channel and color images with three channels (one for the red values at each location in the image, one for the blue values, and one for the green values). Then, regardless of the number of channels, the operation proceeds as described earlier, with a number of feature maps being created from the image, each of which is a combination of the convolutions resulting from all of the channels in the image (or from the channels in the prior layer, if dealing with layers further on in the network).

### Forward pass

Given all this, the full code to compute the output for a convolutional layer, given four-dimensional ndarrays for the input and the parameters, is:

```
def _compute_output_obs(obs: ndarray,
                        param: ndarray) -> ndarray:
    '''
    obs: [channels, img_width, img_height]
    param: [in_channels, out_channels, param_width, param_height]
    '''
    assert_dim(obs, 3)
    assert_dim(param, 4)

    param_size = param.shape[2]
    param_mid = param_size // 2
    obs_pad = _pad_2d_channel(obs, param_mid)

    in_channels = fil.shape[0]
    out_channels = fil.shape[1]
    img_size = obs.shape[1]

    out = np.zeros((out_channels,) + obs.shape[1:])
    for c_in in range(in_channels):
```

```
                for c_out in range(out_channels):
                    for o_w in range(img_size):
                        for o_h in range(img_size):
                            for p_w in range(param_size):
                                for p_h in range(param_size):
                                    out[c_out][o_w][o_h] += \
                                        param[c_in][c_out][p_w][p_h]
                                        * obs_pad[c_in][o_w+p_w][o_h+p_h]
        return out

    def _output(inp: ndarray,
                param: ndarray) -> ndarray:
        '''
        obs: [batch_size, channels, img_width, img_height]
        param: [in_channels, out_channels, param_width, param_height]
        '''
        outs = [_compute_output_obs(obs, param) for obs in inp]

        return np.stack(outs)
```

Note that _pad_2d_channel is a function that pads the input along the channel dimension.

Again, the actual code that does the computation is similar to the code in the simpler 2D case (without channels) shown before, except now we have, for example, fil[c_out][c_in][p_w][p_h] instead of just fil[p_w][p_h], since there are two more dimensions and c_out × c_in more elements in the filter array.

## Backward pass

The backward pass is similar and follows the same conceptual principles as the backward pass in the simple 2D case:

1. For the input gradients, we compute the gradients of each observation individually—padding the output gradient to do so—and then stack the gradients.

2. We also use the padded output gradient for the parameter gradient, but we loop through the observations as well and use the appropriate values from each one to update the parameter gradient.

Here's the code for computing the output gradient:

```
def _compute_grads_obs(input_obs: ndarray,
                       output_grad_obs: ndarray,
                       param: ndarray) -> ndarray:
    '''
    input_obs: [in_channels, img_width, img_height]
    output_grad_obs: [out_channels, img_width, img_height]
    param: [in_channels, out_channels, img_width, img_height]
    '''
    input_grad = np.zeros_like(input_obs)
    param_size = param.shape[2]
    param_mid = param_size // 2
```

```
        img_size = input_obs.shape[1]
        in_channels = input_obs.shape[0]
        out_channels = param.shape[1]
        output_obs_pad = _pad_2d_channel(output_grad_obs, param_mid)

        for c_in in range(in_channels):
            for c_out in range(out_channels):
                for i_w in range(input_obs.shape[1]):
                    for i_h in range(input_obs.shape[2]):
                        for p_w in range(param_size):
                            for p_h in range(param_size):
                                input_grad[c_in][i_w][i_h] += \
                                output_obs_pad[c_out][i_w+param_size-p_w-1][i_h+param_size-p_h-1] \
                                * param[c_in][c_out][p_w][p_h]
        return input_grad

    def _input_grad(inp: ndarray,
                    output_grad: ndarray,
                    param: ndarray) -> ndarray:

        grads = [_compute_grads_obs(inp[i], output_grad[i], param) for i in range(output_grad.shape[0])]

        return np.stack(grads)
```

And here's the parameter gradient:

```
    def _param_grad(inp: ndarray,
                    output_grad: ndarray,
                    param: ndarray) -> ndarray:
        '''
        inp: [in_channels, img_width, img_height]
        output_grad_obs: [out_channels, img_width, img_height]
        param: [in_channels, out_channels, img_width, img_height]
        '''
        param_grad = np.zeros_like(param)
        param_size = param.shape[2]
        param_mid = param_size // 2
        img_size = inp.shape[2]
        in_channels = inp.shape[1]
        out_channels = output_grad.shape[1]

        inp_pad = _pad_conv_input(inp, param_mid)
        img_shape = output_grad.shape[2:]

        for i in range(inp.shape[0]):
            for c_in in range(in_channels):
                for c_out in range(out_channels):
                    for o_w in range(img_shape[0]):
                        for o_h in range(img_shape[1]):
                            for p_w in range(param_size):
                                for p_h in range(param_size):
                                    param_grad[c_in][c_out][p_w][p_h] += \
                                    inp_pad[i][c_in][o_w+p_w][o_h+p_h] \
                                    * output_grad[i][c_out][o_w][o_h]
        return param_grad
```

These three functions—_output, _input_grad, and _param_grad—are just what we need to create a Conv2DOperation, which will ultimately form the core of the Conv2DLayers we'll use in our CNNs! There are just a few more details to work out before we can use this Operation in a working convolutional neural network.

# Using This Operation to Train a CNN

We need to implement a few more pieces before we can have a working CNN model:

1. We have to implement the Flatten operation discussed earlier in the chapter; this is necessary to enable the model to make predictions.

2. We have to incorporate this Operation as well as the Conv2DOpOperation into a Conv2D Layer.

3. Finally, for any of this to be usable, we have to write a faster version of the Conv2D Operation. We'll outline this here and share the details in "Matrix Chain Rule" on page 221.

## The Flatten Operation

There's one other Operation we'll need to complete our convolutional layer: the Flatten operation. The output of a convolution operation is a 3D ndarray for each observation, of dimension (channels, img_height, img_width). However, unless we are passing this data into another convolutional layer, we'll first need to transform it into a *vector* for each observation. Luckily, as described previously, since each of the individual neurons involved encodes whether a particular visual feature is present at that location in the image, we can simply "flatten" this 3D ndarray into a 1D vector and pass it forward without any problem. The Flatten operation shown here does this, accounting for the fact that in convolutional layers, as with any other layer, the first dimension of our ndarray is always the batch size:

```
class Flatten(Operation):
    def __init__(self):
        super().__init__()

    def _output(self) -> ndarray:
        return self.input.reshape(self.input.shape[0], -1)

    def _input_grad(self, output_grad: ndarray) -> ndarray:
        return output_grad.reshape(self.input.shape)
```

That's the last Operation we'll need; let's wrap these Operations up in a Layer.

# The Full Conv2D Layer

The full convolutional layer, then, would look something like this:

```
class Conv2D(Layer):

    def __init__(self,
                 out_channels: int,
                 param_size: int,
                 activation: Operation = Sigmoid(),
                 flatten: bool = False) -> None:
        super().__init__()
        self.out_channels = out_channels
        self.param_size = param_size
        self.activation = activation
        self.flatten = flatten

    def _setup_layer(self, input_: ndarray) -> ndarray:

        self.params = []
        conv_param = np.random.randn(self.out_channels,
                                     input_.shape[1],  # input channels
                                     self.param_size,
                                     self.param_size)
        self.params.append(conv_param)

        self.operations = []
        self.operations.append(Conv2D(conv_param))
        self.operations.append(self.activation)

        if self.flatten:
            self.operations.append(Flatten())

        return None
```

The Flatten operation is optionally added on at the end, depending on whether we want the output of this layer to be passed forward into another convolutional layer or passed into another fully connected layer for predictions.

## A note on speed, and an alternative implementation

As those of you who are familiar with computational complexity will realize, this code is catastrophically slow: to calculate the parameter gradient, we needed to write *seven* nested for loops! There's nothing wrong with doing this, since the purpose of writing the convolution operation from scratch was to solidify our understanding of how CNNs work. Still, it is possible to write convolutions in a completely different way; instead of breaking down that process like we have in this chapter, we can break it down into the following steps:

1. From the input, extract `image_height` × `image_width` × `num_channels` patches of size `filter_height` × `filter_width` from the test set.

2. For each of these patches, perform a dot product of the patch with the appropriate filter connecting the input channels to the output channels.

3. Stack and reshape the results of all of these dot products to form the output.

With a bit of cleverness, we can express almost all of the operations described previously in terms of a batch matrix multiplication, implemented using NumPy's `np.mat mul` function. The details of how to do this are described in Appendix A and are implemented on the book's website (*https://oreil.ly/2H99xkJ*), but suffice it to say that this allows us to write relatively small convolutional neural networks that can train in a reasonable amount of time. This lets us actually run experiments to see how well convolutional neural networks work!

## Experiments

Even using the convolution operation defined by reshaping and the `matmul` functions, it takes about 10 minutes to train this model for one epoch with just one convolutional layer, so we restrict ourselves to demonstrating a model with just one convolutional layer, with 32 channels (a number chosen somewhat arbitrarily):

```
model = NeuralNetwork(
    layers=[Conv2D(out_channels=32,
                param_size=5,
                dropout=0.8,
                weight_init="glorot",
                flatten=True,
                activation=Tanh()),
            Dense(neurons=10,
                activation=Linear())],
            loss = SoftmaxCrossEntropy(),
    seed=20190402)
```

Note that this model has just $32 \times 5 \times 5 = 800$ parameters in the first layer, but these parameters are used to create $32 \times 28 \times 28 = 25{,}088$ neurons, or "learned features." By contrast, a fully connected layer with hidden size 32 would have $784 \times 32 = 25{,}088$ *parameters*, and just 32 neurons.

Some simple trial and error—training this model for just a few hundred batches with different learning rates and observing the resulting validation losses—shows that a learning rate of 0.01 works better than a learning rate of 0.1 now that we have a convolutional layer as our first layer, rather than a fully connected layer. Training this network for one epoch with optimizer `SGDMomentum(lr = 0.01, momentum=0.9)` gives:

```
Validation accuracy after 100 batches is 79.65%
Validation accuracy after 200 batches is 86.25%
Validation accuracy after 300 batches is 85.47%
Validation accuracy after 400 batches is 87.27%
Validation accuracy after 500 batches is 88.93%
Validation accuracy after 600 batches is 88.25%
Validation accuracy after 700 batches is 89.91%
Validation accuracy after 800 batches is 89.59%
Validation accuracy after 900 batches is 89.96%
Validation loss after 1 epochs is 3.453

Model validation accuracy after 1 epoch is 90.50%
```

This shows that we can indeed train a convolutional neural network from scratch that ends up getting above 90% accuracy on MNIST with just one pass through the training set![9]

# Conclusion

In this chapter, you've learned about convolutional neural networks. You started out learning at a high level what they are and about their similarities and differences from fully connected neural networks, and then you went all the way down to seeing how they work at the lowest level, implementing the core multichannel convolution operation from scratch in Python.

Starting at a high level, convolutional layers create roughly an order of magnitude more neurons than the fully connected layers we've seen so far, with each neuron being a combination of just a few features from the prior layer, rather than each neuron being a combination of *all* of the features from the prior layer as they are in fully connected layers. A level below that, we saw that these neurons are in fact grouped into "feature maps," each of which represents whether a particular visual feature—or a particular combination of visual features, in the case of deep convolutional neural networks—is present at a given location in an image. Collectively we refer to these feature maps as the convolutional Layer's "channels."

Despite all these differences from the Operations we saw involved with the Dense layer, the convolution operation fits into the same template as other ParamOperations we've seen:

---

9 The full code can be found in the section for this chapter on the book's GitHub repo (*https://oreil.ly/2H99xkJ*).

- It has an _output method that computes the output given its input and the parameter.

- It has _input_grad and _param_grad methods that, given an output_grad of the same shape as the Operation's output, compute gradients of the same shape as the input and parameters, respectively.

The difference is just that the _input, output, and params are now four-dimensional ndarrays, whereas they were two-dimensional in the case of fully connected layers.

This knowledge should serve as an extremely solid foundation for any future learning about or application of the convolutional neural networks you undertake. Next, we'll cover another common kind of advanced neural network architecture: recurrent neural networks, designed for dealing with data that appears in sequences, rather than simply the nonsequential batches we've dealt with in the cases of houses and images. Onward!

## CHAPTER 6

# Recurrent Neural Networks

In this chapter, we'll cover recurrent neural networks (RNNs), a class of neural network architectures meant for handling sequences of data. The neural networks we've seen so far treated each batch of data they received as a set of independent observations; there was no notion of some of the MNIST digits arriving before or after the other digits, in either the fully connected neural networks we saw in Chapter 4 or the convolutional neural networks we saw in Chapter 5. Many kinds of data, however, are intrinsically ordered, whether time series data, which one might deal with in an industrial or financial context, or language data, in which the characters, words, sentences, and so on are ordered. Recurrent neural networks are designed to learn how to take in *sequences* of such data and return a correct prediction as output, whether that correct prediction is of the price of a financial asset on the following day or of the next word in a sentence.

Dealing with ordered data will require three kinds of changes from the fully connected neural networks we saw in the first few chapters. First, it will involve "adding a new dimension" to the ndarrays we feed our neural networks. Previously, the data we fed our neural networks was intrinsically two-dimensional—each ndarray had one dimension representing the number of observations and another representing the number of features;[1] another way to think of this is that *each observation* was a one-dimensional vector. With recurrent neural networks, each input will still have a dimension representing the number of observations, but each observation will be represented as a two-dimensional ndarray: one dimension will represent the length of the sequence of data, and a second dimension will represent the number of features

---

[1] We happened to find it convenient to arrange the observations along the rows and the features along the columns, but we didn't necessarily have to arrange the data that way. The data does, however, have to be two-dimensional.

present at each sequence element. The overall input to an RNN will thus be a three-dimensional ndarray of shape [batch_size, sequence_length, num_features]—a batch of sequences.

Second, of course, to deal with this new three-dimensional input we'll have to use a new kind of neural network architecture, which will be the main focus of this chapter. The third change, however, is where we'll start our discussion in this chapter: we'll have to use a completely different framework with different abstractions to deal with this new form of data. Why? In the cases of both fully connected and convolutional neural networks, each "operation," even if it in fact represented *many* individual additions and multiplications (as in the case of matrix multiplication or a convolution), could be described as a single "minifactory," that on both the forward and backward passes took in one ndarray as input and produced one ndarray as an output (possibly using another ndarray representing the operation's parameters as part of these computations). As it turns out, recurrent neural networks cannot be implemented in this way. Before reading further to find out why, take some time to think about it: what characteristics of a neural network architecture would cause the framework we've built so far to break down? While the answer is illuminating, the full solution involves concepts that go deep into implementation details and are beyond the scope of this book.[2] To begin to unpack this, let's reveal a key limitation of the framework we've been using so far.

## The Key Limitation: Handling Branching

It turns out that our framework couldn't train models with computational graphs like those depicted in Figure 6-1.

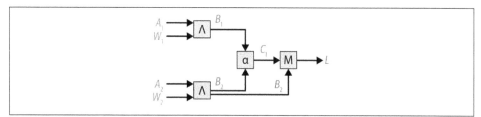

*Figure 6-1. The computational graph that causes our Operation framework to fail: the same quantity is repeated multiple times during the forward pass, meaning that we can't simply send gradients backward in sequence during the backward pass as before*

What's wrong with this? Translating the forward pass into code seems fine (note that we have written Add and Multiply operations here for illustration purposes only):

---

2 Or this edition of the book, at least.

```
a1 = torch.randn(3,3)
w1 = torch.randn(3,3)

a2 = torch.randn(3,3)
w2 = torch.randn(3,3)

w3 = torch.randn(3,3)

# operations
wm1 = WeightMultiply(w1)
wm2 = WeightMultiply(w2)
add2 = Add(2, 1)
mult3 = Multiply(2, 1)

b1 = wm1.forward(a1)
b2 = wm2.forward(a2)
c1 = add2.forward((b1, b2))
L = mult3.forward((c1, b2))
```

The trouble begins when we start the backward pass. Let's say we want to use our usual chain rule logic to calculate the derivative of L with respect to w1. Previously, we would simply call backward on each operation in reverse order. Here, because of the *reuse of b2 during the forward pass*, that approach doesn't work. If we began by calling backward on mult3, for example, we would have gradients for each of its inputs, c1 and b2. However, if we then called backward on add2, we couldn't just feed in the gradient for c1: we would have to also feed in the gradient for b2 somehow, since this also affects the loss L. So, to properly perform the backward pass for this graph, we couldn't just move through the operations in exactly the reverse sequence; we'd have to manually write something like the following:

```
c1_grad, b2_grad_1 = mult3.backward(L_grad)

b1_grad, b2_grad_2 = add2.backward(c1_grad)

# combine these gradients to reflect the fact that b2 is used twice on the
# forward pass
b2_grad = b2_grad_1 + b2_grad_2

a2_grad = wm2.backward(b2_grad)

a1_grad = wm1.backward(b1_grad)
```

At this point we might as well skip using Operations entirely; we can simply save all of the quantities we computed on the forward pass and reuse them on the backward pass, as we were doing in Chapter 2! We could *always* code arbitrarily complicated neural networks by manually defining the individual computations to be done on the forward and backward passes of the network, just as we wrote out the 17 individual operations involved in the backward pass of a two-layer neural network in Chapter 2 (indeed, we'll do something like this later in this chapter inside "RNN cells"). What we were trying to do with `Operations` was to build a flexible framework that let us describe a neural network in high-level terms and have all of the low-level computations "just work." While this framework illustrated many key concepts about neural networks, we now see its limitations.

There is an elegant solution to this problem: automatic differentiation, a completely different way of implementing neural networks.[3] We'll cover just enough of this concept here to give you an idea of how it works but won't go further than that building a full-featured automatic differentiation framework would take several chapters just on its own. Furthermore, we'll see how to *use* a high-performance automatic differentiation framework in the next chapter when we cover PyTorch. Still, automatic differentiation is an important enough concept to understand from first principles that before we get into RNNs, we'll design a basic framework for it and show how it solves the problem with reusing objects during the forward pass described in the preceding example.

# Automatic Differentiation

As we've seen, there are some neural network architectures for which the `Operation` framework we've been using so far can't easily compute the gradients of the output with respect to the inputs, as we have to do to be able to train our models. Automatic differentiation allows us to compute these gradients via a completely different route: rather than the `Operations` being the atomic units that make up the network, we define a class that wraps around the data itself and allows the data to keep track of the operations performed on it, so that the data can continually accumulate gradients as it is involved in different operations. To understand better how this "gradient accumulation" would work, let's start to code it up.[4]

## Coding Up Gradient Accumulation

To automatically keep track of gradients, we have to overwrite the Python methods that perform basic operations on our data. In Python, using operators such as + or - actually calls underlying hidden methods such as __add__ and __sub__. For example, here's how that works with +:

---

3 I want to mention an alternative solution to this problem shared by author Daniel Sabinasz on his blog, *deep ideas* (*http://www.deepideas.net*): he represents the operations as a graph and then uses breadth-first search to compute the gradients on the backward pass in the correct order, ultimately building a framework that mimics TensorFlow. His blog posts covering how he does this are extremely clear and well structured.

4 For a deeper dive into how to implement automatic differentiation, see *Grokking Deep Learning* by Andrew Trask (Manning).

```
a = array([3,3])
print("Addition using '__add__':", a.__add__(4))
print("Addition using '+':", a + 4)

Addition using '__add__': [7 7]
Addition using '+': [7 7]
```

We can take advantage of this to write a class that wraps around a typical Python "number" (float or int) and overwrites the add and mul methods:

```
Numberable = Union[float, int]

def ensure_number(num: Numberable) -> NumberWithGrad:
    if isinstance(num, NumberWithGrad):
        return num
    else:
        return NumberWithGrad(num)


class NumberWithGrad(object):

    def __init__(self,
                 num: Numberable,
                 depends_on: List[Numberable] = None,
                 creation_op: str = ''):
        self.num = num
        self.grad = None
        self.depends_on = depends_on or []
        self.creation_op = creation_op

    def __add__(self,
                other: Numberable) -> NumberWithGrad:
        return NumberWithGrad(self.num + ensure_number(other).num,
                              depends_on = [self, ensure_number(other)],
                              creation_op = 'add')

    def __mul__(self,
                other: Numberable = None) -> NumberWithGrad:

        return NumberWithGrad(self.num * ensure_number(other).num,
                              depends_on = [self, ensure_number(other)],
                              creation_op = 'mul')

    def backward(self, backward_grad: Numberable = None) -> None:
        if backward_grad is None: # first time calling backward
            self.grad = 1
        else:
            # These lines allow gradients to accumulate.
            # If the gradient doesn't exist yet, simply set it equal
            # to backward_grad
            if self.grad is None:
                self.grad = backward_grad
            # Otherwise, simply add backward_grad to the existing gradient
            else:
```

```
                self.grad += backward_grad

            if self.creation_op == "add":
                # Simply send backward self.grad, since increasing either of these
                # elements will increase the output by that same amount
                self.depends_on[0].backward(self.grad)
                self.depends_on[1].backward(self.grad)

            if self.creation_op == "mul":

                # Calculate the derivative with respect to the first element
                new = self.depends_on[1] * self.grad
                # Send backward the derivative with respect to that element
                self.depends_on[0].backward(new.num)

                # Calculate the derivative with respect to the second element
                new = self.depends_on[0] * self.grad
                # Send backward the derivative with respect to that element
                self.depends_on[1].backward(new.num)
```

There's a lot going on here, so let's unpack this NumberWithGrad class and see how it works. Recall that the goal of such a class is to be able to write simple operations and have the gradients be computed automatically; for example, suppose we write:

```
a = NumberWithGrad(3)

b = a * 4
c = b + 5
```

At this point, how much will increasing a by $\epsilon$ increase the value of c? It should be pretty obvious that it will increase c by $4 \times \epsilon$. And indeed, using the preceding class, if we first write:

```
c.backward()
```

then, without writing a for loop to iterate through the Operations or anything, we can write:

```
print(a.grad)

4
```

How does this work? The fundamental insight incorporated into the previous class is that every time the + or * operations are performed on a NumberWithGrad, a new NumberWithGrad is created, with the first NumberWithGrad as a dependency. Then, when backward is called on a NumberWithGrad, like it is called on c previously, all the gradients for all of the NumberWithGrads used to create c are automatically calculated. So indeed, not only was the gradient for a calculated, but so was the gradient for b:

```
print(b.grad)

1
```

The real beauty of this framework, however, is that it allows the NumberWithGrads to *accumulate* gradients and thus be reused multiple times during a series of computations, and we still end up with the correct gradient. We'll illustrate this with the same series of operations that stumped us before, using a NumberWithGrad multiple times in a series of computations, and then unpack how it works in detail.

## Automatic differentiation illustration

Here's the series of computations in which a is reused multiple times:

```
a = NumberWithGrad(3)

b = a * 4
c = b + 3
d = c * (a + 2)
```

We can work out that if we do these operations, $d = 75$, but as we know, the real question is: how much will increasing the value of a increase the value of d? We can first work out the answer to this question mathematically. We have:

$$d = (4a + 3) \times (a + 2) = 4a^2 + 11a + 6$$

So, using the power rule from calculus:

$$\frac{\partial d}{\partial a} = 8a + 11$$

For $a = 3$, therefore, the value of this derivative should be $8 \times 3 + 11 = 35$. Confirming this numerically:

```
def forward(num: int):
    b = num * 4
    c = b + 3
    return c * (num + 2)

print(round(forward(3.01) - forward(2.99)) / 0.02), 3)

35.0
```

Now, observe that we get the same result when we compute the gradient with our automatic differentiation framework:

```
a = NumberWithGrad(3)

b = a * 4
c = b + 3
d = (a + 2)
e = c * d
e.backward()
```

```
print(a.grad)
35
```

### Explaining what happened

As we can see, the goal with automatic differentiation is to make the *data objects themselves*—numbers, ndarrays, Tensors, and so on—the fundamental units of analysis, rather than the Operations as before.

All automatic differentiation techniques have the following in common:

- Each technique includes a class that wraps around the actual data being computed. Here, we wrap NumberWithGrad around floats and ints; in PyTorch, for example, the analogous class is called Tensor.

- Common operations such as adding, multiplying, and matrix multiplication are redefined so that they always return members of this class; in the preceding case, we ensure the addition of *either* a NumberWithGrad and a NumberWithGrad *or* a NumberWithGrad and a float or an int.

- The NumberWithGrad class must contain information on how to compute gradients, given what happens on the forward pass. Previously, we did this by including a creation_op argument in the class that simply recorded how the NumberWithGrad was created.

- On the backward pass, gradients are passed backward using the underlying data type, not the wrapper. Here, this means gradients are of type float and int, not NumberWithGrad.

- As mentioned at the start of this section, automatic differentiation allows us to reuse quantities computed during the forward pass—in the preceding example, we use a twice with no problem. The key for allowing this is these lines:

  ```
  if self.grad is None:
      self.grad = backward_grad
  else:
      self.grad += backward_grad
  ```

  These lines state that upon receiving a new gradient, backward_grad, a Number WithGrad should either initialize the gradient of NumberWithGrad to be this value, or simply add the value to the NumberWithGrad's existing gradient. This is what allows the NumberWithGrads to accumulate gradients as the relevant objects are reused in the model.

That's all we'll cover of automatic differentiation. Let's now turn to the model structure that motivated this digression, since it requires certain quantities to be reused during the forward pass to make predictions.

---

# Motivation for Recurrent Neural Networks

As we discussed at the beginning of this chapter, recurrent neural networks are designed to handle data that appears in sequences: instead of each observation being a vector with, say, n features, it is now a two-dimensional array of dimension n features by t time steps. This is depicted in Figure 6-2.

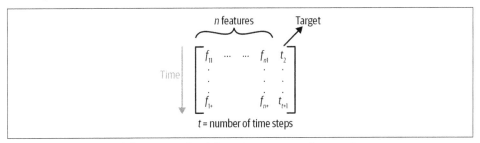

*Figure 6-2. Sequential data: at each of the t time steps we have n features*

In the following few sections, we'll explain how RNNs accommodate data of this form, but first let's try to understand why we need them. What would be the limitations of simply using a normal feed-forward neural network to deal with this kind of data? One way would be to represent each time step as an independent set of features. For example, one observation could have the features from time $t$ = 1 with the value of the target from time $t$ = 2, the next observation could have the features from time $t$ = 2 with the value of the target from time $t$ = 3, and so on. If we wanted to use data from *multiple* time steps to make each prediction rather than data from just one time step, we could use the features from $t$ = 1 and $t$ = 2 to predict the target at $t$ = 3, the features from $t$ = 2 and $t$ = 3 to predict the target at $t$ = 4, and so on.

However, treating each time step as independent ignores the fact that the data is ordered sequentially. How would we ideally want to use the sequential nature of the data to make better predictions? The solution would look something like this:

1. Use features from time step $t$ = 1 to make predictions for the corresponding target at $t$ = 1.

2. Use features from time step $t$ = 2 *as well as the information from $t$ = 1, including the value of the target at $t$ = 1*, to make predictions for $t$ = 2.

3. Use features from time step $t$ = 3 *as well as the accumulated information from $t$ = 1 and $t$ = 2* to make predictions at $t$ = 3.

4. And so on, at each step using the information from all prior time steps to make a prediction.

To do this, it seems that we'd want to pass our data through the neural network one sequence element at a time, with the data from the first time step being passed through first, then the data from the next time step, and so on. In addition, we'll want our neural network to "accumulate information" about what it has seen before as the new sequence elements are passed through. We'll spend the rest of this chapter discussing in detail precisely how recurrent neural networks do this. As we'll see, while there are several variants of recurrent neural networks, they all share a common underlying structure in the way they process data sequentially; we'll spend most of our time discussing this structure and at the end discuss the ways in which the variants differ.

# Introduction to Recurrent Neural Networks

Let's start our discussion of RNNs by reviewing, at a high level, how data is passed through a "feed-forward" neural network. In this type of network, data is passed forward through a series of *layers*. For a single observation, the output of each layer is the neural network's "representation" of that observation at that layer. After the first layer, that representation consists of features that are combinations of the original features; after the next layer, it consists of combinations of these representations, or "features of features" of the original features, and so on for subsequent layers in the network. After each forward pass, then, the network contains in the outputs of each of its layers many representations of the original observation. This is encapsulated in Figure 6-3.

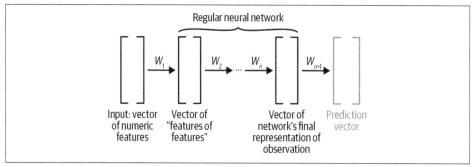

*Figure 6-3. A regular neural network passing an observation forward and transforming it into different representations after each layer*

When the next set of observations is passed through the network, however, these representations are discarded; the key innovation of recurrent neural networks and all of their variants is to *pass these representations back into the network* along with the next set of observations. Here's how that procedure would look:

---

1.  In the first time step, t = 1, we would pass through the observation from the first time step (along with randomly initialized representations, perhaps). We would output a prediction for t = 1, along with representations at each layer.

2.  In the next time step, we would pass through the observation from the second time step, t = 2, along with the representations computed during the first time step (which, again, are just the outputs of the neural network's layers), and combine these somehow (it is in this combining step that the variants of RNNs we'll learn about differ). We would use these two pieces of information to output a prediction for t = 2 as well as the *updated* representations at each layer, which are now a function of the inputs passed in at both t = 1 *and* t = 2.

3.  In the third time step, we would pass through the observation from t = 3, as well as the representations that now incorporate the information from t = 1 and t = 2, and use this information to make predictions for t = 3, as well as additional updated representations at each layer, which now incorporate information from time steps 1–3.

This process is depicted in Figure 6-4.

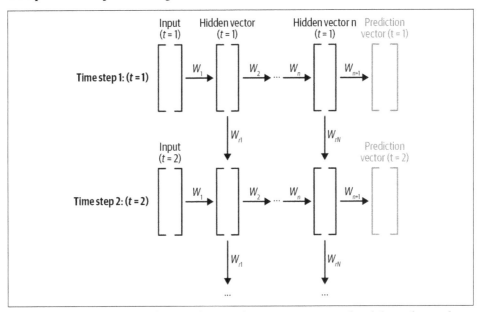

*Figure 6-4. Recurrent neural networks pass the representations of each layer forward into the next time step*

We see that each layer has a representation that is "persistent," getting updated over time as new observations are passed through. Indeed, this fact is why RNNs are not amenable to the Operation framework we've written for the prior chapters: the ndarray that represents this state for each layer is continually updated and reused many times in order to make one set of predictions for a single sequence of data using an RNN. Because we can't use the framework from the prior chapter, we'll have to reason from first principles about what classes to build to handle RNNs.

## The First Class for RNNs: RNNLayer

Based on the description of how we want RNNs to work, we know at the very least that we'll need an RNNLayer class that passes a sequence of data forward one sequence element at a time. Let's now get into the details of how such a class should work. As we've mentioned in this chapter, RNNs will deal with data in which each observation is two-dimensional, with dimensions (sequence_length, num_features); and since it is always more efficient computationally to pass data forward in batches, RNNLayer will have to take in three-dimensional ndarrays, of size (batch_size, sequence_length, num_features). I explained in the prior section, however, that we want to feed our data through our RNNLayers one sequence element at a time; how can we do this if our input, data, is (batch_size, sequence_length, num_fea tures)? Here's how:

1. Select a two-dimensional array from the second axis, starting with data[:, 0, :]. This ndarray will have shape (batch_size, num_features).

2. Initialize a "hidden state" for the RNNLayer that will continually get updated with each sequence element passed in, this time of shape (batch_size, hid den_size). This ndarray will represent the layer's "accumulated information" about the data that has been passed in during the prior time steps.

3. Pass these two ndarrays forward through the first time step in this layer. We'll end up designing RNNLayer to output ndarrays of different dimensionality than the inputs, just like regular Dense layers can, so the output will be of shape (batch_size, num_outputs). In addition, update the neural network's represen tation for each observation: at each time step, our RNNLayer should *also* output an ndarray of shape (batch_size, hidden_size).

4. Select the next two-dimensional array from data: data[:, 1, :].

5. Pass this data, as well as the values of the RNN's representations outputted at the first time step, into the second time step at this layer to get another output of shape (batch_size, num_outputs), as well as updated representations of shape (batch_size, hidden_size).

6. Continue until all sequence_length time steps have been passed through the layer. Then concatenate all the results together to get an output from that layer of shape (batch_size, sequence_length, num_outputs).

This gives us an idea of how our RNNLayers should work—and we'll solidify this understanding when we code it up—but it also hints that we'll need another class to handle receiving the data and updating the layer's hidden state at each time step. For this we'll use the RNNNode, the next class we'll cover.

## The Second Class for RNNs: RNNNode

Based on the description from the prior section, an RNNNode should have a forward method with the following inputs and outputs:

- Two ndarrays as inputs:
  - One for the data inputs to the network, of shape [batch_size, num_fea tures]
  - One for the representations of the observations at that time step, of shape [batch_size, hidden_size]
- Two ndarrays as outputs:
  - One for the outputs of the network at that time step, or shape [batch_size, num_outputs]
  - One for the *updated* representations of the observations at that time step, of shape: [batch_size, hidden_size]

Next, we'll show how the two classes, RNNNode and RNNLayer, fit together.

## Putting These Two Classes Together

The RNNLayer class will wrap around a list of RNNNodes and will (at least) contain a forward method that has the following inputs and outputs:

- Input: a batch of sequences of observations of shape [batch_size, sequence_length, num_features]
- Output: the neural network output of those sequences of shape [batch_size, sequence_length, num_outputs]

Figure 6-5 shows the order that data would move forward through an RNN with two RNNLayers with five RNNNodes each. At each time step, inputs initially of dimension feature_size are passed successively forward through the first RNNNode in each RNNLayer, with the network ultimately outputting a prediction at that time step of dimension output_size. In addition, each RNNNode passes a "hidden state" forward to the next RNNNode within each layer. Once data from each of the five time steps has been passed forward through all the layers, we will have a final set of predictions of shape (5, output_size), where output_size should be the same dimension as the targets. These predictions would then be compared to the target, and the loss gradient would be computed, kicking off the backward pass. Figure 6-5 summarizes this, showing the order in which the data would flow through the 5 × 2 RNNNodes from first (1) to last (10).

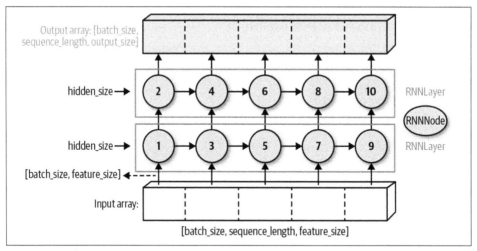

*Figure 6-5. The order in which data would flow through an RNN with two layers that was designed to process sequences of length 5*

Alternatively, data could flow through the RNN in the order shown in Figure 6-6. Whatever the order, the following must occur:

- Each layer needs to process its data at a given time step before the next layer—for example, in Figure 6-5, 2 can't happen before 1, and 4 can't happen before 3.

- Similarly, each layer has to process all of its time steps in order—in Figure 6-5, for example, 4 can't happen before 2, and 3 can't happen before 1.

- The last layer has to output dimension `feature_size` for each observation.

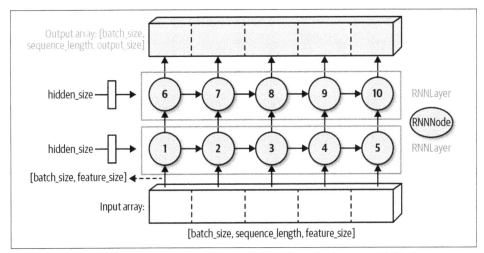

*Figure 6-6. Another order in which data could flow through the same RNN during its forward pass*

This all covers how the forward pass through an RNN would work. What about the backward pass?

## The Backward Pass

Backpropagation through recurrent neural networks is often described as a separate algorithm called "backpropagation through time." While this does indeed describe what happens during backpropagation, it makes things sound a lot more complicated than they are. Keeping in mind the explanation of how data flows forward through an RNN, we can describe what happens on the backward pass this way: we pass data backward through the RNN by passing gradients backward through the network in reverse of the order that we passed inputs forward on the forward pass—which, indeed, is the same thing we do in regular feed-forward networks.

Looking at the diagrams in Figures 6-5 and 6-6, on the forward pass:

1. We start with a batch of observations, each of shape (`feature_size`, `sequence_length`).

2. These inputs are broken up into the individual `sequence_length` elements and passed into the network one at a time.

3. Each element gets passed through all the layers, ultimately getting transformed into an output of size `output_size`.

4. At the same time, the layer passes the hidden state forward into the layer's computation at the next time step.

5. This continues for all `sequence_length` time steps, resulting in a total output of size (`output_size, sequence_length`).

Backpropagation simply works the same way, but in reverse:

1. We start with a *gradient* of shape [`output_size, sequence_length`], representing how much each element of the output (also of size [`output_size, sequence_length`]) ultimately impacts the loss computed for that batch of observations.

2. These gradients are broken up into the individual `sequence_length` elements and passed *backward* through the layers *in reverse order.*

3. The gradient for an individual element is passed backward through all the layers.

4. At the same, the layers pass the *gradient of the loss with respect to the hidden state at that time step* backward into the layers' computations at the prior time steps.

5. This continues for all `sequence_length` time steps, until the gradients have been passed backward to every layer in the network, thus allowing us to compute the gradient of the loss with respect to each of the weights, just as we do in the case of regular feed-forward networks.

This parallelism between the backward and forward pass is highlighted in Figure 6-7, which shows how data flows through an RNN during the backward pass. You'll notice, of course, that it is the same as Figure 6-5 but with the arrows reversed and the numbers changed.

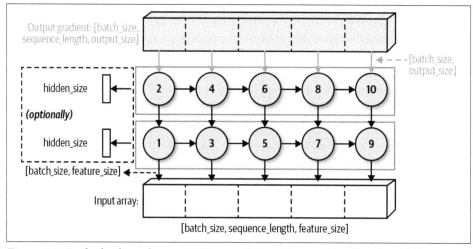

*Figure 6-7. In the backward pass, RNNs pass data in the opposite direction of the way the data is passed during the forward pass*

This highlights that, at a high level, the forward and backward passes for an RNNLayer are very similar to those of a layer in a normal neural network: they both receive ndarrays of a certain shape as input, output ndarrays of another shape, and on the backward pass receive an output gradient of the same shape as their output and produce an input gradient of the same shape as their input. There is a key difference in the way the weight gradients are handled in RNNLayers versus other layers, however, so we'll briefly cover that before we shift to coding this all up.

### Accumulating gradients for the weights in an RNN

In recurrent neural networks, just as in regular neural networks, each layer will have *one set of weights*. That means that the same set of weights will affect the layer's output at all sequence_length time steps; during backpropagation, therefore, the same set of weights will receive sequence_length different gradients. For example, in the circle labeled "1" in the backpropagation shown in Figure 6-7, the second layer will receive a gradient for the last time step, while in the circle labeled "3," the layer will receive a gradient for the second-to-last time step; both of these will be driven by the same set of weights. Thus, during backpropagation, we'll have to *accumulate gradients* for the weights over a series of time steps, which means that however we choose to store the weights, we'll have to update their gradients using something like the following:

```
weight_grad += grad_from_time_step
```

This is different from the Dense and Conv2D layers, in which we just stored the parameters in a param_grad argument.

We've laid out how RNNs work and the classes we want to build to implement them; now let's start figuring out the details.

# RNNs: The Code

Let's start with several of the ways the implementation of RNNs will be similar to that of the other neural networks we've covered in this book:

1. An RNN still passes data forward through a series of layers, which send outputs forward on the forward pass and gradients backward on the backward pass. Thus, for example, whatever the equivalent of our NeuralNetwork class ends up being will still have a list of RNNLayers as a layers attribute, and the forward pass will consist of code like:

```
def forward(self, x_batch: ndarray) -> ndarray:

    assert_dim(ndarray, 3)

    x_out = x_batch
    for layer in self.layers:
```

```
        x_out = layer.forward(x_out)

    return x_out
```

2. The `Loss` for RNNs is the same as before: an `ndarray` output is produced by the last `Layer` and compared with `y_batch`, a single value is computed, and a gradient of this value with respect to the input to the `Loss` is returned with the same shape as `output`. We'll have to modify the softmax function to work appropriately with `ndarrays` of shape [`batch_size, sequence_length, feature_size`], but we can handle that.

3. The `Trainer` is mostly the same: we cycle through our training data, selecting batches of input data and batches of output data, and continually feed them through our model, producing loss values that tell us whether our model is learning and updating the weights after each batch has been fed through. Speaking of which…

4. Our `Optimizer` remains the same as well. As we'll see, we'll have to update how we extract the `params` and `param_grads` at each time step, but the "update rules" (which we captured in the `_update_rule` function in our class) remain the same.

The `Layers` themselves are where things get interesting.

# The RNNLayer Class

Previously, we gave `Layers` a set of `Operations` that passed data forward and sent gradients backward. `RNNLayers` will be completely different; they now must maintain a "hidden state" that continually gets updated as new data gets fed in and gets "combined" with the data somehow at each time step. How *exactly* should this work? We can use Figures 6-5 and 6-6 as guides here: they suggest that each `RNNLayer` should have a `List` of `RNNNodes` as an attribute, and then each sequence element from the layer's input should get passed through each `RNNNode`, one element at a time. Each `RNNNode` will take in this sequence element, as well as the "hidden state" for that layer, and produce an output for the layer at that time step as well as updating the layer's hidden state.

To clarify all this, let's dive in and start coding it up: we'll cover, in order, how an `RNNLayer` should be initialized, how it should send data forward during the forward pass, and how it should send data backward during the backward pass.

### Initialization

Each `RNNLayer` will start with:

- An `int` `hidden_size`

---

- An int output_size
- An ndarray start_H of shape (1, hidden_size), representing the layer's hidden state

In addition, just like in regular neural networks, we'll set self.first = True when we initialize the layer; the first time we pass data into the forward method we'll pass the ndarray we receive into an _init_params method, initialize the parameters, and set self.first = False.

With our layer initialized, we are ready to describe how to send data forward.

### The forward method

The bulk of the forward method will consist of taking in an ndarray x_seq_in of shape (batch_size, sequence_length, feature_size) and feeding it through the layer's RNNNodes in sequence. In the following code, self.nodes are the RNNNodes for the layer, and H_in is the hidden state for the layer:

```
sequence_length = x_seq_in.shape[1]

x_seq_out = np.zeros((batch_size, sequence_length, self.output_size))

for t in range(sequence_length):

    x_in = x_seq_in[:, t, :]

    y_out, H_in = self.nodes[t].forward(x_in, H_in, self.params)

    x_seq_out[:, t, :] = y_out
```

One note on the hidden state H_in: the hidden state for an RNNLayer is typically represented in a vector, but the operations in each RNNNode require the hidden state to be an ndarray of size (batch_size, hidden_size). So, at the beginning of each forward pass, we simply "repeat" the hidden state:

```
batch_size = x_seq_in.shape[0]

H_in = np.copy(self.start_H)

H_in = np.repeat(H_in, batch_size, axis=0)
```

After the forward pass, we take the average value across the observations making up the batch to get the updated hidden state for that layer:

```
self.start_H = H_in.mean(axis=0, keepdims=True)
```

Also, we can see from this code that an RNNNode will have to have a forward method that takes in two arrays of shapes:

- (batch_size, feature_size)
- (batch_size, hidden_size)

and returns two arrays of shapes:

- (batch_size, output_size)
- (batch_size, hidden_size)

We'll cover RNNNodes (and their variants) in the next section. But first let's cover the backward method for the RNNLayer class.

## The backward method

Since the forward method outputted x_seq_out, the backward method will receive a gradient of the same shape as x_seq_out called x_seq_out_grad. Moving in the opposite direction from the forward method, we feed this gradient *backward* through the RNNNodes, ultimately returning x_seq_in_grad of shape (batch_size, sequence_length, self.feature_size) as the gradient for the entire layer:

```
h_in_grad = np.zeros((batch_size, self.hidden_size))

sequence_length = x_seq_out_grad.shape[1]

x_seq_in_grad = np.zeros((batch_size, sequence_length, self.feature_size))

for t in reversed(range(sequence_length)):

    x_out_grad = x_seq_out_grad[:, t, :]

    grad_out, h_in_grad = \
        self.nodes[t].backward(x_out_grad, h_in_grad, self.params)

    x_seq_in_grad[:, t, :] = grad_out
```

From this, we see that RNNNodes should have a backward method that, following the pattern, is the opposite of the forward method, taking in two arrays of shapes:

- (batch_size, output_size)
- (batch_size, hidden_size)

and returning two arrays of shapes:

- (batch_size, feature_size)
- (batch_size, hidden_size)

And that's the working of an RNNLayer. Now it seems like the only thing left is to describe the core of recurrent neural networks: the RNNNodes where the actual computations happen. Before we do, let's clarify the role of RNNNodes and their variants within RNNs as a whole.

## The Essential Elements of RNNNodes

In most treatments of RNNs, the first thing discussed is the workings of what we are here calling RNNNodes. However, we cover these last because the most important concepts to understand about RNNs are those that we've described in the diagrams and code thus far in this chapter: the way the data is structured and the way it and the hidden states are routed between layers and through time. As it turns out, there are multiple ways we can implement RNNNodes, the actual processing of the data from a given time step, and updating of the layer's hidden state. One way produces what is usually thought of as a "regular" recurrent neural network, which we'll refer to here by another common term: a "vanilla RNN." However, there are other, more complicated ways that produce different variants of RNNs; one of these, for example, is a variant with RNNNodes called GRUs, which stands for "Gated Recurrent Units." Often, GRUs and other RNN variants are described as being significantly different from vanilla RNNs; however, it is important to understand that *all* RNN variants share the structure of the layers that we've seen so far—for example, they all pass data forward in time in the same way, updating their hidden state(s) at each time step. The only way they differ is in the internal workings of these "nodes."

To reinforce this point: if we implemented a GRULayer instead of an RNNLayer, the code would be exactly the same! The following code would still form the core of the forward pass:

```
sequence_length = x_seq_in.shape[1]

x_seq_out = np.zeros((batch_size, sequence_length, self.output_size))

for t in range(sequence_length):

    x_in = x_seq_in[:, t, :]

    y_out, H_in = self.nodes[t].forward(x_in, H_in, self.params)

    x_seq_out[:, t, :] = y_out
```

The only difference is that each "node" in self.nodes would be a GRUNode instead of an RNNNode. The backward method, similarly, would be identical.

This is also almost entirely true for the most well-known variant on vanilla RNNs: LSTMs, or "Long Short Term Memory" cells. The only difference with these is that LSTMLayers require *two* quantities to be "remembered" by the layer and updated as sequence elements are passed forward through time: in addition to a "hidden state," there is a "cell state" stored in the layer that allows it to better model long-term dependencies. This leads to some minor differences in how we would implement an LSTMLayer as opposed to an RNNLayer; for example, an LSTMLayer would have two ndarrays to store the layer's state throughout the time steps:

- An ndarray start_H of shape (1, hidden_size), representing the layer's hidden state
- An ndarray start_C of shape (1, cell_size), representing the layer's cell state

Each LSTMNode, therefore, should take in the input, as well as both the hidden state *and* the cell state. On the forward pass, this will look like:

```
y_out, H_in, C_in = self.nodes[t].forward(x_in, H_in, C_in self.params)
```

as well as:

```
grad_out, h_in_grad, c_in_grad = \
    self.nodes[t].backward(x_out_grad, h_in_grad, c_in_grad, self.params)
```

in the backward method.

There are many more variants than the three mentioned here, some of which, such as LSTMs with "peephole connections," have a cell state in addition to only a hidden state, and some of which maintain only a hidden state.[5] Still, a layer made up of LSTMPeepholeConnectionNodes would fit into an RNNLayer in the same way as the variants we've seen so far and would thus have the same forward and backward methods. This basic structure of RNN—the way data is routed forward through layers, as well as forward through time steps, and then routed in the opposite direction during the backward pass—is what makes recurrent neural networks unique. The actual structural differences between a vanilla RNN and an LSTM-based RNN, for example, are relatively minor, even though they can have dramatically different performance.

With that, let's look at the implementation of an RNNNode.

## "Vanilla" RNNNodes

RNNs receive data one sequence element at a time; for example, if we are predicting the price of oil, at each time step, the RNN will receive information about the features we are using to predict the price at that time step. In addition, the RNN will have in its "hidden state" an encoding representing cumulative information about what has happened at prior time steps. We want to combine these two pieces of data—the fea-

---

5 See the Wikipedia page on LSTMs for more examples of LSTM variants (*https://oreil.ly/2TysrXj*).

tures at the time step, and the cumulative information from all the prior time steps—into a prediction at that time step, as well as an updated hidden state.

To understand how RNNs should accomplish this, recall what happens in a regular neural network. In a feed-forward neural network, each layer receives a set of "learned features" from the prior layer, each of which is a combination of the original features that the network has "learned" is useful. The layer then multiplies these features by a weight matrix that allows the layer to learn features that are combinations of the features the layer received as input. To level set and normalize the output, respectively, we add a "bias" to these new features and feed them through an activation function.

In recurrent neural networks, we want our updated hidden state to be a combination of both the input and the old hidden state. Thus, similar to what happens in regular neural networks:

1. We first concatenate the input and the hidden state. Then we multiply this value by a weight matrix, add a bias, and feed the result through the Tanh activation function. This is our updated hidden state.

2. Next, we multiply this new hidden state by a weight matrix that transforms the hidden state into an output with the dimension that we want. For example, if we are using this RNN to predict a single continuous value at each time step, we'll multiply the hidden state by a weight matrix of size (hidden_size, 1).

Thus, our updated hidden state will be a function of both the input received at that time step as well as the prior hidden state, and the output will be the result of feeding this updated hidden state through the operations of a fully connected layer.

Let's code this up.

## RNNNode: The code

The following code implements the steps described a moment ago. Note that, just as we'll do with GRUs and LSTMs a bit later (and as we did with the simple mathematical functions we showed in Chapter 1), we save all the quantities computed on the forward pass as attributes stored in the Node so we can use them to compute the backward pass:

```
def forward(self,
            x_in: ndarray,
            H_in: ndarray,
            params_dict: Dict[str, Dict[str, ndarray]]
            ) -> Tuple[ndarray]:
    '''
    param x: numpy array of shape (batch_size, vocab_size)
    param H_prev: numpy array of shape (batch_size, hidden_size)
    return self.x_out: numpy array of shape (batch_size, vocab_size)
```

```
            return self.H: numpy array of shape (batch_size, hidden_size)
        '''
        self.X_in = x_in
        self.H_in = H_in

        self.Z = np.column_stack((x_in, H_in))

        self.H_int = np.dot(self.Z, params_dict['W_f']['value']) \
                            + params_dict['B_f']['value']

        self.H_out = tanh(self.H_int)

        self.X_out = np.dot(self.H_out, params_dict['W_v']['value']) \
                            + params_dict['B_v']['value']

        return self.X_out, self.H_out
```

Another note: since we're not using `ParamOperations` here, we'll need to store the parameters differently. We'll store them in a dictionary `params_dict`, which refers to the parameters by name. Furthermore, each parameter will have two keys: `value` and `deriv`, which will store the actual parameter values and their associated gradients, respectively. Here, in the forward pass, we simply use the `value` key.

### RNNNodes: The backward pass

The backward pass through an `RNNNode` simply computes the value of the gradients of the loss with respect to the inputs to the `RNNNode`, given gradients of the loss with respect to the outputs of the `RNNNode`. We can do this using logic similar to that which we worked out in Chapters 1 and 2: since we can represent an `RNNNode` as a series of operations, we can simply compute the derivative of each operation evaluated at its input, and successively multiply these derivatives together with the ones that have come before (taking care to handle matrix multiplication correctly) to end up with `ndarrays` representing the gradients of the loss with respect to each of the inputs. The following code accomplishes this:

```
    def forward(self,
                x_in: ndarray,
                H_in: ndarray,
                params_dict: Dict[str, Dict[str, ndarray]]
                ) -> Tuple[ndarray]:
        '''
        param x: numpy array of shape (batch_size, vocab_size)
        param H_prev: numpy array of shape (batch_size, hidden_size)
        return self.x_out: numpy array of shape (batch_size, vocab_size)
        return self.H: numpy array of shape (batch_size, hidden_size)
        '''
        self.X_in = x_in
        self.H_in = H_in
```

```
self.Z = np.column_stack((x_in, H_in))

self.H_int = np.dot(self.Z, params_dict['W_f']['value']) \
                           + params_dict['B_f']['value']

self.H_out = tanh(self.H_int)

self.X_out = np.dot(self.H_out, params_dict['W_v']['value']) \
                           + params_dict['B_v']['value']

return self.X_out, self.H_out
```

Note that just as in our `Operations` from before, the shapes of the inputs to the `back ward` function must match the shapes of the outputs of the `forward` function, and the shapes of the outputs of the `backward` function must match the shapes of the inputs to the `forward` function.

## Limitations of "Vanilla" RNNNodes

Remember: the purpose of RNNs is to model dependencies in sequences of data. Thinking of modeling the price of oil as our canonical example, this means that we should be able to uncover the relationship between the sequence of features we've seen in the last several time steps and what will happen with the price of oil in the next time step. But how long should "several" be? For the price of oil, we might imagine that the relationship between what happened yesterday—one time step before—would be most important for predicting the price of oil tomorrow, with the day before being less important, and the importance generally decaying as we move backward in time.

While this is true for many real-world problems, there are domains to which we'd like to apply RNNs where we would want to learn extremely long-range dependencies. *Language modeling* is the canonical example here—that is, building a model that can predict the next character, word, or word part, given a theoretically extremely long series of past words or characters (since this is a particularly prevalent application, we'll discuss some details specific to language modeling later in this chapter). For this, vanilla RNNs are usually insufficient. Now that we've seen their details, we can understand why: at each time step, the hidden state is multiplied by *the same weight matrix* across all time steps in the layer. Consider what happens when we multiply a number by a value x over and over again: if x < 1, the number decreases exponentially to 0, and if x > 1, the number increases exponentially to infinity. Recurrent neural networks have the same issues: over long time horizons, because the same set of weights is multiplied by the hidden state at each time step, the gradient for these weights tends to become either extremely small or extremely large. The former is known as the *vanishing gradient problem* and the latter is known as the *exploding gradient problem*. Both make it hard to train RNNs to model the very long term dependencies (50–100 time steps) needed for high-quality language modeling. The two commonly used modifications of the vanilla RNN architectures we'll cover next both significantly mitigate this problem.

## One Solution: GRUNodes

Vanilla RNNs can be described as taking the input and hidden state, combining them, and using the matrix multiplication to determine how to "weigh" the information contained in the hidden state against the information in the new input to predict the output. The insight that motivates more advanced RNN variants is that to model long-term dependencies, such as those that exist in language, *we sometimes receive information that tells us we need to "forget" or "reset" our hidden state.* A simple example is a period "." or a colon ":"—if a language model receives one of these, it knows that it should forget the characters that came before and begin modeling a new pattern in the sequence of characters.

A first, simple variant on vanilla RNNs that leverages this insight is GRUs or Gated Recurrent Units, so named because the input and the prior hidden state are passed through a series of "gates."

1. The first gate is similar to the operations that take place in vanilla RNNs: the input and hidden state are concatenated together, multiplied by a weight matrix, and then passed through a sigmoid operation. We can think of the output of this as the "update" gate.

2. The second gate is interpreted as a "reset" gate: the input and hidden state are concatenated, multiplied by a weight matrix, passed through a sigmoid operation, *and then multiplied by the prior hidden state.* This allows the network to "learn to forget" what was in the hidden state, given the particular input that was passed in.

3. The output of the second gate is then multiplied by another matrix and passed through the Tanh function, with the output being a "candidate" for the new hidden state.

4. Finally, the hidden state is updated to be the update gate times the "candidate" for the new hidden state, plus the old hidden state times 1 minus the update gate.

We'll cover two advanced variants on vanilla RNNs in this chapter: GRUs and LSTMs. LSTMs are more popular and were invented long before GRUs. Nevertheless, GRUs are a simpler version of LSTMs, and more directly illustrate how the idea of "gates" can enable RNNs to "learn to reset" their hidden state given the input they receive, which is why we cover them first.

---

## GRUNodes: A diagram

Figure 6-8 depicts GRUNode as a series of gates. Each gate contains the operations of a Dense layer: multiplication by a weight matrix, adding a bias, and feeding the result through an activation function. The activation functions used are either sigmoid, in which case the range of the result falls between 0 and 1, or Tanh, in which case the range falls between –1 and 1; the range of each intermediate ndarray produced next is shown under the name of the array.

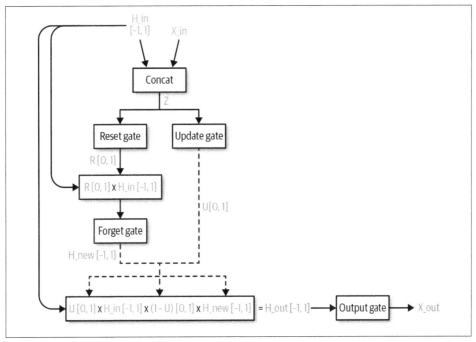

*Figure 6-8. The flow of data forward through a GRUNode, passing through gates and producing X_out and H_out*

In Figure 6-8 as in Figures 6-9 and 6-10, the inputs to the node are colored green, the intermediate quantities computed are colored blue, and the outputs are colored red. All the weights (not directly shown) are contained in the gates.

Note that to backpropagate through this, we would have to represent this solely as a series of Operations, compute the derivative of each Operation with respect to its input, and multiply the results together. We don't show that explicitly here, instead showing gates (which are really groups of three operations) as a single block. Still, at this point, we know how to backpropagate through the Operations that make up each gate, and the notion of "gates" is used throughout descriptions of recurrent neural networks and their variants, so we'll stick with that representation here.

Indeed, Figure 6-9 shows a representation of a vanilla RNNNode, using gates.

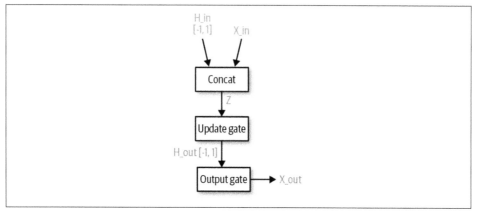

*Figure 6-9. The flow of data forward through an RNNNode, passing through just two gates and producing X_out and H_out*

Thus, another way to think of the Operations we previously described as making up a vanilla RNNNode is as passing the input and hidden state through two gates.

### GRUNodes: The code

The following code implements the forward pass for a GRUNode as described earlier:

```
def forward(self,
            X_in: ndarray,
            H_in: ndarray,
            params_dict: Dict[str, Dict[str, ndarray]]) -> Tuple[ndarray]:
    '''
    param X_in: numpy array of shape (batch_size, vocab_size)
    param H_in: numpy array of shape (batch_size, hidden_size)
    return self.X_out: numpy array of shape (batch_size, vocab_size)
    return self.H_out: numpy array of shape (batch_size, hidden_size)
    '''
    self.X_in = X_in
    self.H_in = H_in

    # reset gate
    self.X_r = np.dot(X_in, params_dict['W_xr']['value'])
    self.H_r = np.dot(H_in, params_dict['W_hr']['value'])

    # update gate
    self.X_u = np.dot(X_in, params_dict['W_xu']['value'])
    self.H_u = np.dot(H_in, params_dict['W_hu']['value'])

    # gates
    self.r_int = self.X_r + self.H_r + params_dict['B_r']['value']
    self.r = sigmoid(self.r_int)
```

```
        self.u_int = self.X_r + self.H_r + params_dict['B_u']['value']
        self.u = sigmoid(self.u_int)

        # new state
        self.h_reset = self.r * H_in
        self.X_h = np.dot(X_in, params_dict['W_xh']['value'])
        self.H_h = np.dot(self.h_reset, params_dict['W_hh']['value'])
        self.h_bar_int = self.X_h + self.H_h + params_dict['B_h']['value']
        self.h_bar = np.tanh(self.h_bar_int)

        self.H_out = self.u * self.H_in + (1 - self.u) * self.h_bar

        self.X_out = (
    np.dot(self.H_out, params_dict['W_v']['value']) \
    + params_dict['B_v']['value']
    )

        return self.X_out, self.H_out
```

Note that we don't explicitly concatenate X_in and H_in, since—unlike in an RNNNode, where they are always used together—we use them independently in GRUNodes; specifically, we use H_in independently of X_in in the line self.h_reset = self.r * H_in.

The backward method can be found on the book's website (*https://oreil.ly/2P0lG1G*); it simply steps backward through the operations that make up a GRUNode, calculating the derivative of each operation with respect to its input and multiplying the results together.

## LSTMNodes

Long Short Term Memory cells, or LSTMs, are the most popular variant of vanilla RNN cells. Part of the reason for this is that they were invented in the early days of deep learning, back in 1997,[6] whereas investigation into LSTM alternatives such as GRUs has just accelerated in the last several years (GRUs were proposed in 2014, for example).

Like GRUs, LSTMs are motivated by the desire to give the RNN the ability to "reset" or "forget" its hidden state as it receives new input. In GRUs, this is achieved by feeding the input and hidden state through a series of gates, as well as computing a "proposed" new hidden state using these gates—self.h_bar, computed using the gate self.r—and then computing the final hidden state using a weighted average of the proposed new hidden state and the old hidden state, controlled by an update gate:

---

6 See the original LSTM paper, "Long Short-Term Memory" (*https://oreil.ly/2YYZvwT*), by Hochreiter et al. (1997).

```
self.H_out = self.u * self.H_in + (1 - self.u) * self.h_bar
```

LSTMs, by contrast, *use a separate "state" vector, the "cell state," to determine whether to "forget" what is in the hidden state.* They then use two other gates to control the extent to which they should reset or update *what is in the cell state*, and a fourth gate to determine the extent to which the hidden state gets updated based on the final cell state.[7]

### LSTMNodes: Diagram

Figure 6-10 shows a diagram of an LSTMNode with the operations represented as gates.

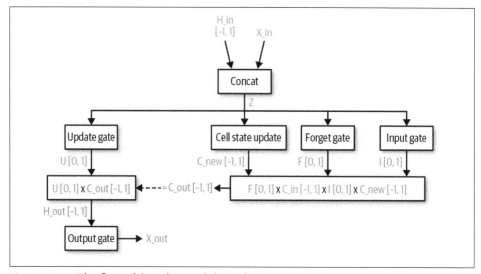

*Figure 6-10. The flow of data forward through an LSTMNode, passing through a series of gates and outputting updated cell states and hidden states C_out and H_out, respectively, along with an actual output X_out*

### LSTMs: The code

As with GRUNodes, the full code for an LSTMNode, including the backward method and an example showing how these nodes fit into an LSTMLayer, is included on the book's website (*https://oreil.ly/2P0lG1G*). Here, we just show the forward method:

```
def forward(self,
    X_in: ndarray,
    H_in: ndarray,
    C_in: ndarray,
    params_dict: Dict[str, Dict[str, ndarray]]):
```

---

7 At least the standard variant of LSTMs; as mentioned, there are other variants such as "LSTMs with peephole connections" whose gates are arranged differently.

```
'''
param X_in: numpy array of shape (batch_size, vocab_size)
param H_in: numpy array of shape (batch_size, hidden_size)
param C_in: numpy array of shape (batch_size, hidden_size)
return self.X_out: numpy array of shape (batch_size, output_size)
return self.H: numpy array of shape (batch_size, hidden_size)
return self.C: numpy array of shape (batch_size, hidden_size)
'''

self.X_in = X_in
self.C_in = C_in

self.Z = np.column_stack((X_in, H_in))
self.f_int = (
  np.dot(self.Z, params_dict['W_f']['value']) \
  + params_dict['B_f']['value']
  )
self.f = sigmoid(self.f_int)

self.i_int = (
  np.dot(self.Z, params_dict['W_i']['value']) \
  + params_dict['B_i']['value']
  )
self.i = sigmoid(self.i_int)

self.C_bar_int = (
  np.dot(self.Z, params_dict['W_c']['value']) \
  + params_dict['B_c']['value']
  )
self.C_bar = tanh(self.C_bar_int)
self.C_out = self.f * C_in + self.i * self.C_bar

self.o_int = (
  np.dot(self.Z, params_dict['W_o']['value']) \
  + params_dict['B_o']['value']
  )
self.o = sigmoid(self.o_int)
self.H_out = self.o * tanh(self.C_out)

self.X_out = (
  np.dot(self.H_out, params_dict['W_v']['value']) \
  + params_dict['B_v']['value']
  )

return self.X_out, self.H_out, self.C_out
```

And that's the last element of our RNN framework that we needed to start training models! There is one more topic we should cover: how to represent text data in a form that will allow us to feed it into our RNNs.

# Data Representation for a Character-Level RNN-Based Language Model

Language modeling is one of the most common tasks RNNs are used for. How can we reshape a sequence of characters into a training dataset so that an RNN can be trained to predict the next character? The simplest method is to use *one-hot encoding*. This works as follows: first, each letter is represented as a vector with dimension equal to *the size of the vocabulary* or the number of letters in the overall corpus of text we'll train the network on (this is calculated beforehand and hardcoded as a hyperparameter in the network). Then each letter is represented as a vector with a 1 in the position representing that letter and 0s everywhere else. Finally, the vectors for each letter are simply concatenated together to get an overall representation for the sequence of letters.

Here's a simple example of how this would look with a vocabulary of four letters, a, b, c, and d, where we arbitrarily call a the first letter, b the second letter, and so on:

$$abcdb \rightarrow \begin{bmatrix} \begin{bmatrix} 1 \\ 0 \\ 0 \\ 0 \end{bmatrix} \begin{bmatrix} 0 \\ 1 \\ 0 \\ 0 \end{bmatrix} \begin{bmatrix} 0 \\ 0 \\ 1 \\ 0 \end{bmatrix} \begin{bmatrix} 0 \\ 0 \\ 0 \\ 1 \end{bmatrix} \begin{bmatrix} 0 \\ 1 \\ 0 \\ 0 \end{bmatrix} \end{bmatrix} = \begin{bmatrix} 1 & 0 & 0 & 0 & 0 \\ 0 & 1 & 0 & 0 & 1 \\ 0 & 0 & 1 & 0 & 0 \\ 0 & 0 & 0 & 1 & 0 \end{bmatrix}$$

This 2D array would take the place of one observation of shape (`sequence_length`, `num_features`) = (5, 4) in a batch of sequences. So if our text was "abcdba"—of length 6—and we wanted to feed sequences of length 5 into our array, the first sequence would be transformed into the preceding matrix, and the second sequence would be:

$$bcdba \rightarrow \begin{bmatrix} \begin{bmatrix} 0 \\ 1 \\ 0 \\ 0 \end{bmatrix} \begin{bmatrix} 0 \\ 0 \\ 1 \\ 0 \end{bmatrix} \begin{bmatrix} 0 \\ 0 \\ 0 \\ 1 \end{bmatrix} \begin{bmatrix} 0 \\ 1 \\ 0 \\ 0 \end{bmatrix} \begin{bmatrix} 1 \\ 0 \\ 0 \\ 0 \end{bmatrix} \end{bmatrix} = \begin{bmatrix} 0 & 0 & 0 & 0 & 1 \\ 1 & 0 & 0 & 1 & 0 \\ 0 & 1 & 0 & 0 & 0 \\ 0 & 0 & 1 & 0 & 0 \end{bmatrix}$$

These would be then concatenated together to create an input to the RNN of shape (`batch_size`, `sequence_length`, `vocab_size`) = (2, 5, 4). Continuing in this way, we can take raw text and transform it into a batch of sequences to be fed into an RNN.

In the Chapter 6 notebook (*https://oreil.ly/2P0lG1G*) on the book's GitHub repo, we code this up as part of an `RNNTrainer` class that can take in raw text, preprocess it using the techniques described here, and feed it into an RNN in batches.

---

# Other Language Modeling Tasks

We didn't emphasize this earlier in the chapter, but as you can see from the preceding code, all RNNNode variants allow an RNNLayer to output a different number of features than it received as input. The last step of all three nodes is to multiply the network's final hidden state by a weight matrix we access via params_dict[W_v]; the second dimension of this weight matrix will determine the dimensionality of the Layer's output. This allows us to use the same architecture for different language modeling tasks simply by changing an output_size argument in each Layer.

For example, so far we've just considered building a language model via "next character prediction"; in this case, our output size will be equal to the size of the vocabulary: output_size = vocab_size. For something like sentiment analysis, however, sequences we pass in may simply have a label of "0" or "1"—positive or negative. In this case, not only will we have output_size = 1, but we'll compare the output to the target only after we pass in the entire sequence. This will look like what is depicted in Figure 6-11.

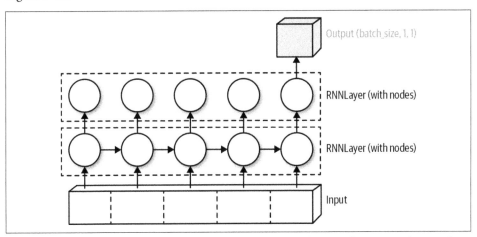

*Figure 6-11. For sentiment analysis, RNNs will compare their predictions with actual values and produce gradients just for the output of the last sequence element; then backpropagation will proceed as usual, with each of the nodes that isn't the last one simply receiving an "X_grad_out" array of all zeros*

Thus, this framework can easily accommodate different language modeling tasks; indeed, it can accommodate any modeling task in which the data is sequential and can be fed into the network one sequence element at a time.

Before we conclude, we'll cover an infrequently discussed aspect of RNNs: that these different kinds of layers—GRULayers, LSTMLayers, and other variants—can be mixed and matched.

## Combining RNNLayer Variants

Stacking different kinds of RNNLayers is straightforward: each RNN outputs an ndar ray of shape (batch_size, sequence_length, output_size), which can be fed into the next layer. As was the case in Dense layers, we don't have to specify an input_shape; we simply set up the weights based on the first ndarray the layer receives as input to be the appropriate shape given the input. An RNNModel can thus have a self.layers attribute of:

```
[RNNLayer(hidden_size=256, output_size=128),
 RNNLayer(hidden_size=256, output_size=62)]
```

As with our fully connected neural networks, we just have to be sure that the last layer produces an output of the desired dimensionality; here, if we are dealing with a vocabulary of size 62 and doing next character prediction, our last layer must have an output_size of 62, just as the last layer in our fully connected neural networks deal-ing with the MNIST problem had to have dimension 10.

Something that should be clear after reading this chapter but that isn't often covered in treatments of RNNs is that, because each kind of layer we've seen has the same underlying structure taking in sequences of dimension feature_size and outputting sequences of dimension output_size, we can easily stack different kinds of layers. For example, on the book's website (*https://oreil.ly/2P0lG1G*), we train an RNNModel with a self.layers attribute of:

```
[GRULayer(hidden_size=256, output_size=128),
 LSTMLayer(hidden_size=256, output_size=62)]
```

In other words, the first layer passes its input forward through time using GRUNodes, and then passes an ndarray of shape (batch_size, sequence_length, 128) into the next layer, which subsequently passes them through its LSTMNodes.

## Putting This All Together

A classic exercise to illustrate the effectiveness of RNNs is to train them to write text in a particular style; on the book's website (*https://oreil.ly/2P0lG1G*), we have an end-to-end code example, with the model defined using the abstractions described in this chapter, that learns to write text in the style of Shakespeare. The only component we haven't shown is an RNNTrainer class that iterates through the training data, prepro-cesses it, and feeds it through the model. The main difference between this and the Trainer we've seen previously is that with RNNs, once we select a batch of data to be fed through—with each element of the batch simply a string—we must first prepro-cess it, one-hot encoding each letter and concatenating the resulting vectors into a sequence to transform each string of length sequence_length into an ndarray of shape (sequence_length, vocab_size). To form the batches that get will fed into our RNN, *these* ndarrays will then be concatenated together to form the batch of size (sequence_length, vocab_size, batch_size).

But once the data has been preprocessed and the model defined, RNNs are trained in the same way as other neural networks we've seen: batches are iteratively fed through, the model's predictions are compared to the targets to generate the loss, and the loss is backpropagated through the operations that make up the model to update the weights.

# Conclusion

In this chapter, you learned about recurrent neural networks, a special kind of neural network architecture designed for processing sequences of data, rather than individual operations. You learned how RNNs are made up of layers that pass data forward in time, updating their hidden states (and their cell states, in the case of LSTMs) as they go. You saw the details of advanced RNN variants, GRUs and LSTMs, and how they pass data forward through a series of "gates" at each time step; nevertheless, you learned that these advanced variants fundamentally process the sequences of data in the same way and thus have the same structure to their layers, differing only in the specific operations they apply at each time step.

Hopefully this multifaceted topic is now less of a black box. In Chapter 7, I'll conclude the book by turning to the practical side of deep learning, showing how to implement everything we've talked about thus far using the PyTorch framework, a high-performance, automatic differentiation–based framework for building and training deep learning models. Onward!

# PyTorch

In Chapters 6 and 5, you learned how convolutional and recurrent neural networks worked by implementing them from scratch. Nevertheless, while understanding how they work is necessary, that knowledge alone won't get them to work on a real-world problem; for that, you need to be able to implement them in a high-performance library. We could devote an entire book to building a high-performance neural network library, but that would be a much different (or simply much longer) book, for a much different audience. Instead, we'll devote this last chapter to introducing PyTorch, an increasingly popular neural network framework based on automatic differentiation, which we introduced at the beginning of Chapter 6.

As in the rest of the book, we'll write our code in a way that maps to the mental models of how neural networks work, writing classes for Layers, Trainers, and so on. In doing so, we won't be writing our code in line with common PyTorch practices, but we'll include links on the book's GitHub repo (*https://oreil.ly/2N4H8jz*) for you to learn more about expressing neural networks the way PyTorch was designed to express them. Before we get there, let's start by learning the data type at the core of PyTorch that enables its automatic differentiation and thus its ability to express neural network training cleanly: the Tensor.

## PyTorch Tensors

In the last chapter, we showed a simple NumberWithGrad accumulate gradients by keeping track of the operations performed on it. This meant that if we wrote:

```
a = NumberWithGrad(3)

b = a * 4
c = b + 3
d = (a + 2)
```

```
e = c * d
e.backward()
```

then `a.grad` would equal 35, which is actually the partial derivative of `e` with respect to `a`.

PyTorch's `Tensor` class acts like an `"ndarrayWithGrad"`: it is similar to `NumberWith Grad`, except with arrays (like `numpy`) instead of just `float`s and `int`s. Let's rewrite the preceding example using a PyTorch `Tensor`. First we'll initialize a `Tensor` manually:

```
a = torch.Tensor([[3., 3.,],
                  [3., 3.]], requires_grad=True)
```

Note a couple of things here:

1. We can initialize a `Tensor` by simply wrapping the data contained in it in a `torch.Tensor`, just as we did with `ndarray`s.

2. When initializing a `Tensor` this way, we have to pass in the argument `requires_grad=True` to tell the `Tensor` to accumulate gradients.

Once we've done this, we can perform computations as before:

```
b = a * 4
c = b + 3
d = (a + 2)
e = c * d
e_sum = e.sum()
e_sum.backward()
```

You can see that there's an extra step here compared to the `NumberWithGrad` example: we have to *sum* `e` before calling `backward` on its sum. This is because, as we argued in the first chapter, it doesn't make sense to think of "the derivative of a number with respect to an array": we can, however, reason about what the partial derivative of `e_sum` with respect to each element of `a` would be—and indeed, we see that the answer is consistent with what we found in the prior chapters:

```
print(a.grad)
```

```
tensor([[35., 35.],
        [35., 35.]], dtype=torch.float64)
```

This feature of PyTorch enables us to define models simply by defining the forward pass, computing a loss, and calling `.backward` on the loss to automatically compute the derivative of each of the `parameters` with respect to that loss. In particular, we don't have to worry about reusing the same quantity multiple times in the forward pass (which was the limitation of the `Operation` framework we used in the first few chapters); as this simple example shows, gradients will automatically be computed correctly once we call `backward` on the output of our computations.

In the next several sections, we'll show how the training framework we laid out earlier in the book can be implemented with PyTorch's data types.

# Deep Learning with PyTorch

As we've seen, deep learning models have several elements that work together to produce a trained model:

- A Model, which contains Layers
- An Optimizer
- A Loss
- A Trainer

It turns out that with PyTorch, the Optimizer and the Loss are one-liners, and the Model and Layers are straightforward as well. Let's cover each of these elements in turn.

## PyTorch Elements: Model, Layer, Optimizer, and Loss

A key feature of PyTorch is the ability to define models and layers as easy-to-use objects that handle sending gradients backward and storing parameters automatically, simply by having them inherit from the torch.nn.Module class. You'll see how these pieces come together later in this chapter; for now, just know that PyTorchLayer can be written as:

```
from torch import nn, Tensor

class PyTorchLayer(nn.Module):

    def __init__(self) -> None:
        super().__init__()

    def forward(self, x: Tensor,
                inference: bool = False) -> Tensor:
        raise NotImplementedError()
```

and PyTorchModel can also be written this way:

```
class PyTorchModel(nn.Module):

    def __init__(self) -> None:
        super().__init__()

    def forward(self, x: Tensor,
                inference: bool = False) -> Tensor:
        raise NotImplementedError()
```

In other words, each subclass of a `PyTorchLayer` or a `PyTorchModel` will just need to implement __init__ and forward methods, which will allow us to use them in intuitive ways.[1]

### The inference flag

As we saw in Chapter 4, because of dropout, we need the ability to change our model's behavior depending on whether we are running it in training mode or in inference mode. In PyTorch, we can switch a model or layer from training mode (its default behavior) to inference mode by running `m.eval` on the model or layer (any object that inherits from `nn.Module`). Furthermore, PyTorch has an elegant way to quickly change the behavior of all subclasses of a layer using the `apply` function. If we define:

```
def inference_mode(m: nn.Module):
    m.eval()
```

then we can include:

```
if inference:
    self.apply(inference_mode)
```

in the forward method of each subclass of `PyTorchModel` or `PyTorchLayer` we define, thus getting the flag we desire.

Let's see how this comes together.

## Implementing Neural Network Building Blocks Using PyTorch: DenseLayer

We now have all the prerequisites to start implementing the Layers we've seen previously, but with PyTorch operations. A `DenseLayer` layer would be written as follows:

```
class DenseLayer(PyTorchLayer):
    def __init__(self,
                 input_size: int,
                 neurons: int,
                 dropout: float = 1.0,
                 activation: nn.Module = None) -> None:
        super().__init__()
        self.linear = nn.Linear(input_size, neurons)
        self.activation = activation
        if dropout < 1.0:
```

---

[1] Writing Layers and Models in this way isn't the most common or recommended use of PyTorch; we show it here because it most closely maps to the concepts we've covered so far. To see a more common way to build neural network building blocks with PyTorch, see this introductory tutorial from the official documentation (*https://oreil.ly/SKB_V*).

```
    self.dropout = nn.Dropout(1 - dropout)


def forward(self, x: Tensor,
            inference: bool = False) -> Tensor:
    if inference:
        self.apply(inference_mode)

    x = self.linear(x) # does weight multiplication + bias
    if self.activation:
        x = self.activation(x)
    if hasattr(self, "dropout"):
        x = self.dropout(x)

    return x
```

Here, with nn.Linear, we see our first example of a PyTorch operation that automatically handles backpropagation for us. This object not only handles the weight multiplication and the addition of a bias term on the forward pass but also causes x's gradients to accumulate so that the correct derivatives of the loss with respect to the parameters can be computed on the backward pass. Note also that since all PyTorch operations inherit from nn.Module, we can call them like mathematical functions: in the preceding case, for example, we write self.linear(x) rather than self.lin ear.forward(x). This also holds true for the DenseLayer itself, as we'll see when we use it in the upcoming model.

## Example: Boston Housing Prices Model in PyTorch

Using this Layer as a building block, we can implement the now-familiar housing prices model from Chapters 2 and 3. Recall that this model simply had one hidden layer with a sigmoid activation; in Chapter 3, we implemented this within our object-oriented framework that had a class for the Layers and a model that had a list of length 2 as its layers attribute. Similarly, we can define a HousePricesModel class that inherits from PyTorchModel as follows:

```
class HousePricesModel(PyTorchModel):

    def __init__(self,
                 hidden_size: int = 13,
                 hidden_dropout: float = 1.0):
        super().__init__()
        self.dense1 = DenseLayer(13, hidden_size,
                                 activation=nn.Sigmoid(),
                                 dropout = hidden_dropout)
        self.dense2 = DenseLayer(hidden_size, 1)

    def forward(self, x: Tensor) -> Tensor:

        assert_dim(x, 2)
```

```
        assert x.shape[1] == 13

        x = self.dense1(x)
        return self.dense2(x)
```

We can then instantiate this via:

```
pytorch_boston_model = HousePricesModel(hidden_size=13)
```

Note that it is not conventional to write a separate Layer class for PyTorch models; it is more common to simply define models in terms of the individual operations taking place, using something like the following:

```
class HousePricesModel(PyTorchModel):

    def __init__(self,
                 hidden_size: int = 13):
        super().__init__()
        self.fc1 = nn.Linear(13, hidden_size)
        self.fc2 = nn.Linear(hidden_size, 1)

    def forward(self, x: Tensor) -> Tensor:

        assert_dim(x, 2)

        assert x.shape[1] == 13

        x = self.fc1(x)
        x = torch.sigmoid(x)
        return self.fc2(x)
```

When building PyTorch models on your own in the future, you may want to write your code in this way rather than creating a separate Layer class—and when *reading* others' code, you'll almost always see something similar to the preceding code.

Layers and Models are more involved than Optimizers and Losses, which we'll cover next.

## PyTorch Elements: Optimizer and Loss

Optimizers and Losses are implemented in PyTorch as one-liners. For example, the SGDMomentum loss we covered in Chapter 4 can be written as:

```
import torch.optim as optim

optimizer = optim.SGD(pytorch_boston_model.parameters(), lr=0.001)
```

In PyTorch, models are passed into the Optimizer as an argument; this ensures that the optimizer is "pointed at" the correct model's parameters so it knows what to update on each iteration (we did this using the Trainer class earlier).

Furthermore, the mean squared error loss we saw in Chapter 2 and the SoftmaxCros sEntropyLoss we discussed in Chapter 4 can simply be written as:

```
mean_squared_error_loss = nn.MSELoss()
softmax_cross_entropy_loss = nn.CrossEntropyLoss()
```

Like the preceding Layers, these inherit from nn.Module, so they can be called in the same way as Layers.

Note that even though the word *softmax* is not in the name of the nn.CrossEntropyLoss class, the softmax operation is indeed performed on the inputs, so that we can pass in "raw outputs" from the neural network rather than outputs that have already passed through the softmax function, just as we did before.

These Losses inherit from nn.Module, just like the Layers from earlier, so they can be called the same way, using loss(x) instead of loss.forward(x), for example.

## PyTorch Elements: Trainer

The Trainer pulls all of these elements together. Let's consider the requirements for the Trainer. We know that it has to implement the general pattern for training neural networks that we've seen many times throughout this book:

1. Feed a batch of inputs through the model.
2. Feed the outputs and targets into a loss function to compute a loss value.
3. Compute the gradient of the loss with respect to all of the parameters.
4. Use the Optimizer to update the parameters according to some rule.

With PyTorch, this all works the same way, except there are two small implementation caveats:

- By default, Optimizers will retain the gradients of the parameters (what we referred to as param_grads earlier in the book) after each iteration of a parameter update. To clear these gradients before the next parameter update, we'll call self.optim.zero_grad.

- As illustrated previously in the simple automatic differentiation example, to kick off the backpropagation, we'll have to call `loss.backward` after computing the loss value.

This leads to the following sequence of code that is seen throughout PyTorch training loops, and will in fact be used in the PyTorchTrainer class. As the `Trainer` class from prior chapters did, `PyTorchTrainer` will take in an `Optimizer`, a `PyTorchModel`, and a `Loss` (either `nn.MSELoss` or `nn.CrossEntropyLoss`) for a batch of data (`X_batch`, `y_batch`); with these objects in place as `self.optim`, `self.model`, and `self.loss`, respectively, the following five lines of code train the model:

```
# First, zero the gradients
self.optim.zero_grad()

# feed X_batch through the model
output = self.model(X_batch)

# Compute the loss
loss = self.loss(output, y_batch)

# Call backward on the loss to kick off backpropagation
loss.backward()

# Call self.optim.step() (as before) to update the parameters
self.optim.step()
```

Those are the most important lines; still, here's the rest of the code for the PyTorch Trainer, much of which is similar to the code for the `Trainer` that we saw in prior chapters:

```
class PyTorchTrainer(object):
    def __init__(self,
                 model: PyTorchModel,
                 optim: Optimizer,
                 criterion: _Loss):
        self.model = model
        self.optim = optim
        self.loss = criterion
        self._check_optim_net_aligned()

    def _check_optim_net_aligned(self):
        assert self.optim.param_groups[0]['params']\
        == list(self.model.parameters())

    def _generate_batches(self,
                          X: Tensor,
                          y: Tensor,
                          size: int = 32) -> Tuple[Tensor]:

        N = X.shape[0]
```

```
    for ii in range(0, N, size):
        X_batch, y_batch = X[ii:ii+size], y[ii:ii+size]

        yield X_batch, y_batch


def fit(self, X_train: Tensor, y_train: Tensor,
        X_test: Tensor, y_test: Tensor,
        epochs: int=100,
        eval_every: int=10,
        batch_size: int=32):

    for e in range(epochs):
        X_train, y_train = permute_data(X_train, y_train)

        batch_generator = self._generate_batches(X_train, y_train,
                                                  batch_size)

        for ii, (X_batch, y_batch) in enumerate(batch_generator):

            self.optim.zero_grad()
            output = self.model(X_batch)
            loss = self.loss(output, y_batch)
            loss.backward()
            self.optim.step()

        output = self.model(X_test)
        loss = self.loss(output, y_test)
        print(e, loss)
```

 Since we're passing a Model, an Optimizer, and a Loss into the Trainer, we need to check that the parameters that the Optimizer refers to are in fact the same as the model's parameters; _check_optim_net_aligned does this.

Now training the model is as simple as:

```
net = HousePricesModel()
optimizer = optim.SGD(net.parameters(), lr=0.001)
criterion = nn.MSELoss()

trainer = PyTorchTrainer(net, optimizer, criterion)

trainer.fit(X_train, y_train, X_test, y_test,
            epochs=10,
            eval_every=1)
```

This code is nearly identical to the code we used to train models using the framework we built in the first three chapters. Whether you're using PyTorch, TensorFlow, or

Theano under the hood, the elements of training a deep learning model remain the same!

Next, we'll explore more features of PyTorch by showing how to implement the tricks to improve training that we saw in Chapter 4.

## Tricks to Optimize Learning in PyTorch

We learned four tricks to accelerate learning in Chapter 4:

- Momentum
- Dropout
- Weight initialization
- Learning rate decay

These are all easy to implement in PyTorch. For example, to include momentum in our optimizer, we can simply include a `momentum` keyword in `SGD`, so that the optimizer becomes:

```
optim.SGD(model.parameters(), lr=0.01, momentum=0.9)
```

Dropout is similarly easy. Just as PyTorch has a built-in `Module` `nn.Linear(n_in, n_out)` that computes the operations of a `Dense` layer from before, the `Module` `nn.Dropout(dropout_prob)` implements the `Dropout` operation, with the caveat that the probability passed in is by default the probability of *dropping* a given neuron, rather than keeping it as it was in our implementation from before.

We don't need to worry about weight initialization at all: the weights in most PyTorch operations involving parameters, including `nn.Linear`, are automatically scaled based on the size of the layer.

Finally, PyTorch has an `lr_scheduler` class that can be used to decay the learning rate over the epochs. The key import you need to get started is from `torch.optim import lr_scheduler`.[2] Now you can easily use these techniques we covered from first principles in any future deep learning project you work on!

---

[2] In the book's GitHub repo (*https://oreil.ly/301qxRk*), you can find an example of code that implements exponential learning rate decay as part of a `PyTorchTrainer`. The documentation for the `ExponentialLR` class used there can be found on the PyTorch website (*https://oreil.ly/2Mj9IhH*).

# Convolutional Neural Networks in PyTorch

In Chapter 5, we systematically covered how convolutional neural networks work, focusing in particular on the multichannel convolution operation. We saw that the operation transforms the pixels of input images into layers of neurons organized into feature maps, where each neuron represents whether a given visual feature (defined by a convolutional filter) is present at that location in the image. The multichannel convolution operation had the following shapes for its two inputs and its output:

- The data input shape [batch_size, in_channels, image_height, image_width]
- The parameters input shape [in_channels, out_channels, filter_size, filter_size]
- The output shape [batch_size, out_channels, image_height, image_width]

In terms of this notation, the multichannel convolution operation in PyTorch is:

```
nn.Conv2d(in_channels, out_channels, filter_size)
```

With this defined, wrapping a ConvLayer around this operation is straightforward:

```
class ConvLayer(PyTorchLayer):
    def __init__(self,
                 in_channels: int,
                 out_channels: int,
                 filter_size: int,
                 activation: nn.Module = None,
                 flatten: bool = False,
                 dropout: float = 1.0) -> None:
        super().__init__()

        # the main operation of the layer
        self.conv = nn.Conv2d(in_channels, out_channels, filter_size,
                              padding=filter_size // 2)

        # the same "activation" and "flatten" operations from before
        self.activation = activation
        self.flatten = flatten
        if dropout < 1.0:
            self.dropout = nn.Dropout(1 - dropout)

    def forward(self, x: Tensor) -> Tensor:

        # always apply the convolution operation
        x = self.conv(x)

        # optionally apply the convolution operation
        if self.activation:
```

```
    x = self.activation(x)
if self.flatten:
    x = x.view(x.shape[0], x.shape[1] * x.shape[2] * x.shape[3])
if hasattr(self, "dropout"):
    x = self.dropout(x)

return x
```

 In Chapter 5, we automatically padded the output based on the filter size to keep the output image the same size as the input image.
PyTorch does not do that; to achieve the same behavior we had
before, we add an argument to the nn.Conv2d operation setting
padding = filter_size // 2.

From there, all we have to do is define a PyTorchModel with its operations in the
__init__ function and the sequence of operations defined in the forward function to
begin to train. Next is a simple architecture we can use on the MNIST dataset we saw
in Chapters 4 and 5, with:

- A convolutional layer that transforms the input from 1 "channel" to 16 channels
- Another layer that transforms these 16 channels into 8 (with each channel still
  containing 28 × 28 neurons)
- Two fully connected layers

The pattern of several convolutional layers followed by a smaller number of fully connected layers is common for convolutional architectures; here, we just use two of
each:

```
class MNIST_ConvNet(PyTorchModel):
    def __init__(self):
        super().__init__()
        self.conv1 = ConvLayer(1, 16, 5, activation=nn.Tanh(),
                               dropout=0.8)
        self.conv2 = ConvLayer(16, 8, 5, activation=nn.Tanh(), flatten=True,
                               dropout=0.8)
        self.dense1 = DenseLayer(28 * 28 * 8, 32, activation=nn.Tanh(),
                               dropout=0.8)
        self.dense2 = DenseLayer(32, 10)

    def forward(self, x: Tensor) -> Tensor:
        assert_dim(x, 4)

        x = self.conv1(x)
        x = self.conv2(x)

        x = self.dense1(x)
        x = self.dense2(x)
        return x
```

Then we can train this model the same way we trained the HousePricesModel:

```
model = MNIST_ConvNet()
criterion = nn.CrossEntropyLoss()
optimizer = optim.SGD(model.parameters(), lr=0.01, momentum=0.9)

trainer = PyTorchTrainer(model, optimizer, criterion)

trainer.fit(X_train, y_train,
            X_test, y_test,
            epochs=5,
            eval_every=1)
```

There is an important caveat related to the nn.CrossEntropyLoss class. Recall that in the custom framework from previous chapters, our Loss class expected an input of the same shape as the target. To get this, we one-hot encoded the 10 distinct values of the target in the MNIST data so that, for each batch of data, the target had shape [batch_size, 10].

With PyTorch's nn.CrossEntropyLoss class—which works exactly the same as our SoftmaxCrossEntropyLoss from before—we don't have to do that. This loss function expects two Tensors:

- A prediction Tensor of size [batch_size, num_classes], just as our Softmax CrossEntropyLoss class did before
- A target Tensor of size [batch_size] with num_classes different values

So in the preceding example, y_train is simply an array of size [60000] (the number of observations in the training set of MNIST), and y_test simply has size [10000] (the number of observations in the test set).

Now that we're dealing with larger datasets, we should cover another best practice. It is clearly very memory inefficient to load the entire training and testing sets into memory to train the model, as we're doing with X_train, y_train, X_test, and y_test. PyTorch has a way around this: the DataLoader class.

## DataLoader and Transforms

Recall that in our MNIST modeling in Chapter 2, we applied a simple preprocessing step to the MNIST data, subtracting off the global mean and dividing by the global standard deviation to roughly "normalize" the data:

```
X_train, X_test = X_train - X_train.mean(), X_test - X_train.mean()
X_train, X_test = X_train / X_train.std(), X_test / X_train.std()
```

Still, this required us to first fully read these two arrays into memory; it would be much more efficient to perform this preprocessing on the fly, as batches are fed into the neural network. PyTorch has built-in functions that do this, and they are especially commonly used with image data—transformations via the `transforms` module, and a `DataLoader` via `torch.utils.data`:

```
from torchvision.datasets import MNIST
import torchvision.transforms as transforms
from torch.utils.data import DataLoader
```

Previously, we read in the entire training set into `X_train` via:

```
mnist_trainset = MNIST(root="../data/", train=True)
X_train = mnist_trainset.train_data
```

We then performed transformations on `X_train` to get it to a form where it was ready for modeling.

PyTorch has some convenience functions that allow us to compose many transformations to each batch of data as it is read in; this allows us both to avoid reading the entire dataset into memory and to use PyTorch's transformations.

We first define a list of transformations to perform on each batch of data read in. For example, the following transformations convert each MNIST image to a `Tensor` (most PyTorch datasets are "PIL images" by default, so `transforms.ToTensor()` is often the first transformation in the list), and then "normalize" the dataset—subtracting off the mean and then dividing by the standard deviation—using the overall MNIST mean and standard deviation of 0.1305 and 0.3081, respectively:

```
img_transforms = transforms.Compose([
    transforms.ToTensor(),
    transforms.Normalize((0.1305,), (0.3081,))
])
```

 `Normalize` actually subtracts the mean and standard deviation *from each channel* of the input image. Thus, it is common when dealing with color images with three input channels to have a `Normalize` transformation that has two tuples of three numbers each—for example, `transforms.Normalize((0.1, 0.3, 0.6), (0.4, 0.2, 0.5))`, which would tell the `DataLoader` to:

- Normalize the first channel using a mean of 0.1 and a standard deviation of 0.4

- Normalize the second channel using a mean of 0.3 and a standard deviation of 0.2

- Normalize the third channel using a mean of 0.6 and a standard deviation of 0.5

Second, once these transformations have been applied, we apply these to the `dataset` as we read in batches:

```
dataset = MNIST("../mnist_data/", transform=img_transforms)
```

Finally, we can define a `DataLoader` that takes in this dataset and defines rules for successively generating batches of data:

```
dataloader = DataLoader(dataset, batch_size=60, shuffle=True)
```

We can then modify the `Trainer` to use the `dataloader` to generate the batches used to train the network instead of loading the entire dataset into memory and then manually generating them using the `batch_generator` function, as we did before. On the book's website (*https://oreil.ly/2N4H8jz*),[3] I show an example of training a convolutional neural network using these `DataLoader`s. The main change in the `Trainer` is simply changing the line:

```
for X_batch, y_batch in enumerate(batch_generator):
```

to:

```
for X_batch, y_batch in enumerate(train_dataloader):
```

In addition, instead of feeding in the entire training set into the `fit` function, we now feed in `DataLoader`s:

```
trainer.fit(train_dataloader = train_loader,
            test_dataloader = test_loader,
            epochs=1,
            eval_every=1)
```

Using this architecture and calling the `fit` method, as we just did, gets us to about 97% accuracy on MNIST after one epoch. More important than the accuracy, however, is that you've seen how to implement the concepts we reasoned through from first principles into a high-performance framework. Now that you understand both the underlying concepts and the framework, I encourage you to modify the code in the book's GitHub repo (*https://oreil.ly/2N4H8jz*) and try out other convolutional architectures, other datasets, and so on.

CNNs were one of two advanced architectures we covered earlier in the book; let's now turn to the other one and show how to implement the most advanced RNN variant we've covered, LSTMs, in PyTorch.

## LSTMs in PyTorch

We saw in the last chapter how to code LSTMs from scratch. We coded an `LSTMLayer` to take in an input `ndarray` of size [`batch_size`, `sequence_length`, `feature_size`], and output an `ndarray` of size [`batch_size`, `sequence_length`, `feature_size`]. In addition, each layer took in a hidden state and a cell state, each initialized with shape

---

3 Look in the "CNNs using PyTorch" section.

[1, hidden_size], expanded to shape [batch_size, hidden_size] when a batch is passed in, and then collapsed back down to [1, hidden_size] after the iteration is complete.

Based on this, we define the __init__ method for our LSTMLayer as:

```python
class LSTMLayer(PyTorchLayer):
    def __init__(self,
                 sequence_length: int,
                 input_size: int,
                 hidden_size: int,
                 output_size: int) -> None:
        super().__init__()
        self.hidden_size = hidden_size
        self.h_init = torch.zeros((1, hidden_size))
        self.c_init = torch.zeros((1, hidden_size))
        self.lstm = nn.LSTM(input_size, hidden_size, batch_first=True)
        self.fc = DenseLayer(hidden_size, output_size)
```

As with convolutional layers, PyTorch has an nn.lstm operation for implementing LSTMs. Note that in our custom LSTMLayer we store a DenseLayer in the self.fc attribute. You may recall from the last chapter that the last step of an LSTM cell is putting the final hidden state through the operations of a Dense layer (a weight multiplication and addition of a bias) to transform the hidden state into dimension out put_size for each operation. PyTorch does things a bit differently: the nn.lstm operation simply outputs the hidden states for each time step. Thus, to enable our LSTMLayer to output a different dimension than its input—as we would want all of our neural network layers to be able to do—we add a DenseLayer at the end to transform the hidden state into dimension output_size.

With this modification, the forward function is now straightforward, looking similar to the forward function of the LSTMLayer from Chapter 6:

```python
def forward(self, x: Tensor) -> Tensor:

    batch_size = x.shape[0]

    h_layer = self._transform_hidden_batch(self.h_init,
                                           batch_size,
                                           before_layer=True)
    c_layer = self._transform_hidden_batch(self.c_init,
                                           batch_size,
                                           before_layer=True)

    x, (h_out, c_out) = self.lstm(x, (h_layer, c_layer))

    self.h_init, self.c_init = (
        self._transform_hidden_batch(h_out,
                                     batch_size,
                                     before_layer=False).detach(),
```

```
    self._transform_hidden_batch(c_out,
                                 batch_size,
                                 before_layer=False).detach()
    )

x = self.fc(x)

return x
```

The key line here, which should look familiar given our implementation of LSTMs in Chapter 6, is:

```
x, (h_out, c_out) = self.lstm(x, (h_layer, c_layer))
```

Aside from that, there's some reshaping of the hidden and cell states before and after the self.lstm function via a helper function self._transform_hidden_batch. You can see the full function in the book's GitHub repo (*https://oreil.ly/2N4H8jz*).

Finally, wrapping a model around this is easy:

```
class NextCharacterModel(PyTorchModel):
    def __init__(self,
                 vocab_size: int,
                 hidden_size: int = 256,
                 sequence_length: int = 25):
        super().__init__()
        self.vocab_size = vocab_size
        self.sequence_length = sequence_length

        # In this model, we have only one layer,
        # with the same output size as input_size
        self.lstm = LSTMLayer(self.sequence_length,
                              self.vocab_size,
                              hidden_size,
                              self.vocab_size)

    def forward(self,
                inputs: Tensor):
        assert_dim(inputs, 3) # batch_size, sequence_length, vocab_size

        out = self.lstm(inputs)

        return out.permute(0, 2, 1)
```

The nn.CrossEntropyLoss function expects the first two dimensions to be the batch_size and the distribution over the classes; the way we've been implementing our LSTMs, however, we have the distribution over the classes as the last dimension (vocab_size) coming out of the LSTMLayer. To prepare the final model output to be fed into the loss, therefore, we move the dimension containing the distribution over letters to the second dimension using out.permute(0, 2, 1).

Finally, in the book's GitHub repo (*https://oreil.ly/2N4H8jz*), I show how to write a class LSTMTrainer to inherit from PyTorchTrainer and use it to train a NextCharacterModel to generate text. We use the same text preprocessing that we did in Chapter 6: selecting sequences of text, one-hot encoding the letters, and grouping the sequences of one-hot encoded letters into batches.

That wraps up how to translate the three neural network architectures for supervised learning we saw in this book—fully connected neural networks, convolutional neural networks, and recurrent neural networks—into PyTorch. To conclude, we'll briefly cover how neural networks can be used for the other half of machine learning: *un*-supervised learning.

## Postscript: Unsupervised Learning via Autoencoders

Throughout this book we've focused on how deep learning models can be used to solve *supervised* learning problems. There is, of course, a whole other side to machine learning: unsupervised learning; which involves what is often described as "finding structure in data without labels"; I like to think of it, though, as finding relationships between characteristics in your data that have not yet been measured, whereas supervised learning involves finding relationships between characteristics in your data that have already been measured.

Suppose you had a dataset of images with no labels. You don't know much about these images—for example, you're not sure whether there are 10 distinct digits represented, or 5, or 20 (these images could be from a strange alphabet)—and you want to know the answers to questions like:

- How many distinct digits are there?
- Which digits are visually similar to one another?
- Are there "outlier" images that are distinctly *dis*similar to other images?

To understand how deep learning can help with this, we'll have to take a quick step back and think conceptually about what deep learning models are trying to do.

# Representation Learning

We've seen that deep learning models can learn to make accurate predictions. They do this by transforming the input they receive into representations that are progressively both more abstract and more tuned to directly making predictions for whatever the relevant problem is. In particular, the final layer of the network, directly before the layer with the predictions themselves (which would have just one neuron for a regression problem and *num_classes* neurons for a classification problem), is the network's attempt at creating a representation of the input data that is as useful as possible for the task of making predictions. This is shown in Figure 7-1.

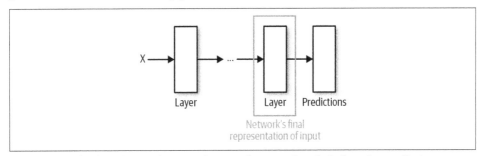

*Figure 7-1. The final layer of a neural network, immediately before the predictions, represents the network's representation of the input that it has found most useful to the task of predicting*

Once trained, then, a model can not only make predictions for new data points, *but also generate representations of these data points*. These could then be used for clustering, similarity analysis, or outlier detection—in addition to prediction.

# An Approach for Situations with No Labels Whatsoever

A limitation with this whole approach is that it *requires labels to train the model to generate the representations in the first place*. The question is: how can we train a model to generate "useful" representations without any labels? If we don't have labels, we need to generate representations of our data using the only thing we do have: the training data itself. This is the idea behind a class of neural network architectures known as autoencoders, which involve training neural networks to *reconstruct* the training data, forcing the network to learn the representation of each data point most helpful for this reconstruction.

## Diagram

Figure 7-2 shows a high-level overview of an autoencoder:

1. One set of layers transforms the data into a compressed representation of the data.

2. Another set of layers transforms this representation into an output of the same size and shape as the original data.

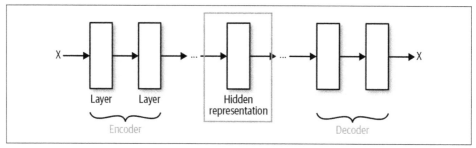

*Figure 7-2. An autoencoder has one set of layers (which can be thought of as the "encoder" network) that maps the input to a lower-dimensional representation, and another set of layers (which can be thought of as the "decoder" network) that maps the lower-dimensional representation back to the input; this structure forces the network to learn a lower-dimensional representation that is most useful for reconstructing the input*

Implementing such an architecture illustrates some features of PyTorch we haven't had a chance to introduce yet.

## Implementing an Autoencoder in PyTorch

We'll now show a simple autoencoder that takes in an input image, feeds it through two convolutional layers and then a Dense layer to generate a representation, and then feeds this representation back through a Dense layer and two convolutional layers to generate an output of the same size as the input. We'll use this to illustrate two common practices when implementing more advanced architectures in PyTorch. First, we can include PyTorchModels as attributes of another PyTorchModel, just as we defined PyTorchLayers as attributes of such models previously. In the following example, we'll implement our autoencoder as having two PyTorchModels as attributes: an Encoder and a Decoder. Once we train the model, we'll be able to use the trained Encoder as its own model to generate the representations.

We define the Encoder as:

```
class Encoder(PyTorchModel):
    def __init__(self,
                 hidden_dim: int = 28):
        super(Encoder, self).__init__()
        self.conv1 = ConvLayer(1, 14, activation=nn.Tanh())
        self.conv2 = ConvLayer(14, 7, activation=nn.Tanh(), flatten=True)

        self.dense1 = DenseLayer(7 * 28 * 28, hidden_dim, activation=nn.Tanh())

    def forward(self, x: Tensor) -> Tensor:
```

```
        assert_dim(x, 4)

        x = self.conv1(x)
        x = self.conv2(x)
        x = self.dense1(x)

        return x
```

And we define the `Decoder` as:

```
class Decoder(PyTorchModel):
    def __init__(self,
                 hidden_dim: int = 28):
        super(Decoder, self).__init__()
        self.dense1 = DenseLayer(hidden_dim, 7 * 28 * 28, activation=nn.Tanh())

        self.conv1 = ConvLayer(7, 14, activation=nn.Tanh())
        self.conv2 = ConvLayer(14, 1, activation=nn.Tanh())

    def forward(self, x: Tensor) -> Tensor:
        assert_dim(x, 2)

        x = self.dense1(x)

        x = x.view(-1, 7, 28, 28)
        x = self.conv1(x)
        x = self.conv2(x)

        return x
```

 If we were using a stride greater than 1, we wouldn't simply be able to use a regular convolution to transform the encoding into an output, as we do here, but instead would have to use a *transposed convolution*, where the image size of the output of the operation would be larger than the image size of the input. See the `nn.ConvTrans pose2d` operation in the PyTorch documentation (*https://oreil.ly/306qiV7*) for more.

Then the `Autoencoder` itself can wrap around these and become:

```
class Autoencoder(PyTorchModel):
    def __init__(self,
                 hidden_dim: int = 28):
        super(Autoencoder, self).__init__()

        self.encoder = Encoder(hidden_dim)

        self.decoder = Decoder(hidden_dim)

    def forward(self, x: Tensor) -> Tensor:
        assert_dim(x, 4)
```

```
encoding = self.encoder(x)
x = self.decoder(encoding)

return x, encoding
```

The `forward` method of the `Autoencoder` illustrates a second common practice in PyTorch: since we'll ultimately want to see the hidden representation that the model produces, the `forward` method returns *two* elements: this "encoding," `encoding`, along with the output that will be used to train the network, `x`.

Of course, we would have to modify our `Trainer` class to accommodate this; specifically, `PyTorchModel` as currently written outputs only a single `Tensor` from its `forward` method. As it turns out, modifying it so that it returns a `Tuple` of `Tensors` by default, even if that `Tuple` is only of length 1, will both be useful—enabling us to easily write models like the `Autoencoder`—and not difficult. All we have to do is three small things: first, make the function signature of the `forward` method of our base `PyTorchModel` class:

```
def forward(self, x: Tensor) -> Tuple[Tensor]:
```

Then, at the end of the `forward` method of any model that inherits from the `PyTorch Model` base class, we'll write `return x,` instead of `return x` as we were doing before.

Second, we'll modify our `Trainer` to always take as output the first element of whatever the model returns:

```
output = self.model(X_batch)[0]
...
output = self.model(X_test)[0]
```

There is one other notable feature of the `Autoencoder` model: we apply a `Tanh` activation function to the last layer, meaning the model output will be between –1 and 1. With any model, the model outputs should be on the same scale as the target they are compared to, and here, the target is our input itself. So we should scale our input to range from a minimum of –1 and a maximum of 1, as in the following code:

```
X_train_auto = (X_train - X_train.min())
                / (X_train.max() - X_train.min()) * 2 - 1
X_test_auto = (X_test - X_train.min())
                / (X_train.max() - X_train.min()) * 2 - 1
```

Finally, we can train our model using training code, which by now should look familiar (we somewhat arbitrarily use 28 as the dimensionality of the output of the encoding):

```
model = Autoencoder(hidden_dim=28)
criterion = nn.MSELoss()
optimizer = optim.SGD(model.parameters(), lr=0.01, momentum=0.9)
```

```
trainer = PyTorchTrainer(model, optimizer, criterion)

trainer.fit(X_train_auto, X_train_auto,
            X_test_auto, X_test_auto,
            epochs=1,
            batch_size=60)
```

Once we run this code and train the model, we can look at both the reconstructed images and the image representations simply by passing X_test_auto through the model (since the forward method was defined to return two quantities):

```
reconstructed_images, image_representations = model(X_test_auto)
```

Each element of reconstructed_images is a [1, 28, 28] Tensor and represents the neural network's best attempt to reconstruct the corresponding original image after passing it through an autoencoder architecture that forced the image through a layer with lower dimensionality. Figure 7-3 shows a randomly chosen reconstructed image alongside the original image.

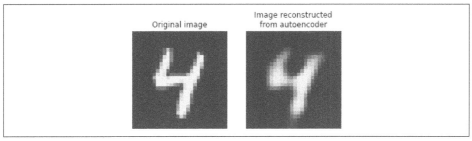

*Figure 7-3. An image from the MNIST test set alongside the reconstruction of that image after it was fed through the autoencoder*

Visually, the images look similar, telling us that the neural network does indeed seem to have taken the original images, which were 784 pixels, and mapped them to a space of lower dimensionality—specifically, 28—such that most of the information about the 784-pixel image is encoded in this vector of length 28. How can we examine the whole dataset to see whether the neural network has indeed learned the structure of the image data without seeing the labels? Well, "the structure of the data" here means that the underlying data is in fact images of 10 distinct handwritten digits. Thus, images close to a given image in the new 28-dimensional space should ideally be of the same digit, or at least visually be very similar, since visual similarity is how we as humans distinguish between different images. We can test whether this is the case by applying a dimensionality reduction technique invented by Laurens van der Maaten when he was a graduate student under Geoffrey Hinton (who was one of the "founding fathers" of neural networks): *t-Distributed Stochastic Neighbor Embedding*, or t-SNE. t-SNE performs its dimensionality reduction in a way that is analogous to how neural networks are trained: it starts with an initial lower-dimensional representation and then updates it so that, over time, it approaches a solution with the property that points that are "close together" in the high-dimensional space are "close together" in the low-dimensional space, and vice versa.[4]

We'll try the following:

- Feed the 10,000 images through t-SNE and reduce the dimensionality to 2.
- Visualize the resulting two-dimensional space, coloring the different points by their *actual* label (which the autoencoder did not see).

Figure 7-4 shows the result.

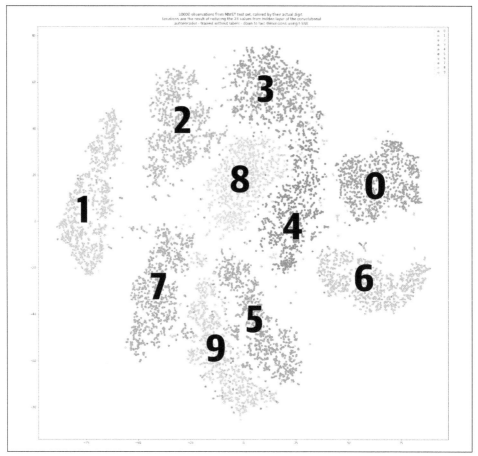

*Figure 7-4. Result of running t-SNE on 28-dimensional learned space of the autoencoder*

---

4 The original 2008 paper is "Visualizing Data using t-SNE" (*https://oreil.ly/2KIAaOt*), by Laurens van der Maaten and Geoffrey Hinton.

It appears that images of each digit are largely grouped together in their own separate cluster; this shows that training our autoencoder architecture to learn to reconstruct the original images from just a lower-dimensional representation has indeed enabled it to discover much of the underlying structure of these images without seeing any labels.[5] And not only are the 10 digits represented as distinct clusters, but visually similar digits are also closer together: at the top and slightly to the right, we have clusters of the digits 3, 5, and 8, and at the bottom we see 4 and 9 clustered tightly together, with 7 not far away. Finally, the most distinct digits—0, 1, and 6—form the most distinct clusters.

## A Stronger Test for Unsupervised Learning, and a Solution

What we've just seen is a fairly weak test for whether our model has learned an underlying structure to the space of input images—by this point, it shouldn't be too surprising that a convolutional neural network can learn representations of images of digits with the property that visually similar images have similar representations. A stronger test would be to examine if the neural network has discovered a "smooth" underlying space: a space in which *any* vector of length 28, rather than just the vectors resulting from feeding real digits through the encoder network, can be mapped to a realistic-looking digit. It turns out that our autoencoder cannot do this; Figure 7-5 shows the result of generating five random vectors of length 28 and feeding them through the decoder network, using the fact that the Autoencoder contained a Decoder as an attribute:

```
test_encodings = np.random.uniform(low=-1.0, high=1.0, size=(5, 28))
test_imgs = model.decoder(Tensor(test_encodings))
```

*Figure 7-5. Result of feeding five randomly generated vectors through the decoder*

You can see that the resulting images don't look like digits; thus, while our autoencoder can map our data to a lower-dimensional space in a sensible way, it doesn't appear to be able to learn a "smooth" space such as the one described a moment ago.

---

5 Furthermore, we did this without much trying: the architecture here is very straightforward, and we're not using any of the tricks we discussed for training neural networks, such as learning rate decay, since we're training for only one epoch. This illustrates that the underlying idea of using an autoencoder-like architecture to learn the structure of a dataset without labels is a good one in general and didn't just "happen to work" here.

Solving the problem, of training a neural network to learn to represent images in a training set in a "smooth" underlying space, is one of the major accomplishments of *generative adversarial networks* (GANs). Invented in 2014, GANs are most widely known for allowing neural networks to generate realistic-looking images via a training procedure in which two neural networks are trained simultaneously. GANs were truly pushed forward in 2015, however, when researchers used them with deep convolutional architectures in both networks not just to generate realistic-looking 64 × 64 color images of bedrooms but also to generate a large sample of said images from randomly generated 100-dimensional vectors.[6] This signaled that the neural networks really had learned an underlying representation of the "space" of these unlabeled images. GANs deserve a book of their own, so we won't cover them in more detail than this.

## Conclusion

You now have a deep understanding of the mechanics of some of the most popular advanced deep learning architectures out there, as well as how to implement these architectures in one of the most popular high-performance deep learning frameworks. The only thing stopping you from using deep learning models to solve real-world problems is practice. Luckily, it has never been easier to read others' code and quickly get up to speed on the details and implementation tricks that make certain model architectures work on certain problems. A list of recommended next steps is listed in the book's GitHub repo (*https://oreil.ly/2N4H8jz*).

Onward!

---

6 Check out the DCGAN paper, "Unsupervised Representation Learning with Deep Convolutional Generative Adversarial Networks" (*https://arxiv.org/abs/1511.06434*) by Alec Radford et al., as well as this PyTorch documentation (*https://oreil.ly/2TEspgG*).

# Deep Dives

In this section, we dive deep into a few technical areas that are important to understand for completion, but are not essential.

## Matrix Chain Rule

First up is an explanation of why we can substitute $W^T$ for $\frac{\partial v}{\partial u}(X)$ in the chain rule expression from Chapter 1.

Remember that $L$ is literally:

$$\sigma(XW_{11}) + \sigma(XW_{12}) + \sigma(XW_{21}) + \sigma(XW_{22}) + \sigma(XW_{31}) + \sigma(XW_{32})$$

where this is shorthand for the fact that:

$$\sigma(XW_{11}) = \sigma(x_{11} \times w_{11} + x_{12} \times w_{21} + x_{13} \times w_{31})$$

$$\sigma(XW_{12}) = \sigma(x_{11} \times w_{12} + x_{12} \times w_{22} + x_{13} \times w_{32})$$

and so on. Let's zoom in on just one of these expressions. What would it look like if we took the partial derivative of, say, $\sigma(XW_{11})$ with respect to every element of $X$ (which is ultimately what we'll want to do with all six components of $L$)?

Well, since:

$$\sigma(XW_{11}) = \sigma(x_{11} \times w_{11} + x_{12} \times w_{21} + x_{13} \times w_{31})$$

it isn't too hard to see that the partial derivative of this with respect to $x_1$, via a very simple application of the chain rule, is:

$$\frac{\partial \sigma}{\partial u}(XW_{11}) \times w_{11}$$

Since the only thing that $x_{11}$ is multiplied by in the $XW_{11}$ expression is $w_{11}$, the partial derivative with respect to everything else is 0.

So, computing the partial derivative of $\sigma(XW_{11})$ with respect to all of the elements of $X$ gives us the following overall expression for $\frac{\partial \sigma(XW_{11})}{\partial X}$:

$$\frac{\partial \sigma(XW_{11})}{\partial X} = \begin{bmatrix} \frac{\partial \sigma}{\partial u}(XW_{11}) \times w_{11} & \frac{\partial \sigma}{\partial u}(XW_{11}) \times w_{21} & \frac{\partial \sigma}{\partial u}(XW_{11}) \times w_{31} \\ 0 & 0 & 0 \\ 0 & 0 & 0 \end{bmatrix}$$

Similarly, we can, for example, work out the partial derivative of $\sigma(XW_{32})$ with respect to each element of $X$:

$$\begin{bmatrix} 0 & 0 & 0 \\ 0 & 0 & 0 \\ \frac{\partial \sigma}{\partial u}(XW_{32}) \times w_{12} & \frac{\partial \sigma}{\partial u}(XW_{32}) \times w_{22} & \frac{\partial \sigma}{\partial u}(XW_{32}) \times w_{32} \end{bmatrix}$$

Now we have all the components to actually compute $\frac{\partial \Lambda}{\partial X}(S)$ directly. We can simply compute six matrices of the same form as the preceding matrices and add the results together.

Note that once again the math gets messy, though not advanced. You can skip the following calculations and move straight to the conclusion, which is ultimately a simple expression. But working through the calculations will give you a greater appreciation for how surprisingly simple the conclusion is. And what else is life for but appreciating things?

There are just two steps here. First, we'll actually write out explicitly that $\frac{\partial \Lambda}{\partial X}(S)$ is a sum of the six matrices just described:

$$\frac{\partial \Lambda}{\partial X}(S) = \frac{\partial \sigma(XW_{11})}{\partial X} + \frac{\partial \sigma(XW_{12})}{\partial X} + \frac{\partial \sigma(XW_{21})}{\partial X} + \frac{\partial \sigma(XW_{22})}{\partial X} + \frac{\partial \sigma(XW_{31})}{\partial X} + \frac{\partial \sigma(XW_{32})}{\partial X} =$$

$$\begin{bmatrix} \frac{\partial \sigma}{\partial u}(XW_{11}) \times w_{11} & \frac{\partial \sigma}{\partial u}(XW_{11}) \times w_{21} & \frac{\partial \sigma}{\partial u}(XW_{11}) \times w_{31} \\ 0 & 0 & 0 \\ 0 & 0 & 0 \end{bmatrix} +$$

$$\begin{bmatrix} \frac{\partial \sigma}{\partial u}(XW_{12}) \times w_{12} & \frac{\partial \sigma}{\partial u}(XW_{12}) \times w_{22} & \frac{\partial \sigma}{\partial u}(XW_{12}) \times w_{32} \\ 0 & 0 & 0 \\ 0 & 0 & 0 \end{bmatrix} +$$

$$\begin{bmatrix} 0 & 0 & 0 \\ \frac{\partial \sigma}{\partial u}(XW_{21}) \times w_{11} & \frac{\partial \sigma}{\partial u}(XW_{21}) \times w_{21} & \frac{\partial \sigma}{\partial u}(XW_{21}) \times w_{31} \\ 0 & 0 & 0 \end{bmatrix} +$$

$$\begin{bmatrix} 0 & 0 & 0 \\ \frac{\partial \sigma}{\partial u}(XW_{22}) \times w_{12} & \frac{\partial \sigma}{\partial u}(XW_{22}) \times w_{22} & \frac{\partial \sigma}{\partial u}(XW_{22}) \times w_{32} \\ 0 & 0 & 0 \end{bmatrix} +$$

$$\begin{bmatrix} 0 & 0 & 0 \\ 0 & 0 & 0 \\ \frac{\partial \sigma}{\partial u}(XW_{31}) \times w_{11} & \frac{\partial \sigma}{\partial u}(XW_{31}) \times w_{21} & \frac{\partial \sigma}{\partial u}(XW_{31}) \times w_{31} \end{bmatrix} +$$

$$\begin{bmatrix} 0 & 0 & 0 \\ 0 & 0 & 0 \\ \frac{\partial \sigma}{\partial u}(XW_{32}) \times w_{12} & \frac{\partial \sigma}{\partial u}(XW_{32}) \times w_{22} & \frac{\partial \sigma}{\partial u}(XW_{32}) \times w_{32} \end{bmatrix}$$

Now let's combine this sum into one big matrix. This matrix won't immediately have any intuitive form, but it is in fact the result of computing the preceding sum:

$$\frac{\partial \Lambda}{\partial X}(S) =$$

$$\begin{bmatrix} \frac{\partial \sigma}{\partial u}(XW_{11}) \times w_{11} + \frac{\partial \sigma}{\partial u}(XW_{12}) \times w_{12} & \frac{\partial \sigma}{\partial u}(XW_{11}) \times w_{21} + \frac{\partial \sigma}{\partial u}(XW_{12}) \times w_{22} & \frac{\partial \sigma}{\partial u}(XW_{11}) \times w_{31} + \frac{\partial \sigma}{\partial u}(XW_{12}) \times w_{32} \\ \frac{\partial \sigma}{\partial u}(XW_{21}) \times w_{11} + \frac{\partial \sigma}{\partial u}(XW_{22}) \times w_{12} & \frac{\partial \sigma}{\partial u}(XW_{21}) \times w_{21} + \frac{\partial \sigma}{\partial u}(XW_{22}) \times w_{22} & \frac{\partial \sigma}{\partial u}(XW_{21}) \times w_{31} + \frac{\partial \sigma}{\partial u}(XW_{22}) \times w_{32} \\ \frac{\partial \sigma}{\partial u}(XW_{31}) \times w_{11} + \frac{\partial \sigma}{\partial u}(XW_{32}) \times w_{12} & \frac{\partial \sigma}{\partial u}(XW_{31}) \times w_{21} + \frac{\partial \sigma}{\partial u}(XW_{32}) \times w_{22} & \frac{\partial \sigma}{\partial u}(XW_{31}) \times w_{31} + \frac{\partial \sigma}{\partial u}(XW_{32}) \times w_{32} \end{bmatrix}$$

Now comes the cool part. Recall that:

$$W = \begin{bmatrix} w_{11} & w_{12} \\ w_{21} & w_{22} \\ w_{31} & w_{32} \end{bmatrix}$$

Well, $W$ is hidden in the preceding matrix—it is just transposed. Recalling that:

$$\frac{\partial \Lambda}{\partial u}(S) = \begin{bmatrix} \frac{\partial \sigma}{\partial u}(XW_{11}) & \frac{\partial \sigma}{\partial u}(XW_{12}) \\ \frac{\partial \sigma}{\partial u}(XW_{21}) & \frac{\partial \sigma}{\partial u}(XW_{22}) \\ \frac{\partial \sigma}{\partial u}(XW_{31}) & \frac{\partial \sigma}{\partial u}(XW_{32}) \end{bmatrix}$$

it turns out that the previous matrix is equivalent to:

$$\frac{\partial \Lambda}{\partial X}(X) = \begin{bmatrix} \frac{\partial \sigma}{\partial u}(XW_{11}) & \frac{\partial \sigma}{\partial u}(XW_{12}) \\ \frac{\partial \sigma}{\partial u}(XW_{21}) & \frac{\partial \sigma}{\partial u}(XW_{22}) \\ \frac{\partial \sigma}{\partial u}(XW_{31}) & \frac{\partial \sigma}{\partial u}(XW_{32}) \end{bmatrix} \times \begin{bmatrix} w_{11} & w_{21} & w_{31} \\ w_{12} & w_{22} & w_{32} \end{bmatrix} = \frac{\partial \Lambda}{\partial u}(S) \times W^T$$

And further, remember that we were looking for something to fill in the question mark in the following equation:

$$\frac{\partial \Lambda}{\partial X}(X) = \frac{\partial \Lambda}{\partial u}(S) \times \text{?}$$

Well, it turns out that thing is $W$. This result falls out like meat falling off the bone.

Note also that this is the same result we saw earlier in one dimension; again, this will turn out to be a result that both explains why deep learning works and allows us to implement it cleanly. Does this mean that we can *actually* replace the question mark in the preceding equation and say that $\frac{\partial v}{\partial X}(X, W) = W^T$? No, not exactly. But if we multiply together two inputs ($X$ and $W$) to get a result $N$ and feed these inputs through some nonlinear function $\sigma$ to end up with an output $S$, then we *can* say the following:

$$\frac{\partial \sigma}{\partial X}(X, W) = \frac{\partial \sigma}{\partial u}(N) \times W^T$$

This mathematical fact is what allows us to compute and express gradient updates efficiently using the notation of matrix multiplication. Furthermore, we could reason similarly to discover that:

$$\frac{\partial \sigma}{\partial W}(X, W) = X^T \times \frac{\partial \sigma}{\partial u}(N)$$

# Gradient of the Loss with Respect to the Bias Terms

Next, we'll go into detail on why, when computing the derivative of the loss with respect to the bias terms in a fully connected neural network, we sum along `axis=0`.

The addition of a bias term in a neural network occurs in the following context: we have a batch of data represented by a matrix of dimension $n$ rows (the batch size) by $f$ columns (the number of features), and we add a single number to each of the $f$ features. For example, in the neural network example from Chapter 2, we have 13 features, and the bias term $B$ has 13 numbers; the first number will be added to every row in the first column of `M1 = np.dot(X, weights[W1])`, the second number will be added to every row in the second column, and so on. Further on in the network, $B2$ will contain one number, which will simply be added to every row in the single column of `M2`. Thus, since the same numbers will be added to each *row* of the matrix, on the backward pass we need to sum the gradients along the dimension representing the rows that each bias element was added to. This is why we sum the expressions for `dLdB1` and `dLdB2` along `axis=0`; for example, `dLdB1 = (dLdN1 × dN1dB1).sum(axis=0)`. Figure A-1 provides a visual explanation of all this, with some commentary.

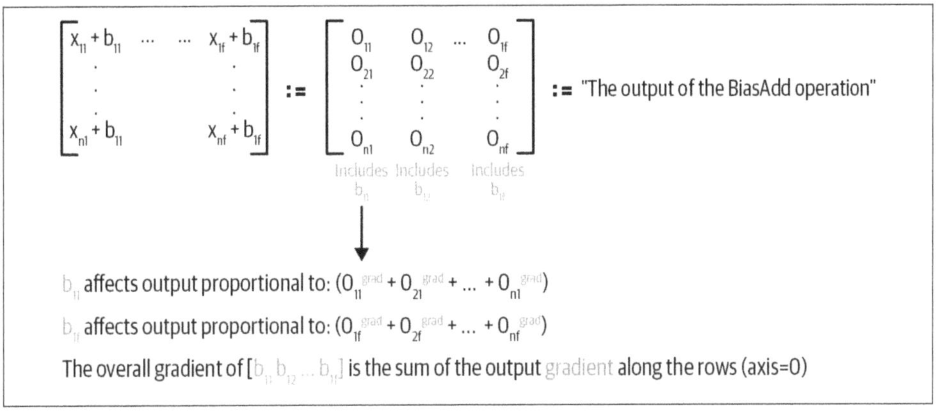

Figure A-1. A summary of why computing the derivative of the output of the fully connected layer with respect to the bias involves summing along axis = 0

# Convolutions via Matrix Multiplication

Finally, we'll show how to express the batch, multichannel convolution operation in terms of a batch matrix multiplication to implement it efficiently in NumPy.

To understand how the convolution works, consider what happens in the forward pass of a fully connected neural network:

- We receive an input of size [batch_size, in_features].
- We multiply it by a parameter of size [in_features, out_features].
- We get a resulting output of size [batch_size, out_features].

In a convolutional layer, by contrast:

- We receive an input of size [batch_size, in_channels, img_height, img_width].
- We convolve it with a parameter of size [in_channels, out_channels, param_height, param_width].
- We get a resulting output of size [batch_size, in_channels, img_height, img_width].

The key to making the convolution operation look more like a regular feed-forward operation is to *first extract* img_height × img_width *"image patches" from each channel of the input image*. Once these patches are extracted, the input can be reshaped so that the convolution operation can be expressed as a batch matrix multiplication using NumPy's np.matmul function. First:

```
def _get_image_patches(imgs_batch: ndarray,
                       fil_size: int):
    '''
    imgs_batch: [batch_size, channels, img_width, img_height]
    fil_size: int
    '''
    # pad the images
    imgs_batch_pad = np.stack([_pad_2d_channel(obs, fil_size // 2)
                               for obs in imgs_batch])
    patches = []
    img_height = imgs_batch_pad.shape[2]

    # For each location in the image...
    for h in range(img_height-fil_size+1):
        for w in range(img_height-fil_size+1):

            # ...get an image patch of size [fil_size, fil_size]
            patch = imgs_batch_pad[:, :, h:h+fil_size, w:w+fil_size]
            patches.append(patch)
```

```
# Stack, getting an output of size
# [img_height * img_width, batch_size, n_channels, fil_size, fil_size]
return np.stack(patches)
```

Then we can compute the output of the convolution operation in the following way:

1. Get image patches of size [batch_size, in_channels, img_height x img_width, filter_size, filter_size].

2. Reshape this to be [batch_size, img_height × img_width, in_channels × filter_sizex filter_size].

3. Reshape parameter to be [in_channels × filter_size × filter_size, out_channels].

4. After we do a batch matrix multiplication, the result will be [batch_size, img_height × img_width, out_channels].

5. Reshape this to be [batch_size, out_channels, img_height, img_width].

```
def _output_matmul(input_: ndarray,
                   param: ndarray) -> ndarray:
    '''
    conv_in: [batch_size, in_channels, img_width, img_height]
    param: [in_channels, out_channels, fil_width, fil_height]
    '''

    param_size = param.shape[2]
    batch_size = input_.shape[0]
    img_height = input_.shape[2]
    patch_size = param.shape[0] * param.shape[2] * param.shape[3]

    patches = _get_image_patches(input_, param_size)

    patches_reshaped = (
      patches
      .transpose(1, 0, 2, 3, 4)
      .reshape(batch_size, img_height * img_height, -1)
      )

    param_reshaped = param.transpose(0, 2, 3, 1).reshape(patch_size, -1)

    output = np.matmul(patches_reshaped, param_reshaped)

    output_reshaped = (
      output
      .reshape(batch_size, img_height, img_height, -1)
      .transpose(0, 3, 1, 2)
    )

    return output_reshaped
```

That's the forward pass! For the backward pass, we have to calculate both the parameter gradient and the input gradients. Again, we can use the way this is done in a fully connected neural network as a guide. Starting with the parameter gradient, the gradient of a fully connected neural network is:

```
np.matmul(self.inputs.transpose(1, 0), output_grad)
```

This should motivate how we implement the backward pass through the convolution operation: here, the input shape is [batch_size, in_channels, img_height, img_width], and the output *gradient* received will be [batch_size, out_channels, img_height, img_width]. Considering that the shape of the parameter is [in_channels, out_channels, param_height, param_width], we can effect this transformation with the following steps:

1. First, we'll have to extract image patches from the input image, resulting in the same output from last time, of shape [batch_size, in_channels, img_height × img_width, filter_size, filter_size].

2. Then, using the multiplication from the fully connected case as a motivation, reshape it to be of shape [in_channels × param_height × param_width, batch_size × img_height × img_width].

3. Then, reshape the output—originally of shape [batch_size, out_channels, img_height, img_width]—to be of shape [batch_size × img_height × img_width, out_channels].

4. Multiply these together to get an output of shape [in_channels × param_height × param_width, out_channels].

5. Reshape this to get the final parameter gradient, of shape [in_channels, out_channels, param_height, param_width].

This process is implemented as follows:

```
def _param_grad_matmul(input_: ndarray,
                       param: ndarray,
                       output_grad: ndarray):
    '''
    input_: [batch_size, in_channels, img_width, img_height]
    param: [in_channels, out_channels, fil_width, fil_height]
    output_grad: [batch_size, out_channels, img_width, img_height]
    '''

    param_size = param.shape[2]
    batch_size = input_.shape[0]
    img_size = input_.shape[2] ** 2
    in_channels = input_.shape[1]
    out_channels = output_grad.shape[1]
    patch_size = param.shape[0] * param.shape[2] * param.shape[3]
```

```
patches = _get_image_patches(input_, param_sizes)

patches_reshaped = (
    patches
    .reshape(batch_size * img_size, -1)
    )

output_grad_reshaped = (
    output_grad
    .transpose(0, 2, 3, 1)
    .reshape(batch_size * img_size, -1)
)

param_reshaped = param.transpose(0, 2, 3, 1).reshape(patch_size, -1)

param_grad = np.matmul(patches_reshaped.transpose(1, 0),
                       output_grad_reshaped)

param_grad_reshaped = (
    param_grad
    .reshape(in_channels, param_size, param_size, out_channels)
    .transpose(0, 3, 1, 2)
)

return param_grad_reshaped
```

In addition, we follow a very similar set of steps to get the input gradient, motivated by mimicking the operation in the fully connected layer, which is:

```
np.matmul(output_grad, self.param.transpose(1, 0))
```

The following code computes the input gradient:

```
def _input_grad_matmul(input_: ndarray,
                       param: ndarray,
                       output_grad: ndarray):

    param_size = param.shape[2]
    batch_size = input_.shape[0]
    img_height = input_.shape[2]
    in_channels = input_.shape[1]

    output_grad_patches = _get_image_patches(output_grad, param_size)

    output_grad_patches_reshaped = (
        output_grad_patches
        .transpose(1, 0, 2, 3, 4)
        .reshape(batch_size * img_height * img_height, -1)
    )

    param_reshaped = (
        param
        .reshape(in_channels, -1)
```

```
)

    input_grad = np.matmul(output_grad_patches_reshaped,
                           param_reshaped.transpose(1, 0))

    input_grad_reshaped = (
        input_grad
        .reshape(batch_size, img_height, img_height, 3)
        .transpose(0, 3, 1, 2)
    )

    return input_grad_reshaped
```

These three functions form the core of the Conv2DOperation, specifically its _output, _param_grad, and _input_grad methods, which you can see in the lincoln library (*https://oreil.ly/2KPdFay*) within the book's GitHub repo.

# Index

dense layers, 83
derivatives
  code describing, 8
  defined, 7
  diagram representing, 7
  of functions with multiple inputs, 19
  of functions with multiple vector inputs,
    23-25
  mathematical description, 7
dot products, 21
downsampling, 136
dropout
  adjusting framework to accommodate, 123
  benefits of, 122
  defined, 122
  experimenting with, 124
  implementing, 122

# E
early stopping, 95
epochs, 94
exploding gradient problem, 183
extensions
  dropout, 122-125
  intuition about neural networks, 100-102
  learning rate decay, 116-118
  MNIST dataset experiment, 110-113
  momentum, 113-115
  overview of, 99
  in PyTorch, 204
  softmax cross entropy loss, 102-110
  weight initialization, 118-121

# F
feature engineering, 43
feature maps, 131
features
  characteristics mapping to, 43
  creating new from existing, 21-23
filters, 132
Flatten layer, 135, 153
foundational mental models
  backward pass, 33-39
  chain rule, 11-14
  chain rule example, 14-17
  computational graph with 2D matrix inputs,
    29-32
  creating new features from existing, 21-23
  derivatives, 7-9

derivatives of functions with multiple
    inputs, 19
derivatives of functions with multiple vector
    inputs, 23-25
functions, 2-6
functions with multiple inputs, 17-19
functions with multiple vector inputs, 20
nested functions, 9-11
overview of, 1
vector functions and their derivatives, 26-29
fully connected layers, 84, 134
functions
  code describing, 3-6
  derivatives of with multiple inputs, 19
  derivatives of with multiple vector inputs,
    23
  diagram representing, 2
  mathematical description, 2
  with multiple inputs, 17-19
  with multiple vector inputs, 20

# G
Gated Recurrent Units (GRUs), 184-187
generative adversarial networks (GANs), 219
gradients
  computing, 48
  computing for 1D convolutions, 143
  defined, 25
  describing visually, 37
  exploding gradient problem, 183
  gradient accumulation, 162, 175
  gradient of the loss and bias terms, 225
  history of gradient updates, 92
  parameter gradient, 145, 147
  shape of output and input gradients, 74
  training models using, 53
  vanishing gradient problem, 183
GRUNodes, 184-187

# H
hidden layers, 77
housing prices example, 43, 72, 199

# I
image data, 128
input gradients, 74
input layer, 77

# K

kernels, 132

# L

language modeling, 190-193
Layer class, 81
layers
  assembling building blocks, 79-85
  convolutional layers, 132-138
  dense layers, 83
  diagram of, 77
  Flatten layer, 135, 153
  fully connected layers, 84
  neurons in, 78
  overview of, 77
Leaky ReLU activation function, 109
learning rate, 101
learning rate decay
  experimenting with, 118
  motivation for, 116
  types of, 116
linear decay, 116
linear regression
  alternate diagram representing, 48
  code describing, 49
  diagram representing, 46
  limitations of, 58
  mathematical description, 45
  training the model, 47
linear relationships, 128
Long Short Term Memory cells (LSTMs),
    187-189, 209-212
Loss base class, 86
loss calculation, 72, 225
LSTMNodes, 187-189

# M

matrices, 20
matrix chain rule, 221-225
matrix multiplication, 20, 22, 41, 47, 226-230
max-pooling, 136
mean squared error, 48
MNIST dataset, 110, 207
model predictions, 57
model training, defined, 47
models, building and training basic
  linear regression, 45-50
  model assessment, 54-58

nonlinear relationships, 58-65
  supervised learning models, 44
  supervised learning overview, 42-44
  training and assessing neural networks, 65
  training the model, 50-54
models, building and training complicated
  building models, 79-85
  deep learning overview, 72
  full training code, 96
  interaction of layers and classes, 88-91
  layers, 77-79
  NeuralNetwork class, 85-88
  Operation class, 73-76
  Trainer and Optimizer classes, 91-95
momentum
  implementing in Optimizer class, 113
  intuition about, 113
  stochastic gradient descent with, 115
mostly differentiable functions, 3, 10
multichannel convolution operations
  2D convolutions, 147-150
  adding channels, 150-153
  backward pass, 142-146
  batches of inputs, 146
  forward pass, 138-142
  versus regular neural networks, 131
multidimensional arrays, 4

# N

nested functions
  alternate diagram representing, 10
  code describing, 10
  defined, 9
  diagram representing, 9
  mathematical description, 9
neural networks
  backward pass, 63-65
  building from scratch, 58-63, 88-91, 97
  deep convolutional neural networks, 132
  diagram of, 77
  implementing using PyTorch, 198
  intuition about, 100-102
  layers in, 77-79
  multiple mental models of, ix, 1
  Operations in, 73-76
  representation learning and, 127-132
  training and assessing, 65-68
NeuralNetwork class
  code describing, 86, 89

Trainer class, 94-95
training sets, 54
training, defined, 47
transposed convolutions, 215
type-checked functions, 5

## U

unsupervised learning
  generative adversarial networks (GANs),
    219
  implementing autoencoders in PyTorch,
    214-219
  overview of, 212
  representation learning, 213
  unlabeled data, 213

## V

vanilla RNNNodes, 180-184

vanishing gradient problem, 183
vector functions, 26-29
vectors, 20

## W

weight initialization
  experimenting with, 121
  math and code describing, 120
  overview of, 118
weights
  in computational graphs, 29
  in neural networks, 100
  loss gradients and, 53
  versus parameters, 54
  weighted sum of features, 21

## About the Author

**Seth Weidman** is a data scientist who has applied and taught machine learning concepts for several years. He started out as the first data scientist at Trunk Club, where he built lead scoring models and recommender systems, and currently works at Facebook, where he builds machine learning models for its infrastructure team. In between, he taught data science and machine learning for the bootcamps and on the corporate training team at Metis. He is passionate about explaining complex concepts plainly, striving to find the simplicity on the other side of complexity.

## Colophon

The bird on the cover of *Deep Learning from Scratch* is a Barbary partridge (*Alectoris barbara*). The Barbary partridge is native to North Africa, Gibraltar, and the Canary Islands, where it lives in forests, shrublands, and dry areas. It has spread to Portugal, Italy, and Spain as well.

Barbary partridges are rotund and prefer walking to flying. They weigh up to a pound (14–16 ounces) and have an 18-inch wingspan. These birds are light gray except for their reddish-brown necks with white spots, buff-colored bellies, and white and brown striped flanks. Their legs, beaks, and rings around their eyes are red.

Barbary partridges eat seeds, a variety of vegetation, and insects. In the spring, the females lay 10 to 16 eggs in nests on the ground. The species is known for being territorial. They often chirp a jarring *kchek kchek kchek*, making their presence known.

Though the Barbary partridge is not globally threatened, many of the animals on O'Reilly covers are endangered. All of them are important to the world.

The cover illustration is by Karen Montgomery, based on a black and white engraving from *British Birds*. The cover fonts are Gilroy Semibold and Guardian Sans. The text font is Adobe Minion Pro; the heading font is Adobe Myriad Condensed; and the code font is Dalton Maag's Ubuntu Mono.

Milton Keynes UK
Ingram Content Group UK Ltd.
UKHW032142211223
R3475900001B/R34759PG434674UKX00004B/12